JAMMED UP

Jammed Up

Bad Cops, Police Misconduct, and the New York City Police Department

Robert J. Kane and Michael D. White

PREFACE BY CANDACE MCCOY

NEW YORK UNIVERSITY PRESS

New York and London

NEW YORK UNIVERSITY PRESS
New York and London
www.nyupress.org

References to Internet websites (URLs) were accurate at the time of writing.
Neither the author nor New York University Press is responsible for URLs
that may have expired or changed since the manuscript was prepared.

LIBRARY OF CONGRESS CATALOGING-IN-PUBLICATION DATA
Kane, Robert J.
Jammed up : bad cops, police misconduct,
and the New York City Police Department /
Robert J. Kane and Michael D. White ; preface by Candace McCoy.
p. cm.
Includes bibliographical references and index.
ISBN 978-0-8147-4841-1 (cl : alk. paper)
ISBN 978-0-8147-8575-1 (ebook)
ISBN 978-0-8147-7085-6 (ebook)
1. New York (N.Y.). Police Dept. 2. Police misconduct—New York (State)—New York.
3. Police-community relations—New York (State)—New York. 4. Police administration—New York
(State)—New York. I. White, Michael D. (Michael Douglas), 1951- II. Title.
HV8148.N5K36 2012
363.209747'1—dc23   2012024952
New York University Press books are printed on acid-free paper,
and their binding materials are chosen for strength and durability.
We strive to use environmentally responsible suppliers and materials
to the greatest extent possible in publishing our books.

Manufactured in the United States of America

c 10 9 8 7 6 5 4 3 2 1
p 10 9 8 7 6 5 4 3 2 1

This book is dedicated to the memory and legacy of Dr. James J. Fyfe, the original architect of the Bad Cops *study. Few scientists of any discipline can rightfully claim that their research ever saved a single human life. Jim Fyfe's research has saved many human lives. Without a doubt, Jim left this world substantially better off than when he found it.*

CONTENTS

PREFACE

What Bad Cops Tell Us about Good Policing

Candace McCoy

Just as every cop is a criminal,
And all the sinners saints . . .
Just call me Lucifer
'Cause I'm in need of some restraint.
So if you meet me, have some courtesy.
Have some sympathy, and some taste . . .
. . . ah, what's puzzling you
is the nature of my game.
> —"Sympathy for the Devil," The Rolling Stones, 1968

Mick Jagger was not claiming that all cops are criminals; he was saying that *everyone* is. The lyrics of this iconic rock song continue: "I cried out, 'who killed the Kennedys?' when after all, it was you and me." Given a certain set of conditions, any cop can be a criminal or any sinner a saint, but we are all responsible for our actions. Have a little sympathy, Jagger says; it can happen to anybody caught in a bad situation. The solution is to change the situation. Applied to the policing profession, this would mean that we first have to understand and probably change the conditions in which cops work, and also to develop policies and organizational structure that upholds standards of good policing. So: what are those conditions, how do they affect good decisions, and what exactly *is* good policing? Or, as Jagger asked, "what's the nature of the game?"

In this book, Kane and White deeply examine the conditions under which cops become criminals, or at least get "jammed up." They go further, analyzing whether those conditions are primarily attributable to the personal characteristics of the police officers themselves or to the organizational characteristics (and political environment) which define their employer, the New York City Police Department. Not surprisingly, the authors find that *both* individual and organizational variables significantly account for police misconduct—or, put in terms of previous scholarship on the police, "rotten apples commit acts of deviance, and sometimes the entire barrel becomes rotten because the rot spreads." Kane and White add to existing knowledge about police misconduct by showing that organizational policy and practices, not simply individual "bad apples," can be a source of bad policing through no fault of individuals. In other words, sometimes the barrel itself is rotten and induces good apples to do bad things, for instance when a police department requires highly aggressive street patrol in neighborhoods that need a different kind of policing.

Among its other strengths, this book sets these findings into criminological inquiry. It broadens the example of police officer deviance within a hierarchical organization into a larger question that applies to anybody who works in any organization: how much do organizational structure, context, and management policies account for individual acts of employee misconduct? Given recent events on Wall Street, in professional sports, in the finances of defense contractors, in medical and legal malpractice . . . well, it is very clear that Kane and White are on to something really important. In its theoretical base, this book is as much about white-collar crime as it is about brass-collar deviance, and it should be read by criminologists as well as scholars of criminal justice organizations like police departments.

The very term "jammed up" shows how nuanced the dynamics of deviance can be. New York police officers say that a police officer "got jammed up" when the bosses charged an individual officer with a violation of departmental rules, whether minor or middling or severe. But the term has another layer of meaning: the alleged offender has gotten caught up in the department's bureaucratic machinery, which may apply arcane rules or office politics or political pressures to the detriment of fair treatment of the individual officer. The cops know when one of their own is a "schmuck" who should have known better or a "nut job" who needs to be thrown out (or, worst of all, a true "bad guy"). They also know that the bosses have their own set of priorities which might collide with what the street cop sees as good policing, blaming schmucks for being nut jobs or bad guys or vice versa. Another great strength of this book is that Kane and White show how the definition of good policing is malleable and, because the organization poorly defines and explains it and because city politics intervene, saying that an officer got jammed up can imply that the department might seek to deny its own responsibility for creating conditions under which cops are more likely to practice bad policing. Getting jammed up means that you got caught in an act of deviance and also in the cogs of an impersonal machine that turns for its own purposes.

Perhaps I am reading too much into the lyrics here, whether they come from the Rolling Stones or officers of the New York Police Department. But I don't think so. Scholars of the police have described these problems before, but Kane and White describe them more deeply by starting with the extremely well-documented and well-analyzed example of officers terminated from NYPD employment over a 20-year period, compared to a matched sample of officers who were not thrown off the job, and expanding the findings into theoretical inquiry about crime committed within organizations and a normative inquiry into how we should define good policing. Such a multi-layered inquiry deserves equally layered terminology and description.

What is *not* described here, unfortunately, is "good policing." This is not a weakness of the book, since Kane and White take pains to explain that "bad policing" is not simply the opposite of "good policing," but a different thing altogether. This book explores deeply the correlates of policing gone bad, when officers are fired from their jobs, compared to officers who succeed in serving without termination. But this comparison cannot tell us much about whether the job these "good cops" are doing is what we would agree to be "good policing." It simply says how well these officers perform given their police organization's rules, policies, and goals. Whether these amount to good policing is another matter entirely.

It seems that bad cops cannot tell us much about good policing. Instead, Kane and White call for police departments to work in developing a new concept of what good policing would be, and they suggest that this can only come from "the bottom up," i.e., from those cops who are "good" and who inform both their bosses and the public about what it is like to practice their profession and what should be done to improve it. Kane and White do not say what "good policing" is. They simply say that whatever it is, good cops know it.

For instance, the authors mention that their study of officers dismissed from police service, when put in the context of the neighborhoods being policed, showed that citizens living in primarily Latino neighborhoods complained less often about police misconduct, probably because they feared their immigration status would be questioned if they complained. What would officers working in Latino neighborhoods, a great many of them Latino themselves, say about this? Previous research about reforming traditional police structures in favor of community policing has shown that Latino neighborhoods may be ignored in otherwise successful policing innovations.[1] How can we do better? Ask the cops on the beat and the people on the street.

Kane and White say that analysis has to "move beyond bad cops" and define the difference between aggressive policing, good policing, and police misconduct. The latter is conceptually isolated from the others. The first two, furthermore, may not necessarily be highly correlated. Is aggressive policing good policing? "Too much aggressive policing can backfire," they say, "but . . . too little can undermine police legitimacy." Incentives and disincentives in performing police work must go beyond punishment for misconduct on the job and support a new vision of "what is good for the people policed, and how can officers be trained and supervised to do it? What is good for our neighborhoods? What can police do to help protect life?"

These ideas are not new, of course. Dorothy Guyot long ago advocated "policing as if people mattered," in which the organization assigns value to actions that do not necessarily result in arrest, and of course the problem-solving model of policing has become a staple of scholarly and community discussion if not action.[2] Kane and White add to this important discussion by suggesting that the good cops at the bottom of the hierarchy be empowered to develop models of good policing consistent with a "protection of life" mission. The protection of life approach is not new, either. My late husband, James Fyfe, articulated the idea in suggesting that it be implemented with a bottom-up rather than traditional military hierarchical police organizational style.[3] What Kane and White add to these earlier discussions is important: understanding police misconduct from the point of view of the bad apples is insufficient. We have to develop the good apples, and ultimately they will remake the barrel.

John Jay College, Department of Criminal Justice
City University of New York

ACKNOWLEDGMENTS

I am continuously and deeply indebted to Anne-Marie, the true scholar of the family. She is all at once both my inspiration and support network. Without her, there is no book. Liam and Aidan are my daily reminders of what is truly important in life, offering much needed "distractions" when the writer's block sets in. When I initially asked Mike White to write this book with me, I naively thought we were in for an easy ride, turning a final report into an academic press book. Mike (and the review process) quickly reset those expectations, and his intellectual contributions have made this book as much his as it is mine. —RJK

I would like to thank my colleagues and friends who have continued to influence and shape my thoughts on the police, especially my co-author Rob Kane, Charles Katz, and Justin Ready. I am also grateful for the continued support and encouragement from my parents. And my final thanks go to my wife, Alyssa, and my kids, Devon, Gabi, and Logan. Their extraordinary patience with "dad typing on his computer all the time" is deeply appreciated. This book is for them. —MDW

PROLOGUE

"This is car 2119."

"Call Greenpoint Hospital."

"We're bringing in a wounded cop."

"All right?— ."

"25th Precinct."

"Jesus Christ."

"Guess who got shot."

"Serpico."

"You think a cop did it?"

"I know six cops said they'd like to."

"Hello?"

"*New York Times.*"

"Oh, my God!"

Many readers will identify the above as the opening dialogue from the 1973 movie *Serpico*, which dramatized perhaps the most infamous case of organized police corruption in the modern history of the New York City Police Department. As the Knapp Commission noted during its investigation of the so-called Serpico scandal, at the time Frank Serpico reported the corruption to investigative reporters at the *New York Times*, over half of all plainclothes officers in the NYPD were engaged in profit-motivated corruption. Although the movie *Serpico* suggests that the misconduct enterprise was protected by a group of officers who would enforce the rules of the game through violence or the threat of violence (including the alleged shooting of Frank Serpico in retaliation for making the systemic corruption public), the most probable tools of enforcement were what the majority of line officers feared most from their colleagues: social isolation and the "silent treatment."[1] Whether Serpico was set up by fellow police officers to be shot during a drug bust on the night of February 3, 1971 remains debatable. What is unquestionable, however, was the response by the NYPD and New York City at large once the *New York Times* published Serpico's accounts of the corruption activities.

Once the scandal was made public, Mayor John Lindsay convened the Knapp Commission in 1970 to investigate allegations of systemic police corruption in the NYPD. In its report the Commission famously identified two types of corrupt police officers: *Meat Eaters* and *Grass Eaters*. The former represented officers actively engaged in police corruption and who sought out and exploited opportunities to maintain and even expand the corruption enterprise. The latter represented officers who did not necessarily participate in the actual corrupt activities but who accepted money for not reporting the corruption to police command staff. The Knapp Commission argued that during the Serpico era, the NYPD was largely organized around a value system that protected police corruption, and that the department maintained few if any effective strategies for preventing and detecting corrupt activities. In response, Mayor Lindsay appointed Patrick V. Murphy as a reformist police commissioner who made sweeping changes to the bureaucratic structure of the NYPD. Among these were the creation of the field associate program, where a small number of academy graduates from different classes were asked to surreptitiously serve as "undercover anti-corruption investigator(s)" while working their regular (usually precinct-level patrol) assignments.[2] In addition, Murphy created an early warning system designed to identify violence-prone police officers, and he developed field internal affairs units.[3] Finally, and perhaps most important, Murphy prohibited organized crime officers from enforcing laws against "victimless crimes," such as prostitution and illegal gambling, unless complaints about these activities originated from outside the department.[4]

Research for this book largely begins where Serpico left off. It examines patterns of misconduct in the NYPD from 1975 through 1996 and is anchored loosely by the Knapp Commission inquiry and the Mollen Commission investigation that took place 20 years later. Perhaps unlike the Serpico era, the NYPD from 1975 to 1996 was not dominated by a value system that favored police corruption. Though there were a small number of scandals since Serpico, they were relatively isolated, involving a limited number of precincts and/or officers. Even the corruption scandal that led to the formation of the Mollen Commission—though it was widely publicized—did not reach nearly the scope of the Knapp Commission–era scandal.[5] Although our data include a number of officers who were part of the Serpico-era misconduct spectacle (in many cases it took several years to successfully identify and adjudicate the offending officers), most of the officers who were forced to leave the job because of official misconduct (i.e., profit-motivated corruption) co-offended in small groups, and in many cases with people they knew before joining the NYPD.

Given that our study period begins in the wake of the Knapp Commission (1972) report and concludes shortly after the publication of the Mollen Commission (1993) report, in Sherman's (1978) terms this book examines patterns of police misconduct over a single cycle of scandal and reform. We regard this timing as key, for as long as an organization can remain relatively free from public scandal, some deviance is allowed to flourish in the department without being sanctioned by the organization's external environment.[6] Under such conditions, the department is free to determine how to respond to the detected deviance. Thus, to a great extent, this study not only examines the causes of police misconduct among individual officers, which probably did not change much over time; it also examines an organization's *response* to police misconduct between two highly publicized anchor points and during a period of relative calm when the department operated in an environment that was relatively free from public scrutiny.

Jammed Up

An Introduction

Mitchell Tisdale[1] was born and raised in Brooklyn. He lived in a two-parent household with three other siblings. His father worked in the service industry, and despite no criminal history in his family, Mitchell was arrested three times on juvenile delinquency charges prior to his eighteenth birthday. He earned his general equivalency diploma (GED) in lieu of a high school diploma, did not serve in the military, and worked at seven different service-industry jobs before joining the NYPD as a police officer at the age of 24. In addition to the juvenile delinquency findings, Mitchell had four moving violation summons and disciplinary problems in two previous jobs. Nevertheless, he had no financial troubles, he was making timely payments on his auto loan, and pursuant to his NYPD background check, investigators found no reason to recommend against his appointment to the department.

At the time of his appointment to the NYPD, Mitchell was married with one child while still residing in Brooklyn. In the police academy Mitchell earned acceptable ratings on all aspects of training (academic, physical fitness, tactics); upon graduation, he was assigned to a Brooklyn patrol precinct. In his fourth year of service, Mitchell received his first citizen complaint. It was for off-duty profit-motivated misconduct. Mitchell was allegedly involved in a drug-dealing enterprise to supplement his NYPD income. The complaint was unsustained, as NYPD investigators were unable to prove at an acceptable threshold Mitchell's involvement in the drug ring.[2] Six months after the first complaint, Mitchell received his second complaint, this time for off-duty violence. As with the first case, the second complaint was adjudicated as unsustained.

Several months after his second disciplinary case, Mitchell was in a bar while off duty, where he met a woman, with whom he went to a hotel room to engage in a consensual sexual encounter (Mitchell was still married). At some point during their time together, a struggle over Mitchell's off-duty firearm ensued, during which the woman was shot in the neck and killed. Mitchell dressed and fled the scene, leaving the woman's body to be discovered by hotel staff. On his way home from the incident, Mitchell disposed of his off-duty firearm so that it could not be traced to the woman's death. It took just a few days for the NYPD to link the deceased woman at the hotel to Mitchell; and despite initial (and repeated) denials of involvement, Mitchell finally confessed that it was his gun that killed the woman. Although no criminal charges were filed against Mitchell, he was subsequently dismissed from the NYPD for violating several administrative rules, such as "conduct unbecoming a member of service," and "failure to safeguard a firearm." He never made it past the rank of patrol officer.

In the same year that Mitchell Tisdale was hired, Paul Barrett was also hired by the NYPD. Paul, along with his four siblings, was born in Manhattan and raised there by his mother and father. Although Paul did not attend college, his father was a college graduate who worked in the professional sector of the economy. Nobody in his immediate family had ever been arrested, including Paul. Upon receiving his high school diploma, Paul joined the then-new NYPD Cadet Corps—essentially a paid internship within the NYPD that socialized pre-recruits into the administrative practices of the police department. During his time as a cadet, Paul also held three different outside jobs in the service economy; he was never disciplined in those jobs, and he never had a former employer make derogatory comments about his performance. By all official criteria, Paul was a model candidate for the position of police officer. After working three years as a cadet, he entered the police academy and was assigned to a Manhattan patrol precinct when he graduated. During his career with the NYPD, Paul moved from Manhattan to Brooklyn, he never married or had children, and he never carried any bank debt. He received zero citizen complaints and took a career path with an upward trajectory: three different commands with a promotion to Detective, Third Grade in his tenth year of service.

At some point in his eleventh year of service, while investigating a deceased person incident in a Brooklyn apartment, Paul and his partner stole a stack of U.S. savings bonds worth several thousand dollars. He took the savings bonds to a local bank, and posing as the owner (i.e., the deceased person from the apartment), attempted to cash them. The suspicious bank teller stalled Paul while the manager called the NYPD. When officers arrived, they arrested Paul, who was subsequently brought up on federal charges. In the end, Paul was convicted in federal court of conspiracy, and he was dismissed from the NYPD for profit-motivated official corruption (an administrative violation).

Approximately 20 years later, the first author of this volume was sitting in an office on the first floor of Police Headquarters at 1 Police Plaza (1PP) in Manhattan. His task as a university researcher was to identify every police officer whose career had ended due to occupational misconduct from 1975 to 1996. While sorting through yellowed personnel documents from the 1970s that had been stored in file cabinets in various locations throughout 1PP, the researcher happened upon the following entry: "Mitchell Tisdale, dismissed for *Failure to Safeguard a Weapon*." After scouring NYPD documents for months, and having seen the range of "normal" incidents for which officers were usually dismissed (e.g., corruption, abusing a citizen, perjury), the researcher asked himself, "Who gets fired for failing to safeguard a weapon?"

The Origins and Methodology of *Jammed Up*

This volume represents the culmination of perhaps the largest study of police misconduct ever conducted in the United States, with a study period spanning from 1975 through 1996. In 1996, the now-late James J. Fyfe offered his graduate student (the first author of this volume) an opportunity to help design and conduct this study of career-ending misconduct in the New York City Police Department. That study, known as *Bad Cops*,[3] was ultimately funded by the National Institute of Justice and gave the research team unprecedented access to NYPD records and data. That study is the foundation for this book. *Bad Cops* sought to explore the nature and prevalence of police misconduct in the NYPD from 1975 to 1996, as well to identify relevant personal and career history characteristics most responsible for distinguishing between officers who engaged in career-ending misconduct and officers who did not. In the end, the research team collected information on more than 3,000 police officers (half of whom had been separated from the department due to misconduct), hired approximately 20 NYPD employees, who worked on the study in the evenings after their regular shifts ended at 1PP, and spent almost three years post-study assembling data at different units of analyses in order to tell the story of *Bad Cops*. Though we refer the reader to Fyfe and Kane's NIJ final report for complete coverage of the study's methodology, the sheer scope and breadth of the study' s design warrants some discussion here.

The first methodological step involved identifying the population of officers separated from the NYPD between 1975 and 1996 for reasons of misconduct. At the time of the study, the NYPD maintained no central file or database that provided information on employment separations, whether for misconduct or other reasons. Instead, usually one to three times per week, it published Personnel Orders and disseminated them to every departmental unit. These orders reported every change in status (e.g., appointment, promotion, transfer, change in designation, resignation, retirement, vesting, dismissal, termination, or death) of both sworn and non-sworn NYPD personnel. The authors gained access to all Personnel Orders, which were contained in multiple filing cabinets inside Police Headquarters. The Personnel Orders represented a starting point for the identification of separated officers.

In addition to reviewing the Personnel Orders described above, the authors accessed all other available NYPD record sources, most notably the personnel files held by the Personnel Records Unit (PRU). The most substantial part of the personnel file (known as the PA-15 in NYPD vernacular) was a lengthy application and information form completed by all police officer candidates and used as the basis for pre-employment investigations. Also from the PRU the authors accessed files containing officers' performance appraisals during recruit training, annual job performance evaluations, reports of disciplinary actions, information concerning changes in marital status, educational achievement, assignments, sick leave, injuries, and various other noteworthy events (e.g., commendatory letters, departmental recognition, serious vehicle accidents, reports of line of duty injuries). Finally, the authors accessed and coded information from the Central Personnel Index (a computerized database that captures all critical career events), Management Information Systems Division, Internal Affairs Bureau, and the Department Advocate (the prosecutor in serious internal disciplinary actions). The only data that the authors could not gain access to included the results of testing and interviews conducted by the NYPD's Psychological Services Unit—as these were protected by doctor/client confidentiality.

Review of the Personnel Orders produced an original pool of about 3,000 officers who had career-ending events that may have been related to misconduct. The authors then reviewed the personnel history of each of those 3,000 officers to determine whether the cause for separation was related to misconduct.[4] We identified several categories of employment separation that met our criteria for inclusion in the study. First, "dismissal" is the term used to describe the firing of tenured civil servants in New York, including the police. Since dismissal is always a penalty for misconduct, all officers dismissed by the NYPD between 1975 and 1996 were included in the study. Second, the NYPD has traditionally followed a practice whereby it forced some officers to retire or resign under honorable conditions in return for their cooperation in investigating and prosecuting wrongdoing of which they had been a part. The authors reviewed the Personnel Orders as well as the personnel files of all officers whose resignation notices gave any indication that they had been in trouble when they left the department.[5] The lead author questioned internal affairs and Trial Room personnel for their recollections of any such cases.

In addition to identifying categories of inclusion, we also identified several categories of separation that excluded officers from the study. First, any officer who had left the department in good standing—e.g., for employment with another police agency—was excluded from the study. Second, prior to the award of tenure, the NYPD typically does not dismiss officers, because this category of involuntary separation requires some due process, beginning with the specification of charges. Instead, probationary officers typically are "terminated," a designation that only requires a statement from the Police Commissioner that an individual has shown to be an unsatisfactory probationer. Such terminations can occur because of misconduct or because of candidates' failure to satisfactorily meet the police academy's standards for performance in the academic, physical, or firearms and tactics training programs. If the termination occurred because of failures or inadequacies rather than misconduct, the officer was excluded from the study. Approximately 1,000 of the initial 3,000 cases were excluded because of performance failures. Probationary officers, however, whose terminations were obviously rooted in misconduct, including failure to abide by the police academy's disciplinary rules or, quite often, failure to take or pass a drug test, were included in the study.[6] The misconduct "screening" process produced a sample of 1,542 study officers.[7]

To generate a comparison group, the authors first identified the police academy classes to which all study officers belonged (based on start dates). Next, from police academy ledgers we obtained rosters for all relevant academy classes (classes ranged from 1948 to 1996) and then matched each study officer to a randomly selected academy classmate.[8] Note that the matching process did not stratify comparison officers on the basis of static (e.g., race, age, etc.) or other characteristics. The matches were made strictly on the basis of academy class. This procedure allowed us to compare study and comparison officers who had been hired under the same screening requirements, similar social and political contexts, and who likely had similar entry-level experiences with the organization.[9] In the end, the authors derived a sample of 1,543 control officers. These 3,085 officers—half of whom were *jammed up*—are the focus of this book.

What Does It Mean to Be Jammed Up?

Readers familiar with the TV show, *NYPD Blue* (ABC, 1993–2005) can likely recall any number of exchanges among the show's main characters in which they made reference to getting "jammed up"—a ubiquitous shorthand term used to describe when the organization launches an investigation into alleged misconduct (administrative or criminal).[10] Within the New York City Police Department (as with many others in the United States), officers can get *jammed up* by bosses (i.e., supervisors who represent the formal police organization), civilians (citizens who make complaints), and the CCRB (Civilian Complaint Review Board), which has the authority to initiate its own investigations. The previously described cases of Mitchell Tisdale and Paul Barrett illustrate the complexities of defining and studying what it means to be jammed up, particularly when using a retrospective design that requires researchers to work backwards to piece together officers' personal and career histories, and when relying on official police department records to do so. The methodological discussion above highlights the challenges of such an approach. When we entered the NYPD in 1997 to begin the study on which this book is based, we thought we had a fairly valid and reliable a priori definition of police misconduct: behaviors proscribed by administrative policies and/or criminal law for which the offending officer(s) was/were dismissed from employment. We presumed that in order to label an incident as police misconduct, the officer(s) involved must have used their office in some way to gain access to the misconduct opportunity. Very shortly into the study, however, we were faced with a series of questions that challenged some of our most basic presumptions about how to characterize police misconduct. The following are examples of actual misconduct cases we encountered, which illustrate the difficulties of defining the police misconduct construct:

1. An off-duty officer driving his private vehicle stops at a convenience store on Long Island, after having just worked a ten-hour shift in Brooklyn, to steal a six-pack of beer at gun point. Is this police misconduct, or is this a robbery committed by someone who happens to be a police officer? The officer was still wearing his uniform pants and brandished his on-duty firearm to commit the crime. (In fact, it was precisely because the officer was wearing his uniform pants that the store clerk figured out that it was a police officer who had robbed him.)
2. A police officer is disciplined no less than six times in three years for failing to comply with administrative standards and is finally dismissed from employment for losing his NYPD shield (badge). Is this police misconduct? This officer never had been disciplined for official corruption or abuse of authority but while on duty did wear an

unauthorized shield, which he purchased from a pawn shop to escape disciplinary charges. (At some point in his NYPD tenure, he lost the shield that was assigned to him.) A citizen then misidentified him to supervisors because of the false badge number, which the department used to terminate his employment.

3. The NYPD of the 1970s suspended officers for up to ten days for taking a free cup of coffee, but then fired different officers for the same behaviors in the 1990s. What does that say about the organization's reliability in its patterns of adjudicating disciplinary cases over time? After all, the latter officers are included in this study, but the former officers are not. To what extent is career-ending police misconduct a moving target, and to what extent is the definition of career-ending misconduct conditioned by when the misconduct occurred?

4. An officer was fired for abusing his sick time, but then further investigation showed that the officer was found not guilty in a criminal trial during which he was accused of using his position as a police officer to protect drug and prostitution enterprises. Should this officer be classified as being dismissed for administrative rule violations (the sick-time abuse) or serious/illegal misconduct? Most officers charged with abusing sick time are not fired, they are suspended. It seemed clear in this case that NYPD administrators believed this officer was guilty of the criminal charges, and they sought to have his employment terminated.

As challenging as they are in their own right, these cases lead to a set of vexing conceptual quandaries: Do the theories that explain illegal police misconduct also explain administrative non-conformity? To what extent do changes in the value system of the organization over time influence, if not the prevalence of misconduct, then the distribution of misconduct over the study period? If the organization became more or less "strict" in the way it responded to certain types of misconduct over time, does this book represent a study of organizational responses to known police misconduct as much as it does a study of the correlates of police misconduct? We believe that the data collection experience described above gave us valuable insights into the complexity of studying police misconduct and allowed us to consider these difficult questions. It also shaped our discussion of prior research and conventional definitions of police misconduct (see chapter 2) and led to the development of our own classification system of misconduct (see chapter 4).

Selznick[11] wrote that by "institutionalizing"—or integrating—the informal personality orientations of its influential members, large formal organizations tend to define deviance in ways that represent the value systems of individuals, perhaps regardless of any public definitions of deviance. This reasoning suggests the difficulty of using organizational records to identify police misconduct, particularly if the definition by design needs to hold constant across multiple generations. Thus, Selznick presents us with two challenges: (1) the importance of looking "deeper" than official dispositions of "terminated" or "dismissed" to measure misconduct; and (2) the need to maintain a sense of the organization's value system over time so that the definition of career-ending misconduct remains as consistent as possible.

From Selznick and others,[12] this volume assumes that being *jammed up* is as much a behavioral issue as it is an organizational designation. When studying police misconduct using police department records, the definition of misconduct becomes inextricably linked to the organization's response to the misconduct. To some extent, this represents a limitation of studying police misconduct via a quantitative research design. On the other hand, however, studying misconduct by using official records—particularly when the researchers are able to dig deeper than the traditional "termination" and "dismissed" separation designations—allows researchers to understand the kinds of behaviors police organizations are unwilling to tolerate. This is particularly the case if it appears that a person has been labeled a "problem" by the organization and is forced to leave the job for reasons that normally do not lead to separation (e.g., abusing one's sick time).

As an illustration, chapter 4 of this volume reports on the prevalence of career-ending police misconduct over the study period, showing that over the 22-year time span, only 1,543 officers out of a total of 78,000 different officers employed by the department were separated for misconduct. This amounts to a 2 percent rate of career-ending misconduct in the organization over the study period. Despite this overall low rate of career-ending misconduct, the annual rates of misconduct varied greatly. For example, when the city entered a fiscal crisis in the early 1970s and reduced the number of police officers by 11,000, the annual rate of career-ending misconduct declined sharply from slightly over 2 officers per 1,000 to just over 1 officer per 1,000. Does this decline suggest that the "bad" cops were those who were laid off, allowing the organization to retain only the non-problematic officers for employment? Perhaps. A more likely explanation, however (and one that was supported during focus group interviews of police officers during the study), is that, by reducing its workforce from 32,000 to 21,000, the department may have been forced to retain as many officers as possible for coverage purposes. In simple terms, the organization was forced to alter its tolerance for misdeeds committed by its officers.

As Doug Perez[13] aptly noted in his book, *Common Sense about Police Review*, while line supervisors are generally concerned with unit-level discipline, the chief administrator (i.e., the police commissioner) is generally concerned with the proper functioning of the organization at large. This "proper functioning" may relate both to ridding the organization of "problem" officers, and retaining as many sworn personnel as possible during times of economic crisis. During the NYPD's hiring freeze and layoff period of the early to mid-1970s, it may have been the case that officers who normally would have been separated for certain types of misconduct (abuse of authority, abusing sick time, fraternizing with known drug dealers) in more economically stable times were given greater than average suspension sanctions (e.g., 10 to 30 days off) that would punish the offending officers yet allow the department to retain them as needed.

As chapter 4 also shows, when New York City emerged from its fiscal crisis in the late 1970s, allowing the NYPD to hire and rehire enough police officers to bring the department back up to pre-fiscal crisis personnel strength, rates of organizational misconduct during that rapid hiring period sharply increased. As the research team found, many officers hired between 1980 and 1984 were appointed as police officers before the Personnel Division completed their background investigations. Indeed, many of those officers had already gotten into trouble by the time the Personnel Division completed its background investigations of the officers. In Perez's terms, it may be that, while the police commissioner was attempting to increase the human resource capacities of the NYPD for the "proper functioning" of the organization, he may have done so at the expense of quality control.[14] That is, many officers were hired during this time period who, if the background investigations had been completed, never would have been appointed as police officers in the first place.

As the empirical chapters show (chapters 4 and 5), being *jammed up* can mean different things at different times, depending on the needs of the organization. This reality represents both a limitation and an opportunity for the purposes of examining career-ending misconduct using official police department records: While the individual-level predictors of misconduct remain constant over the study period, changes in the organization over time (e.g., hiring and retention practices, the introduction of drug testing, and changes in enforcement strategies) likely have influenced the rates and distribution of career-ending misconduct at the level of the organization.

It should also be noted that, although large formal organizations tend to sanction known deviants with respect to the organization's value system, police departments generally are not as "free market" as other publicly accountable agencies. Police departments tend to be governed more strictly than other organizations by law and civil liability risk. In basic terms, it can be very costly for police departments to retain "bad" cops. Moreover, for serious cases of misconduct (drug dealing, weapons trafficking, protecting gambling enterprises, etc.), both policy and law leave police departments with very little discretion as to how to respond to the offending officer(s). In this sense, and as noted, using official records to identify cases of career-ending misconduct is analogous to using official data to study crime. We develop the greatest understanding of the most serious acts of deviance—i.e., those that are most important about which to learn.

The Remaining "Characters"

In addition to Mitchell Tisdale and Paul Barrett, this book will also introduce as case studies several more police officers who served in the NYPD at various times over the study period and who were forced to leave the job due to misconduct. These include Ricky Tolson, who was appointed to the NYPD in 1968 and worked most of his 15-year career in the Midtown South Division. A Brooklyn native, Tolson had a high school diploma when he entered the NYPD at age 21. He had never been arrested, and by the time he stood trial in federal court, he had been the subject of just one internal investigation early in his career for violating a fairly low-grade administrative rule.

Some time during his twelfth year of service, Tolson became involved with a group of officers—also working in Midtown South—who began stealing drugs from known drug dealers, and then selling them on the open market. Stealing drugs versus buying them is an important distinction to make because, during focus group interviews with NYPD officers at multiple levels of the organization, we (the original research team) learned that many officers placed different values on buying versus stealing drugs—even drugs they intended to sell. Buying drugs with the intention of selling them was often viewed as behavior in which "crooks in uniform" or "assholes" engaged. *Stealing* drugs from known drug dealers (even with the intention of selling them later) was often viewed as less morally objectionable because drug dealers were regarded as lowlife offenders who deserved to be victimized.

Tolson serves almost as the archetypal "corrupt" cop: he worked narcotics in a very busy section of Manhattan under conditions that were largely unsupervised and very frequently undercover; he routinely contacted low-visibility drug offenders, learning their patterns and lifestyle habits; and he engaged in his misbehavior with a small group of similarly "dirty" police officers. It was not clear how long Tolson and his group engaged in their misconduct before getting caught. Tolson's personal history, however, makes him somewhat anomalous in that he had no obvious risk factors for misconduct at the time he was hired, and his background investigators recommended he be given the job as a New York City police officer. Was Tolson a "good" cop who happened to fall in with a group of corrupt officers, or did he always have deviant intentions, which led him to seek out similar officers? This question is addressed more thoroughly in other sections of the book, and particularly in chapters 5 and 7.

In some contrast to Ricky Tolson was Colin Ahearne, a ten-year veteran narcotics officer, who was also convicted in federal court after being arrested by the Drug Enforcement Administration (DEA) on drug trafficking charges. One primary difference between Ricky Tolson and Colin Ahearne was that, while the former stole drugs from drug dealers, the latter bought drugs from the dealers and then sold them on the open market. Ahearne and his co-defendants actually participated in the drug trade and profited from it, making them, in NYPD nomenclature, *criminals* who happened to be employed as police officers. Another primary difference between these two officers was that, at the time of his hiring, Ahearne had two previous arrests for possession of drugs, and after taking the job with the NYPD, he maintained close social ties with "known drug dealers," whom he knew before taking the job. It was with these individuals that Ahearne participated in the drug trade.

Colin Ahearne was one of the many officers hired in the early 1980s when New York City emerged from its fiscal crisis, during which it laid off more than 11,000 sworn police officers and did not hire anyone from 1974 to 1979. During the rapid hiring spree of the early 1980s, the department hired 12,000 new and formerly employed police officers, hundreds of whom were hired without the benefit of full background investigations.

As a result (and as we discuss this more thoroughly in chapter 5), a large group of officers who would ultimately get *jammed up* for serious misconduct never would have been hired had the department learned more about them during the recruitment process. Colin Ahearne serves as a fairly representative example of how poor organizational administration (i.e., hiring people faster than the organization can properly vet them) can contribute to the rates of organizational misbehavior. We return to Ahearne and others like him when we describe how changes in organizational hiring and retention practices can influence patterns of organizational misconduct above and beyond the individual characteristics of those who actually engage in the misconduct.

Rochelle Bearie was hired as a New York City police officer in 1993 during Ray Kelly's first tenure as Commissioner. She was fired just three years later, during the William Bratton era (the last commissioner during our study period) for committing welfare fraud. Bearie came to the NYPD as a 24-year-old, high school-educated, divorced mother of three who probably had little intention of ever becoming a police officer. She was an academy "holdover," meaning that she failed to successfully complete her police academy training on her first try, so the department allowed her to repeat the parts of the academy curriculum she originally did not pass. She was legally receiving public assistance income before joining the police department in 1993, but state and federal law required her to give up public assistance once she entered the police academy as a paid police recruit. For reasons that our data cannot address, Rochelle Bearie continued receiving welfare benefits while she was employed by the NYPD, and three years into her police service her ex-husband (who shared custody of their children) reported to the Internal Affairs Bureau that she was illegally receiving welfare benefits. Because Bearie had been an academy holdover, she was still on probation during her third year at the time the allegations were made against her. As a result, the department terminated her employment for "failure to perform" her duties (an administrative violation, though the underlying misbehavior was welfare fraud) without due process considerations that normally would be given to tenured (non-probationary) members of service.

Female police officers represent a special category of those who engage in misconduct. In our data, female officers made up 16 percent of all officers who were separated for misconduct (compared to 13% representation among comparison officers), and they displayed marked contrasts (in terms of charges) to their male counterparts. For example, men were far more likely to be involved in official profit-motivated misconduct (men = 19%; women = 10%) and off-duty public order/crimes against persons (men = 18%; women = 9%) than women; while women were more likely than men to be jammed up for drug possession (including failed drug tests) (women = 38%; men = 29%) and administrative/probationary failures (women = 36%; men = 24%). On average, female officers who got into trouble tended to be "problems" for the organization, while men tended to be "problems" for the community.

Bridging the Gap between "Bad" Cops and "Good" Policing

With the early Bad Cops work as a foundation, *Jammed Up* makes a number of additional contributions to the study of police misconduct. First, we employ a character-driven model to make our way through more than 20 years of history in the NYPD. Tisdale, Barrett, Tolson, Ahearne, Bearie—as well as other supporting characters—will demonstrate in real terms the major themes of the book. Second, *Jammed Up* includes new multivariate analyses (chapter 5), a strong treatment of ecological and historical context (chapters 3 and 6), and a theoretical chapter which explores the value of several prevailing criminological theories for explaining the cause of police misconduct (chapter 7). Last, and most important, *Jammed Up* seeks to broaden our conceptions of good and bad policing. As the discussion thus far suggests, *Jammed Up* is a book concerned primarily with investigating the multiple dimensions of police misconduct; and although inquiries into "bad" cops and "bad" policing are important, they probably do little to help us understand "good" policing, which many readers may regard as the logical opposite of bad policing. If, however, we strip away the misconduct events that led to the "bad" cops leaving the job, we are left with a group of police officers who scored high on the risk factors of bad policing, but who did not look much different from the comparison group officers on what we might consider to be the indicators of good policing. For example, compared to the comparison officers, the "bad" cops on average had higher instances of pre-employment arrests, were fired from more previous jobs, had more derogatory comments made about them by their prior employers, had lower educational attainment, lower rates of being married, more dependent children, more disciplinary problems in the NYPD leading up to the events that precipitated separation, and had higher rates of absenteeism and sick-time abuse (the meaning of these risk factors are discussed thoroughly in chapter 5). Based on these differences alone, it seems fairly evident that the average "bad" cop engaged in dysfunctional behavior both before and after getting a job as a police officer, and that the continuation of the dysfunctional behaviors ultimately led to their separation.

These risk factors notwithstanding, when it came to the dimensions that many believe are indicators of "good" policing (or at least a good career), the study and comparison officers did not exhibit substantial differences. For example, the two groups achieved very similar academic and physical education ratings during the police academy. About half the officers in both groups remained at the rank of patrol officer during their careers; and less than 10 percent of both groups ever reached the rank of sergeant. The problem with these measures, which probably distorts the actual differences between bad cops and good cops, is that it is much easier to develop quantitative dimensions of bad policing than it is for good policing. At the very least, although the risk factors of bad policing (i.e., misconduct) may help us identify officers at risk for misconduct, the presumed protective factors tell us nothing about how "good" cops benefit the community and the organization as a whole. For these reasons, we argue that a relative absence of bad cops or bad policing does not necessarily translate into good cops or good policing.

That is, the present study does not distinguish bad cops from good cops. Rather, the present study distinguishes bad cops from all the other cops. To move beyond the study of police misconduct (the quintessential definition of bad policing) and into the realm of studying and identifying good policing requires different data collection procedures and a broader conceptualization of what constitutes "good" policing. Indeed, we argue that good and bad policing probably do not exist at opposite ends of the same continuum. Bad policing has one spectrum, and good policing has another. Although this book is mostly concerned with understanding the spectrum of bad policing, we argue that developing an understanding of good policing begins with identifying the dimensions of good policing in substantive terms, rather than as just an absence of misconduct. We further argue that an independent focus on good policing is long overdue, and we try to weave discussions of good policing into the text where possible throughout the book, particularly in chapter 8.

Organization of the Book

This book covers much ground over a more than two-decade period in the New York Police Department. Chapter 2 is a literature review that provides the foundation for the present volume. Specifically, chapter 2 reports on the literature that has attempted to define police misconduct and describe its prevalence. It also reports on the empirical literature that has examined the causes and correlates of police misconduct. Just as important, the chapter highlights what we don't know about police misconduct and sets the stage for the current study. Chapter 3 describes the research setting and provides a historical treatment of police misconduct in the New York City Police Department. It is divided into two primary substantive areas. First, the chapter briefly describes the organizational structure of the NYPD with respect to the units that investigate and adjudicate known cases of misconduct. It then describes how allegations of misconduct make their way through the NYPD disciplinary system. Finally, chapter 3 provides a comprehensive examination of how misconduct has manifested in the NYPD over the study period.

As noted, chapters 4 and 5 provide the empirical foundations of the present study. Chapter 4 examines the prevalence and patterns of career-ending misconduct at the organizational level and provides our definitional framework for misconduct. Specifically, chapter 4 identifies eight categories of career-ending misconduct, ranging from on-duty profit-motivated misconduct to off-duty public order crimes to administrative violations and "failure to perform" designations. Chapter 4 then describes the annual patterns of organizational misconduct over the study period, as well as examining the distribution of misconduct across the eight categories. Notably, chapter 4 also includes a separate discussion of on-duty abuse of authority (i.e., excessive force and/or brutality), given that this form of misconduct was rarely observed in the present data (e.g., 119 cases of on-duty abuse out of a total of 1,543 cases of misconduct). Last, chapter 4 presents results from bivariate analyses examining characteristics of officers who got *jammed up* and their matched counterparts.

Chapter 5 tests the bivariate relationships identified in chapter 4 by employing multivariate techniques to examine the individual-level predictors of police misconduct both for the total sample and for distinct racial/ethnic categories. As noted, because race and ethnicity were the strongest predictors of career-ending misconduct, much of chapter 5 is devoted to explaining this relationship. This is done by interpreting the findings in the context of a few theories of race and justice (tokenism and conflict theory), as well as by examining the extent to which the predictors of misconduct are salient for both white and nonwhite police officers.

In terms of analyses, chapter 5 reports the results of a logistic regression, a multinomial regression, and a CHAID analysis. These multivariate analyses formed the bases of hypothesis testing for the present study.

Chapter 6 is a summary of several journal articles the first author published between 2002 and 2006, which examined the social ecology of police misconduct, the consequences of police misconduct in structurally disadvantaged communities, as well as the crime reduction potentials of arrest-based policing strategies. Chapter 6 is unique in that it not only examines the causes and consequences of police misconduct at the precinct level, it also examines the consequences of overly aggressive policing strategies that often lead to the very behaviors the police are trying to control—i.e., violent crime. This discussion is particularly important because it extends the examination of the NYPD and its practices well into the twenty-first century. It is also in chapter 6 that we begin the transition from focusing exclusively on "bad" cops to a more focused consideration of good policing.

Chapter 7 is devoted to theoretical explanations of police misconduct. The chapter begins with a review of previous theoretical work (of which there is not much), and then explores the application of criminological theory to police misconduct. As noted, the empirical examinations (primarily in chapter 5) do not explicitly test criminological theories, though they are informed by several theoretical frameworks. Chapter 7 describes in detail how mainstream criminological theories such as strain, social learning, control, and life-course perspectives might ground future examinations of police misconduct. Discussions in chapter 7 use as examples findings from chapter 5 to highlight both the prospects and limitations of using criminological theories to explain police misconduct.

Finally, in chapter 8, we summarize the findings, draw some conclusions, and discuss both the strengths and limitations of the research that drove the current study. We also build on Fyfe's research to develop a model of good policing that is distinct from police misconduct—or the absence of it—and that might ground future studies of police behavior.

Beyond Serpico

In the end, *Jammed Up* represents a 22-year journey through the largest police department in the United States. The study begins in the wake of the Serpico scandal and Knapp Commission, and it ends at the time of the Mollen Commission—though several lines of discussion carry us through to present time. As the most extensive study of police misconduct ever undertaken, this book allows us to explore causes and correlates of police misconduct at the individual officer level using advanced multivariate techniques, as well as in its proper organizational and ecological context. Although the present volume attempts to answer research questions through rigorous empirical analyses, it also leaves several of these issues open for discussion, recognizing that there is no single best way to study police malpractice. Whereas we identify the limitations of many prior studies of police misconduct (both on conceptual and methodological grounds), and we intend to fill many of the gaps that currently exist in the literature on police misconduct, we also hope this book highlights some of the subjective nature of trying to identify and define police misconduct, as well as the difficulties of conceptually distinguishing between police deviance and organizational responses to police deviance. We also hope to drive home the critically important distinction between the constructs of good and bad policing. In short, while this book may answer some old questions about police misconduct, at the same time it introduces new ones that we believe provide fertile ground for future research endeavors in two separate lines of inquiry; one for bad cops who get *jammed up* and one for those who excel in the profession—the good cops.

What We Know and Don't Know about Police Misconduct

The owners of the Tenderloin's dives did not usually pay off beat cops. . . . The "heavy sugar" went to the captain by way of his wardman. . . . Clubber Williams commanded the Tenderloin precinct for all but two of the years between 1876 and 1887, when a captain's official salary was $2,750. Yet in 1894, Williams acknowledged a net worth in excess of $300,000.

By late 1949 . . . some of Reardon's fellow cops had taken to calling him the "Connecticut Squire," thanks to his elegant digs he had found for himself in Westport, Connecticut. He was not a subtle operator. Indeed, word of his activities had apparently reached the mayor himself. Foreseeing a scandal, O'Dwyer was said to have urged the department to get rid of "the young plainclothesman out in Brooklyn with piles of money."

In September 1993, New Yorkers listened with morbid fascination to the testimony of a succession of rogue cops. Dowd, perhaps the most gut-wrenching of the bunch, admitted to snorting cocaine in a patrol car and being on the payroll of a drug dealer (for $4,000 a week), among other criminal acts. At the scene of drug shootings, Dowd recalled, he would steal whatever he could and then graciously give the arrest to others; that way, any complaints would land on them.[1]

Police misconduct is not a new problem. In the United States, almost every major police department has had at least one misconduct-related scandal in its history, and some departments have experienced them on an almost cyclical basis. The NYPD, for example, has experienced a persistent pattern of scandal and reform, with blue ribbon commissions being organized about every 20 years since the mid-1800s.[2] The examples above highlight some of the most notorious characters whose misconduct activities were made public and infamous by the Lexow Commisson (1894–1895, Clubber Williams), the so-called Harry Gross scandals (1949, Jimmy Reardon), and the Mollen Commission (1992–1994, Michael Dowd). With these historical patterns as a backdrop, this chapter reviews the current state of knowledge with regard to police misconduct in the United States.

The chapter is broken down into three parts: Defining and Measuring Police Misconduct, Prevalence of Misconduct, and Empirical Evidence on Causes and Correlates of Police Misconduct.[3]

The information presented provides a foundation on which to introduce the current study by highlighting "what we know" about police misconduct, but just as important, the chapter also uncovers "what we don't know."

Defining and Measuring Police Misconduct

Defining police misconduct appears, on first glance, to be a rather simple task. Few among us have problems coming up with examples of police misconduct. Unquestionably, there is widespread consensus that certain activities constitute police misconduct, such as taking bribes, sodomizing a suspect with a broom handle, and planting evidence at a crime scene. Nevertheless, once we move beyond a few clear-cut examples of misconduct, the consensus disappears. Consider the following examples. Given concerns about homeland security and terrorism, has an officer engaged in police misconduct if he stops a car occupied by Middle Eastern men for no other reason than their ethnicity and religion? Has a police officer engaged in police misconduct if he or she uses abusive language toward a citizen? Is it excessive force if an officer uses a Taser on a six-year-old child? What if an officer accepts a free cup of coffee? The classification of these activities as police misconduct is greatly complicated if the officer commits any of these acts while off-duty, or if the act is unrelated to the individual's position (and authority) as a police officer. The discussion below explores these issues through a review of the most commonly identified taxonomy of police deviance.

Police Crime

Not all crime committed by a police officer should be considered police crime.[4] For example, consider the off-duty officer who assaults his wife during a domestic dispute, or the off-duty officer who commits a burglary to support his drug habit. These criminal activities are unrelated to their occupation as police officers. But, unlike the off-duty officer who assaults his wife during a domestic dispute, the on-duty officer who assaults a suspect during an interrogation has committed police crime. The defining feature of police crime—and the common element in the examples described at the beginning of this chapter—is that the officer has used his or her position of trust (and authority) to violate existing criminal statutes.

Consider, for example, Paul Barrett, who was introduced in chapter 1. Recall that Barrett and his partner stole a set of U.S. savings bonds from a deceased person and then tried to cash them at a local bank while posing as the owner. Barrett and his partner never would have had access to the savings bonds had they not responded on behalf of the NYPD to the deceased person call for service. It was their employment as police officers that granted them the opportunity to commit the crimes for which they were ultimately convicted in federal court. It is noteworthy that Barrett and his partner stole the savings bonds while on-duty and attempted to sell them while off-duty, demonstrating how misconduct activities occur across the duty status spectrum.

Police Corruption

Herman Goldstein defined police corruption as "acts involving the misuse of authority by a police officer in a manner designed to produce personal gain for himself or others."[5] Although there is disagreement over the range of activities considered to be corruption, there is consensus on the two key elements: that it involves a misuse of authority, and that it is for personal gain.[6] Examples of corruption include accepting gratuities (e.g., free meals), accepting money to turn a blind eye to illegal activities (e.g., gambling and prostitution), taking money or property from crime scenes, and extorting money from suspects engaged in illegal activity (e.g., shaking down drug dealers). Stoddard[7] outlined a variety of corrupt activities, termed "blue coat crime," ranging from mooching (receiving free coffee, meals, liquor, cigarettes, etc., usually because the officer is underpaid or for possible acts of favoritism later) and chiseling (police demands for free admission to entertainment, price discounts, etc.) to shakedowns (taking expensive items for personal use and attributing it to criminal activity) and premeditated theft (planned burglary).

Sherman noted two types of police corruption: events and arrangements.[8] Officers who engage in corrupt events are generally individuals who practice profit-motivated misconduct with varying degrees of repetition, and most frequently with different victims.[9] Corrupt arrangements tend to involve police officers acting in groups, representing organized corruption involving the same officers and the same victims, and maintaining a standard degree of repetition.[10] Corrupt arrangements were discovered to exist in the NYPD by the Knapp Commission, which identified *pads*, or networks of payoffs to officers at regular, usually monthly, intervals (see quote from the Knapp Commission below).[11] Sherman also argued that corrupt officers go through a "moral career," engaging in increasingly serious misconduct over time.[12] The moral career begins with the acceptance of minor gratuities, such as free meals and coffee, and the officer begins to see these gifts as a normal and routine part of the job.[13] The second and third stages of the moral career involve more serious offenses, with the officer providing something in return for a gift or gratuity.[14] The final stages of the moral career are distinct in that the officer is no longer passively accepting what comes his or her way, but rather is actively and aggressively seeking out opportunities for corruption.[15]

Similarly, the Knapp Commission distinguished between "grass eaters" and "meat eaters," and suggested that the former—who passively accept what is offered and do nothing about it—represent the real problem because they foster the culture that corruption is "acceptable" (meat eaters are those who are in Sherman's final moral career stage and who aggressively seek out opportunities for corruption).[16] Twenty years later, former NYPD officer Michael Dowd developed what became known as the "Dowd test" by getting officers to accept small gifts, then engaging them in more serious acts over time (Dowd was convicted of drug trafficking).

Sherman also outlined different levels of corruption in police departments based on the number of officers involved and degree of organization in the illicit activities.[17] The first level of corruption, Type 1, involves rotten apples and rotten pockets, defined as one or a few officers acting on their own without the support or knowledge of others in the department. The second level, Type 2, involves pervasive unorganized corruption. At this level, the majority of the officers in the department are engaged in corruption, but there is little or no organization to the misconduct (i.e., there is no active cooperation among officers). The third and most serious level, pervasive organized corruption, involves highly organized misconduct that penetrates the highest levels of the department. Although instructive, Sherman's "corrupt organization" index says little about the extent to which police agencies may encourage increasingly organized corruption within the department based on incompetent or indifferent hiring and retention practices. For example, our data will show (chapter 4) that over a 22-year period the NYPD created some of its own misconduct problems by failing to properly screen applicants for the job of police officer. During this time period (i.e., the early to mid-1980s), the rate of organizational misconduct increased markedly over previous generations.

It should be apparent now that the dimensions of misconduct are not necessarily mutually exclusive: Paul Barrett and his partner engaged in both "police corruption" and "police crime"; and the same is true for Ricky Tolson and Colin Ahearne, also introduced in chapter 1. Thus, the "types" of misconduct we describe in this chapter should be considered groupings more than strict categories, as we attempt to provide logical contexts for as many forms of misconduct as possible.

Abuse of Authority

Abuse of authority is defined as "any action by a police officer without regard to motive, intent or malice that tends to injure, insult, or trespass upon human dignity, manifest feelings of inferiority, and/or violate an inherent legal right of a member of the police constituency in the course of performing 'police work'."[18] Barker and Carter outlined three types of abuse of authority: psychological abuse, physical abuse, and legal abuse.[19] Each is described below.

PSYCHOLOGICAL ABUSE

According to Carter, police psychological abuse is verbal abuse, harassment, or ridicule of a citizen by a police officer (i.e., the "third degree"). This form of abuse has historically been rooted in police interview practices, and developed largely in response to the prohibition of the use of physically compelling tactics during interrogations.[20] In the early 1930s, the Wickersham Commission concluded that "the third degree—the inflicting of pain, physical or mental, to extract confessions or statements—is extensively practiced."[21] Del Carmen and Walker noted that, in the wake of the Wickersham report, the U.S. Supreme Court's decision in *Brown v. Mississippi* (1936) banned the police use of physical coercion during interrogations, but this likely led officers to increasingly rely on psychological coercion as a means of obtaining confessions.[22]

PHYSICAL ABUSE

Although psychological abuse has been well documented in the past (i.e., the third degree), the most recent controversial cases have involved physical abuse and violation of one's rights. Often times, these two forms of abuse occur simultaneously. For example, the four officers who beat Rodney King obviously engaged in physical abuse—the 56 baton blows—but they were eventually convicted in federal court for violating King's civil rights. Another example from New York (that occurred after the study period for *Jammed Up*) helps illustrate this form of abuse of authority. On August 9, 1997, Officer Justin Volpe responded to a Brooklyn nightclub to disperse an unruly crowd. Volpe was struck in the head by a black man, who fled the scene, while Abner Louima was arrested by another officer.[23] Volpe—assuming that it was Louima who had struck him—assaulted Louima while he was handcuffed in the back of the patrol car. In the lobby of the station house, Louima was stripped naked from the waist down, then escorted to a bathroom where Volpe used a wooden stick to sodomize Louima. Volpe then jammed the stick into Louima's mouth, breaking his front teeth. Louima required surgery to repair a ripped bladder and punctured lower intestine. After the incident, two commanders were transferred, a desk sergeant was suspended, and 11 other officers were pulled off active duty—all for either implicit involvement, failure to provide information, or impeding the investigation. Five officers were criminally charged in the incident, and two, including Volpe, were sentenced to lengthy prison terms. Three officers were convicted of conspiracy for attempting to conceal details of the crime.[24] This case is a clear (and egregious) example of physical abuse of authority.

LEGAL ABUSE

Generally, legal abuse involves police officers who violate criminal statutes, or the rights of citizens (typically, accused offenders) in order to achieve some organizational goal[25] or to accomplish some presumably noble cause.[26] Carl Klockars observed that this form of misconduct often involves the use of dirty means to achieve what most would regard as noble ends (what Klockars called the *Dirty Harry problem*—see chapter 7).[27] One of its forms is police perjury, which is designed to ensure that an accused offender is adjudicated guilty. It may also involve officers who set up illegal wiretaps in order to surreptitiously gather incriminating information on suspects.

Another type of legal police abuse of authority that has received significant attention recently is racial profiling. Racial profiling is defined as "the process of using certain racial characteristics, such as skin color, as indicators of criminal activity."[28] Racial profiling has been documented most commonly on highways, as motorists are pulled over solely on the basis of their race, though the NYPD has come under recent scrutiny for their use of stop, question, and frisk tactics on pedestrians (see discussion in chapter 3).[29] Early cases of racial profiling emerged in New Jersey and Maryland during the mid-1990s, and allegations of this form of police misconduct have continued to dominate discussions of race and policing across the United States well into the twenty-first century.[30] Racial profiling represents a form of misconduct because the practice involves a violation of one's constitutional protections, especially the Fourth Amendment protection against unreasonable search and seizure and the Fourteenth Amendment equal protection clause. Police officers must have reasonable suspicion to stop a car on the highway. That is, the officer must have a legal and legitimate reason for stopping the car, and quite simply, the color of one's skin does not meet the reasonable suspicion standard.

The Special Case of Off-Duty Misconduct

As previously noted, not all police misconduct occurs when officers are on-duty. Fyfe reported that in New York City, 20 percent of police firearms discharges involved officers who were off-duty, and that the NYPD found cause for disciplinary or criminal action in half those cases.[31] In our data, at least 20 percent of all misconduct cases involved off-duty activities. Moreover, off-duty officers can abuse their police authority while engaged in any number of other activities such as personal disputes, domestic violence, bar fights, drunk driving and related vehicle accidents, acts of vandalism, sex offenses, and larceny. For example, several of the *Jammed Up* study officers were forced to leave the department as a result of abusing their authority at minor traffic accidents they caused while driving their personal vehicles. In a typical case, the officer would collide with another vehicle (usually on one of the bridges that connect Manhattan to the outer boroughs, and very often on the way to work), engage the other motorist in a verbal dispute; and when/if the other motorist engaged the officer verbally in the dispute, the officer would identify him/herself as a New York City Police officer, draw his/her off-duty weapon, and force the other motorist onto the ground. In several of these instances the officer shot the other motorist as part of the dispute. Although clearly an example of misconduct (that resulted in career-ending separation for the officer), the off-duty status of the officer distinguishes it from other types of on-duty misconduct.

Drawing the line between police off-duty conduct that is not job-related and that which is associated with offenders' status as police officers often is not an easy task. For example, in most jurisdictions, police officers have law enforcement authority 24 hours a day, seven days a week, both within the municipalities and counties that employ them and throughout the state. But should the actions officers take off-duty be considered to have occurred in the line of duty? The experiences of the NYPD are especially relevant here. Although the NYPD has long attempted to discourage officers from taking police action in situations that are not imminently life-threatening, there remain controversies about which off-duty actions are legitimate, which are wrongful abuses of police authority, and which are simply aberrations independent of officers' police status (the latter two both being forms of misconduct).

Consider the case of Travis McNamee, an NYPD officer regarded by his commanders and supervisors as emotionally and psychologically unfit for field duty. Consequently, even though he was stationed at a patrol precinct, McNamee had been assigned to station house duty (as the attendant, or "broom") for more than a decade. He was, however, permitted to retain possession of his gun.[32] While off-duty, he used his gun to shoot his estranged wife, causing permanent brain damage, and to kill himself. In a suit brought by McNamee's wife, a jury found that his actions were a predictable result of the department's failure to keep McNamee's gun from him while he was off-duty. Consequently, the shooting was found to be job-related, and the NYPD was found liable for the injuries McNamee inflicted upon his wife. The Second Circuit United States Court of Appeals rejected New York City's appeal in the case, ruling that McNamee's attempt to kill his wife with his police gun was a job-related act for which the NYPD was liable, given their policy and practice of failing to prevent access to duty weapons among emotionally unstable officers. Although often not as egregious as the McNamee case, subsequent chapters will demonstrate that a sizable number of officers in the *Jammed Up* study were, indeed, fired for misconduct that occurred while they were off-duty.

Limitations of Existing Definitions and Classifications of Police Misconduct

The discussion above illustrates that there are a number of ways in which existing classifications of police misconduct are limited. First, police crime does not describe all crimes committed by police officers since many offenses may have nothing to do with officers' employment status.[33] Examples reviewed above include off-duty burglaries, domestic assaults, or tax evasion—all of which certainly are crimes; but absent abuse of the *police* authority to gain the opportunity to commit the crimes, these acts of deviance should not be considered *police* crime.

Second, most conceptions of police corruption focus on profit as the motive, making (as suggested above) corruption not entirely distinguishable from police crime. Each category often includes some overlap with the other. Moreover, Hale noted that there are differing views of whether or not definitions of corruption should include only illegal behaviors.[34] For example, under some definitions, accepting gratuities (e.g., free coffee or soda) would be considered corruption. McMullan noted that any public official is corrupt if he or she accepts compensation for not performing regular duties, or for performing duties normally proscribed by their employment positions.[35] McMullan's formulation recognized that both legal and illegal behavior may be considered corrupt. So, too, does the definition offered by Sherman, who wrote simply that an act of police deviance represents corruption when the act is committed for personal gain.[36]

Whether one considers corruption to include only crime or, more broadly, to also include administrative or ethical violations has important implications for our attempts to classify and simplify the range of behaviors discovered in the *Jammed Up* study. In New York and other cities, for example, police agencies have placed administrative limits on officers' off-duty employment activities. New York officers who violated such limits by, for example, working second jobs for more than the maximum 20 hours allowed by department regulations, or by accepting administratively prohibited private security positions in the patrol precincts to which they were assigned, would be considered corrupt under McMullan's definition. Because such conduct violates only administrative regulations and is not proscribed by law, these actions would not be considered corrupt if only statutory violations were included in this classification.

Additional problems are raised when dealing with officers who have committed crimes that are profit-motivated, but appear to be unrelated to their status as police officers. For example, recall the case of Rochelle Bearie, introduced in chapter 1. Bearie was fired after three years on the job for committing welfare fraud. At the time of her appointment to the NYPD, she was legally receiving benefits but then failed to notify the social service agencies supporting her that she had secured paying employment and was therefore no longer eligible for the benefits. Rochelle Bearie was corrupt in that she committed profit-motivated crimes that were related to her employment; but only the *fact* of her employment—no matter what it may have been—disqualified her for the benefits she was receiving. Bearie's offenses involved no apparent use or abuse of police authority and could have just as easily occurred had she worked in the city's board of education or in any of a range of other non-police employment situations. That is, her activities unquestionably involved corruption and her employment, but they did not involve crime that is unique to the police.

Third, though physical abuse is often considered a single construct,

Fyfe distinguished between extralegal and unnecessary police violence.[37] Fyfe argued that extralegal force, or brutality, represents intentional physical abuse inflicted maliciously and for no legitimate police purpose.[38] Justin Volpe's treatment of Abner Louima meets Fyfe's definition of brutality. By contrast, unnecessary force typically results from police incompetence or carelessness, and is generally not the product of malice. It usually occurs when officers unnecessarily put themselves in harm's way by using poor tactics while approaching potentially violent persons or situations. Then, when potential violence suddenly becomes real, the officers find that their exposed and vulnerable positions have left them no option but to resort to force to defend themselves.[39] Clearly, some forms of unnecessary violence would be considered misconduct by the police department, resulting in discipline for the officer (though see Fyfe's discussion of the split-second syndrome). Last, the recent crossover between brutality and corruption presents problems for existing definitions of misconduct. Consider the cases examined by the Mollen Commission where officers had engaged in profit-motivated misconduct that also included abuses of power such as robbery, kidnapping, and attempted murder.[40]

Prevalence of Police Misconduct

Little is known regarding the true prevalence of police misconduct generally, or in its specific forms, and much of this uncertainty can be traced to two related problems. First, the aforementioned problems in defining and classifying the construct have certainly contributed to problems in determining the prevalence of misconduct. For example, there is variation across departments in what is considered misconduct and what is not (e.g., accepting gratuities is tolerated in many departments but specifically prohibited in others), as well as differences in definitions of specific forms of misconduct (e.g., is a profit-motivated act considered corruption if it violates department policy but not the law?). The absence of clear, uniform definitions has resulted in a fragmented understanding of the frequency of those proscribed activities.

Second, data that capture the frequency and type of officer transgressions generally are not made available to researchers and academics, and police departments have traditionally been unwilling to engage in discussions about those issues. Internal investigations of police officer wrongdoing are vigorously protected by police departments, and only the most publicized (and usually most egregious) misdeeds come to the attention of the public.[41] As a result, much of the empirical work on police misconduct has employed surveys of officers using hypothetical scenario-based research designs (i.e., officer self-report attitudes of what they might do in certain situations), or less than ideal proxy measures of misconduct, most often citizen complaints.[42]

Inconsistent definitions of a construct, combined with limited (and mostly poor) data, is usually a devastating one-two empirical punch for researchers' attempts to measure an event, and police misconduct is no exception to that rule. Nevertheless, when police misconduct is placed in historical context, it seems almost certain that rates of misconduct have dropped over time. With regard to physical abuse of authority, Skolnick and Fyfe stated that, "despite the current publicity given to police brutality, we believe that it has diminished in the past 50 years, even in the last twenty. We need to recall how much worse, how routine, police brutality used to be."[43] The early work of the Wickersham Commission—which found police abuses to be widespread[44]—and the Presidential Commissions from the 1960s—which found that police routinely used excessive force—serve as an important benchmark for current discussions of the prevalence of police misconduct.

Our understanding of the prevalence of physical abuse of authority is perhaps more clear than other forms of misconduct because of available data on police use of force. Despite its central importance to the police role, police use of force is actually quite rare. The Bureau of Justice Statistics concluded that police used some kind of force in less than 1 percent of all police-citizen encounters.[45] Samuel Walker and Charles Katz point out that there are about 1,100 use of force incidents per day, and 360 of those will involve excessive use of force. In the context of more than 700,000 sworn police officers across 18,000 police departments, in more than 43 million police-citizen encounters every year, this excessive force figure represents less than one-third of 1 percent of all police-citizen encounters.[46]

Other research has also indicated that use of force is uncommon, and excessive force is rare. Albert Reiss found that police used "improper" force in less than 3 percent of encounters with suspects;[47] more recently, Robert Worden found improper force was used in just over 1 percent of encounters.[48] Alpert and Dunham calculated a force factor—the difference between the officer's use of force and the suspect's —and found that: (1) in most cases, the officer's force matched the suspect's resistance; and (2) officers followed the force continuum.[49] There is evidence, however, suggesting that some officers are more "violence-prone" than others. The

Christopher Commission identified a group of 44 officers who were disproportionately involved in excessive force incidents.[50] A fair amount of research has investigated whether violence-prone officers have characteristics that set them apart from other officers, and a number of factors stand out: (1) violence-prone officers tend to define their role narrowly, focusing on crime fighting and enforcement; (2) they believe they can perform most effectively when using their authority; and (3) they tend to view the public as unappreciative and hostile.[51]

Although available evidence suggests that serious forms of police misconduct such as physical abuse of authority are rare, this research is by no means definitive. Moreover, when one begins to consider types of misconduct that are more easily hidden (e.g., profit-motivated corruption) and lesser forms of misconduct such as administrative violations that may or may not be considered illegal, the true prevalence of police misconduct remains virtually unknown.

Evidence on the Correlates of Police Misconduct

Studies attempting to identify factors associated with police misconduct have focused on community and organizational variables, as well as upon personal characteristics of police officers. This research serves as an important guide for the *Jammed Up* study.

Community and Organizational Correlates of Police Misconduct

Consideration of the types of misconduct in police departments reveals that there are geographic differences that have persisted over time. In large eastern cities, for example, the trouble most frequently affecting police is profit-motivated misconduct, perhaps best illustrated by the NYPD corruption scandals that anchor the *Jammed Up* study.[52] In western jurisdictions, police deviance has more often involved on-duty physical abuse, best exemplified by the Rodney King incident.[53] There are some exceptions to this generality,[54] but the literature is replete with observations that confirm it.[55] These patterns are explored further below.

In New York, Daley, Kelly, Maas, McAlary, the Mollen Commission, Murphy and Pate, Schecter and Phillips have all reported on corruption and efforts to deal with it,[56] as have the Philadelphia Police Study Task Force and Rubinstein in their analyses of Philadelphia police.[57] Despite the history of corruption scandals in New York City, Chevigny stated that "[t]he NYPD is not a notably abusive department," and that a thriving "lawyer who specializes in damage actions for police brutality in

Los Angeles told [him] that he would starve if he had to practice in New York."[58,59] In 1931, the blue ribbon Chicago Police Committee conducted one of many studies of corruption in that city's police department.[60] Kappeler, Sluder, and Alpert write at length regarding violence in the Los Angeles Police Department and corruption in the New York City and Washington, DC Police Departments.[61]

The presence of brutality and the apparent absence of money corruption during the recent history of the Los Angeles Police Department (with the exception of the Rampart scandal about a decade ago) has been documented by Bobb and colleagues, the Christopher Commission, Domanick, Gates, Rothmiller and Goldman, and Skolnick and Fyfe.[62] Although the Los Angeles County Sheriff's Department recently suffered a narcotics-related corruption scandal, the major focus of the Kolts Commission's study and subsequent reports has been brutality and other abusive behavior,[63] as it was in Cohen's study of policing in neighboring Long Beach.[64]

There are several likely explanations for this variation in types of misconduct between older, eastern (and eastern-style) cities—and their police departments—and more recently settled areas in the western United States. First, this apparent geographic variation may actually be cultural, having more to do with cities' histories and populations than with location. For example, many of the people who populate eastern inner cities have emigrated from places characterized by great oppression and have settled "among their own," in distinct ethnic communities. Wilson argues that such persons were taught by their experience in other places to distrust government and to regard "[g]overnmental integrity [as] an implausible abstraction."[65] The underground cultures and economies that developed in these conditions frequently are characterized by graft and gratuities to untrustworthy public officials in return for permission to break laws they had no part in enacting and that they regard as arbitrary.

Second, the prevalence of profit-motivated corruption may be tied to the socioeconomic and crime-related features of older eastern cities. The sometimes severe poverty, high rates of crime and violence, and alienation in some areas of older, eastern cities are often associated with profitable markets for drugs and other illegal goods—services that simply do not exist in more homogenous and uniformly prosperous jurisdictions where legitimate opportunities are in greater supply. Officers—especially young suburbanites who may not identify with or understand underclass problems and cultures, and who may wrongly stereotype all of their clientele as criminal—may exploit these markets through theft, bribery, and direct involvement in drug dealing.[66] Moreover, in western cities that are similar to eastern cities in terms of demographics and developmental history —such as Seattle, Portland, San Francisco, Oakland, and Denver— police misconduct has more commonly involved profit-motivated corruption rather than use of force.[67] In these, and in diverse eastern jurisdictions— Boston, Chicago, Newark, New York, Philadelphia, and Washington, DC —there typically exists a tradition of Wilson's "Watchman Style" of policing, in which officers exercise great discretion in fitting their activities to distinct ethnic and racial communities characterized by highly decentralized political leadership.[68]

Third, the tendency toward profit-motivated misconduct may be tied to the "old world" legal traditions of eastern jurisdictions. Specifically, police are mandated to enforce locally unpopular laws enacted by distant and rural dominated state legislatures (e.g., limiting gambling; sale and consumption of liquor; prostitution).[69] In such cases, officers may be likely to cede to the will of their local constituents, and to engage in pervasive organized corruption[70] that serves as a de facto licensing of these activities in return for bribes and kickbacks.[71] The "pads" or highly organized monthly payments by gamblers to New York City vice officers exposed by Officer Frank Serpico[72] and the Knapp Commission are perhaps the best-known modern example of this form of profit-motivated misconduct.[73] Moreover, these laws have historically reflected a narrow, colonial-era, religious view of propriety not found in newer western cities. In fact, the Knapp Commission cited routine violation of these "blue laws"—which prohibited virtually all commerce on Sundays—as a major source of profit-motivated misconduct.[74]

Last, until very recently, the residents of recently developed western areas typically have been homogenous immigrants who have left other parts of the United States in search of the good life and good government. In post–World War II Los Angeles, Chevigny and Domanick suggest that a major job of the police was to see that rapid western growth and migration were unimpeded by crime or the obtrusive presence of people some might see as undesirable.[75] Hence, police misconduct in furtherance of these objectives—harassment, brutality, unlawful arrests—were tolerated. Conversely, profit-motivated misconduct was sought out and punished so vigorously by the department's leadership that it virtually disappeared. In Wilson's terms, William Parker's Los Angeles Police Department (like the formerly corrupt Oakland Police Department he studied) shifted from "Watchman" to "Legalistic" policing.[76]

In addition to these more general geographic patterns, there are several empirical studies that have explored organizational and environmental correlates of misconduct. Herbert identified six different subcultural factors—called "normative orders"—that explained variations in police behavior at the organizational group level.[77] Although Herbert did not specifically apply these normative orders to misconduct, he noted that they "provide guidelines and justifications for" police activity;[78] and this argument applies equally well to both legitimate and illegitimate police behavior. Klinger adopted a negotiated order framework that can be used to explain how the acceptance of and participation in misconduct may be more likely to develop in socially disorganized communities.[79] In his "ecology of patrol" model, Klinger argues that officers' perceptions of crime (i.e., what is normal and accepted) and victim deservedness are affected by the level of crime and deviance to which they are exposed.[80] Kane argues that Klinger's model may be extended to explain levels of police misconduct:

> It is therefore reasonable to theorize that deviance levels may also help explain patterns of police misconduct across communities: In police districts where demand for service and victim deservedness are high, and where officers regard much of the deviance as normal crime, police malpractice may also come to be regarded as "normal" within such settings as officers experience conflict and legitimacy problems between themselves and citizens.[81]

Kane continued these discussions in his examination of whether variations in social ecological conditions in New York City police precincts predicted patterns of misconduct.[82] Drawing on the social disorganization literature and racial threat perspective, Kane found that dimensions of structural disadvantage and population mobility, as well as changes in the size of the Latino population, explained changes in police misconduct over time.[83] These issues are explored in much greater detail in chapter 6.

Individual-Level Correlates of Police Misconduct

Several researchers have conducted largely empirically driven examinations that have attempted to link static characteristics and life histories to police misconduct.[84] For example, Waugh, Ede, and Alley reported that female officers in Queensland, Australia were less likely than males to be subjects of complaints,[85] a finding supported by Hickman, Piquero, and

Greene in Philadelphia.[86] Felkenes found that female officers' adherence to the "siege mentality" in the Los Angeles Police Department was substantively equivalent to male officers' adherence, which may suggest that organizational culture exerts similar effects across officer subgroups.[87] Several studies have found that male officers are often more aggressive enforcers than female officers[88] and that males are more likely than females to use force in the course of their work.[89,90] Although some research has found that African American officers are more likely than white officers to engage in misconduct,[91] the link between race and misconduct has been confounded by both patterns of differential rule enforcement and assignments. That is, in many urban police departments, African American officers have been more commonly assigned to duties and/or geographies in which opportunities for misconduct were greater than average. Research on deadly force and police exposure to violence has also identified confounding variables that explain racial disparities in shooting rates.[92] More recently, Fyfe and colleagues reported that black officers' disparate rates of disciplinary action also were associated with differential patterns of assignment, rank, and off-duty behavior.[93]

Research has also examined the link between education and misconduct, showing mixed results.[94] Kappeler, Sapp, and Carter reported that college-educated officers received fewer citizen complaints than non-college-educated officers.[95] Truxillo, Bennett, and Collins, however, found that although college training was moderately (and significantly) associated with both promotions in rank and supervisory ratings on job knowledge dimensions, neither a two-year nor four-year college degree was associated with fewer disciplinary problems among officers.[96]

Some researchers have tested associations between life and career histories and occupational deviance among police officers. In one of the few identified large-scale studies of police misconduct, Cohen and Chaiken examined the background characteristics of 1,915 New York City police officers who had been hired in 1957.[97] Using data from police files collected in 1968—more than a decade after the officers had joined the department (a methodological approach that is similar to the *Jammed Up* study)—Cohen and Chaiken sought to identify predictors of police performance among the 1,608 officers who were still employed by the department.[98] They reported that a number of variables were unrelated to measures of police performance, including civil service exam score, IQ, prior arrests for petty crimes, reported history of a psychological disorder, military service (and commendations), father's occupation, marital status, number of children, financial debt, and number of summonses written.[99] However, the authors reported that records of dismissal in prior jobs and military discipline were associated with internal police rules violations. Cohen and Chaiken also found that officers who scored well in the police academy and on probationary evaluations were more likely than others to have advanced through the ranks and win awards; and they were less likely to have engaged in misconduct or to have been disciplined.[100] More recently, the Mollen Commission found a relatively high prevalence of prior arrests among suspended and dismissed officers, supporting Cohen and Chaiken's results.[101,102]

Conclusion about our Knowledge of Police Misconduct

This chapter serves two important functions. First, any discussion of a social phenomenon must recognize and review what is already known about that phenomenon. This knowledge base on police misconduct serves as a foundation for ongoing research efforts on the topic, and acts as a launching point for new research questions, hypotheses, and directions for future inquiries. Second, and just as important, this chapter serves to identify what we do not know about the phenomenon. In the case of police misconduct, our knowledge deficits are considerable. A brief review of what we know and don't know about police misconduct helps set the stage for introduction of the *Jammed Up* study and its findings.

We Know Our Current Definitions Are Not Very Good

We have identified and reviewed a number of limitations with existing definitions and classifications of misconduct. Although there is consensus on the key elements of major forms of misconduct such as corruption and physical abuse of authority, our understanding and ability to distinguish between various forms of misconduct become much less clear if any of the following occurs:

1. the misdeed occurs while the officer is off-duty;
2. the misdeed is not at all related to the individual's position as a police officer;
3. the misdeed violates department policy but is not criminal;
4. the misdeed results from carelessness or incompetence, rather than malice;
5. the misdeed is considered by some to be misconduct, but not by others (e.g., gratuities);

6. the misdeed involves multiple forms of misconduct (brutality and corruption combined).

In simple terms, there is need for a new framework that offers mutually exclusive and meaningful classifications of the various forms of misconduct. An improved understanding of police misconduct must begin with better definitions of the problem.[103]

We Don't Know How Often Misconduct Occurs

We have no reasonable estimate of how often misconduct occurs. The aforementioned definition problems certainly contribute to our inability to determine its prevalence, but a larger issue is that data which would allow researchers to assess the prevalence of misconduct are very hard to come by. It seems plausible that the most egregious forms of misconduct are rare. Available data from BJS surveys suggest that use of force in general, and excessive force specifically, occurs in fewer than 1 percent of police encounters. The important work by activist and civil rights groups such as Amnesty International and the American Civil Liberties Union also serves an important monitoring function on serious forms of misconduct. Technology helps too—through real-time news coverage, cell phone cameras, video cameras on patrol cars— all of which enhances surveillance of police activities. Still, we don't know how often police departments investigate their officers for misdeeds, what those misdeeds involve, what types of punishments officers receive for their transgressions, and specifically, how many officers are fired for their improper behavior. Open access to police department misconduct and disciplinary data is needed to address these questions. Kane concisely described the reasons for the current state of affairs, as well as the implications of this mind-set for accountability:

> Currently, however, police departments operate under a paradigm where the burden of proof rests on the members of the public to justify adequately why they want access to police data. The paradigm should change such that the burden of proof is on police departments to justify why the information should be kept unavailable to the public. Until this paradigm shifts, police accountability in the United States will remain stalled, and members of the public will continue to be harmed unnecessarily by the police.[104]

We Know Our Current Empirical Studies Have Serious Methodological Deficiencies

Police departments' reluctance to provide access to internal investigations of officer misconduct has handcuffed researchers and forced them to rely on alternative methodologies and data. These alternative research designs have typically centered on two data sources: either citizen complaints against officers or the use of scenario-based methodologies, whereby officers read the scenario and self-report their thoughts, perceptions, and likely responses. The limitations of these approaches are well known and have been reviewed earlier. The one exception to this is special commissions created in the wake of misconduct scandals which have reviewed official police data and heard testimony on officers' misdeeds. Notably, these commissions are rare and likely provide a glimpse into a very small spectrum of police misconduct, transgressions that are either very serious, or for one reason or another, have come into public view. While researchers should be lauded for their efforts to study police misconduct, the bottom line is that the body of empirical work has provided a fragmented, incomplete understanding of the phenomenon.

We Don't Know Much about What Differentiates Bad Cops from Their Peers

More than 30 years ago, Cohen and Chaiken conducted one of the most important examinations of factors related to police performance and misconduct.[105] Their findings have served as the foundation for many departments' efforts to screen out applicants with checkered pasts, and this theme occasionally has been supported by more recent post-hoc examinations of troublesome officers.[106] However, even in police departments characterized by systemic opportunities for corruption and/or abuse, it is likely that most officers do their work without, themselves, engaging in misconduct.[107] Thus, officers' individual characteristics, as well as career experiences, may distinguish deviant officers from their colleagues, but reliable empirical links between misconduct and individual-level factors are scarce. As a result, our ability to identify, up front, who is at greatest risk to engage in police misconduct—and who is not—is quite limited.

Setting the Stage

An Historical Look at the New York Police Department

We begin with a historical look at how career-ending misconduct has manifested itself in the NYPD over two previous generations. Specifically, this chapter sets aside questions regarding the *prevalence* of misconduct in the organization over time (that is described in chapter 4), and focuses on the primary *characteristics* of misconduct over the different eras included in the study period. These "eras" can be loosely delineated by the major political, economic, and policy shifts that have likely influenced the changing patterns of misconduct within the organization, apart from the characteristics of the individual officers who engaged in the behavior.

To set a context for the examination of organizational misconduct, the chapter first describes the processes by which the NYPD has come to label behaviors of officers as *mis*behaviors. To this end, the first section offers a brief overview of the NYPD's organizational structure with a focus on Internal Affairs and the Department's disciplinary system. It then describes the major historical events that occurred in the police department and the city during the 22-year study period, including the Knapp Commission findings and the city's fiscal crisis during the 1970s; the hiring spree, emergence of drug testing, and the "Buddy Boys" scandal during the 1980s; and the continued expansion of drug testing and the Mollen Commission findings in the 1990s; as well as the initial years of the Giuliani/Bratton administrations. Within that evolving milieu, we examine the extent—if any—to which the observable patterns of misconduct may have changed over the study period.

The NYPD's Organizational Structure

The NYPD is the largest police agency in the United States, and by virtually any measure, it is massive. With a personnel complement that has reached as high as 41,000 officers in addition to 14,500 civilian employees, the NYPD is more than three times as large as the Chicago Police Department, the nation's second largest agency. The department was founded in 1845 and is headed by a single police commissioner, who is appointed by the city's mayor. With rare exceptions, new NYPD academy graduates are assigned to work uniformed duty in one of the 76 precincts after the completion of field training. It is the precincts that supply the core police services of preventive patrol and responding to calls.

Although patrol typically is described as the "backbone" of policing, it represents the department's point of access, or entry level, and historically has been the assignment that many officers have sought to leave after gaining a few years of experience.[1] Officers who leave patrol can follow a variety of career paths that include serving in police academy/field training units, proactive investigative units (e.g., organized crime and narcotics), Detective Bureau/warrants squads, as well as several staff units, such as Headquarters, crime laboratory, and the Internal Affairs Bureau.

The Internal Affairs Bureau

The NYPD's Internal Affairs Bureau (IAB) is itself larger than most U.S. police departments. In 2000, IAB processed 25,091 "logs" or complaints, 1,203 of which involved allegations that, if sustained, could result in criminal charges or dismissal.[2] As the Knapp Commission suggested, however, limiting internal investigations to inquiries into alleged misconduct that has already occurred greatly limits the effectiveness of police integrity control efforts.[3] Hence, the commission recommended that the NYPD adopt more proactive strategies and tactics that, like traditional police undercover operations, would create the circumstances in which potential or suspected offenders would be given opportunities to engage in corruption. In adopting these recommendations, the IAB created a subunit called the Intelligence Section, which has used a variety of techniques and strategies for preventing and detecting misconduct.

Perhaps the most interesting and controversial mission of the Intelligence Section is the Field Operative Program. This involves officers and other personnel who are assigned to departmental units but who, unknown to their colleagues, surreptitiously report to IAB on serious misconduct and on conditions that are conducive to corruption. In addition, the Intelligence Section uses integrity tests and the EDIT program (see below) to proactively identify officers inclined to engage in police misconduct.

INTEGRITY TESTS

Following traffic enforcement corruption scandals in the 1950s, members of the NYPD's internal affairs units intermittently were assigned to drive civilian autos and to violate traffic laws in the presence of officers suspected of extorting traffic offenders. This limited operation has since evolved into an extensive program of integrity testing. IAB notes:

> An integrity test is an artificial situation created by investigators to present an opportunity for a reaction by the subject member(s)

of the service. During the test, the subject is given the opportunity to perform or fail to perform in a manner consistent with legal and Department guidelines. Such tests may be conducted randomly in response to a pattern of allegations, or targeted toward a specific investigation.[4]

IAB conducts hundreds of integrity tests annually and classifies the results of these tests into four types. *Passes* are those in which test subjects perform as required by law and department regulations. *Procedural failures* are those in which officers or other employees are found to disobey department rules by, for example, treating citizens inappropriately. *Criminal failures* are those in which employees take wrongful advantage of opportunities to commit crimes. *Supervisory failures* are those in which commanders or supervisors fail in their responsibilities by, for example, discouraging or turning away citizens (actually IAB officers) who wish to lodge complaints against officers or to complain about police service.

EDIT PROGRAM

The EDIT Program (Enforcement, Debriefing, Intelligence, and Testing) is an operation in which IAB conducts its own enforcement operations, debrief[s] arrestees, and gain[s] valuable intelligence in those areas that have traditionally been corruption-prone.[5] Often, this occurs after patterns of allegations are identified,[6] and/or involves arrests of people who are believed to be involved in corrupt relations with police officers. After their arrests, these individuals are debriefed with the intention of turning them on corrupt officers (e.g., gaining their cooperation in building cases against corrupt officers in return for promises of leniency). For example, in 1999, IAB conducted 280 EDIT operations involving 498 arrests; in 2000, EDIT's 262 operations resulted in 455 arrests; in 2001, EDIT conducted 300 operations with 543 arrests. Thus, IAB probably is one of the few such units that makes cases against citizens as well as police. Certainly, it has been a major source of the disciplinary actions that resulted in the involuntary separations studied in this report.

The NYPD's Disciplinary System

This study does not describe the totality of the NYPD's disciplinary mechanisms. Instead, it focuses on separation from the service, which is the mechanism by which the present study "captured" the *jammed up* officers. Punishments for rule violations that may be administered to NYPD officers range from verbal reprimands through suspensions and lost vacation days to involuntary separation. Because of the interactions and interdependence of these processes, the frequency and nature of punishment are affected by changes in earlier disciplinary outcomes. These have varied and evolved over time, often in ways that are hard to quantify. Consequently, some temporal variation in disciplinary practices should be expected. In addition, the NYPD includes two tiers of punitive discipline: *command discipline* and formal *charges and specifications.*

Command Discipline

Command discipline is a semi-formal, non-judicial system designed to help commanding officers address minor deficiencies and correct employees' behavior without blemishing their records with the permanent stigma that may attach to charges and specifications. The command discipline system has roots in the early 1970s recognition that supervisors were reluctant to take punitive disciplinary action against officers because formal charges—then the only available variety—became permanent features of officers' records for even minor administrative misconduct. Given the choice between doing nothing about minor misconduct and permanently marking an officer's record with a complaint (which virtually guaranteed permanent relegation to patrol duty and exclusion from any specialized assignments), most supervisors and commanders chose to do nothing.

The command discipline system is highly decentralized, and allows local commanders to punish officers for specified acts of minor misconduct that carry penalties of no more than ten days' loss of pay (e.g., tardiness; negligent vehicle accidents, or loss of department property; absence from assignment; wearing an improper uniform or equipment). Following informal interviews with the uniformed or civilian employees involved, commanders decide upon and impose penalties, which officers and civilian employees may decline. When they do so, their cases go for formal proceedings at the department's Trial Room.

In 1995, in conjunction with attempts to decentralize disciplinary authority and to enhance local commanders' accountability, the NYPD made additional categories of misconduct subject to command discipline (e.g., loss of shield, failure to safeguard a prisoner) and the maximum penalty applicable under command discipline was increased from loss of five days' vacation to ten. Dismissible offenses are not subject to command discipline, so that this system does not account for any of the involuntary separations in this study.

Charges and Specifications

More serious and/or chronic violations, as well as refusals or appeals of command discipline findings or penalties,[7] are the province of the NYPD's formal disciplinary system, which is where most of the officers we studied were found guilty of the offenses that led to their separations.[8] Much like a military court martial system, this process includes administrative proceedings that commence with the service upon an employee of formal charges and specifications. Like criminal or civil actions, department charges are open to negotiation from both parties, which may obviate the need for administrative hearings.

The Department Advocate generally prosecutes these cases on behalf of the NYPD.[9] The Advocate's position is an attorney's assignment, and has been held by both uniformed officers and non-sworn employees. Since 1995, all supervisors have been required to consult with attorneys assigned to the Department Advocate's Office and receive their approval before charges may be filed. In much the same way that assistant district attorneys consult with arresting officers, the Advocate's staff is charged to confirm that a sufficient legal basis exists for each charge and that all appropriate investigative steps have been completed. The Department Advocate may decide not to proceed with charges and specifications, recommending instead either command discipline or no charges at all.

Trial Room proceedings are open to the public and follow rules of evidence and procedure that differ from those found in criminal or civil courts, mainly because they allow the admission of hearsay evidence. Department trials are heard by the Deputy Commissioner, Trials (an attorney) or one of his Assistant Deputy Commissioners (also attorneys). Accused employees are permitted counsel, and usually have attorneys provided by their labor organizations. Cross-examination is permitted, and all proceedings are stenographically recorded. The Trial Commissioner then presents a written report and recommendation to the Police Commissioner, who renders the final decision, both as to the finding of fact and, when guilty verdicts result, the penalty. There is no arbitration system for police administrative disciplinary actions in New York, so that appeals must be to the courts. Although we made no attempt to search systematically for the results of any such appeals, both general experience and our data collection efforts suggest that reversals of NYPD dismissals and terminations are rare.

The Nature of Organizational Misconduct in the NYPD: 1975–1996

Any 20-year slice of the NYPD's history includes a variety of noteworthy events.[10] The period we studied began at the tail end of an era of great turmoil and uncertainty in the NYPD. During 1971–1973, several officers were assassinated by the radical Black Liberation Army, who engaged in 20 or more exchanges of gunfire with NYPD officers.[11] At the same time, the corruption scandals of the early 1970s were being closed out with the criminal and administrative trials of many of the officers who had been implicated in the investigations of the Knapp Commission and of the Special Investigations Unit of the NYPD's Narcotics Division. Our study period ended immediately after the Mollen corruption scandal, amid accusations that the department's aggressive law enforcement tactics were encouraging officers to use excessive force to accomplish their new order maintenance mandates.

In this section, we describe the primary characteristics of police misconduct during several important historical contexts that likely characterized much of the NYPD's culture. We launch this examination with a discussion of the Knapp Commission era, which predates our data by a few years, because so much of what came after Knapp in terms of policy and practice in the NYPD had its roots in both the findings and recommendations of that blue ribbon commission. Moreover, the Serpico scandal that led to the Knapp Commission has become not only an archetype of organized police corruption but also the standard by which all subsequent public scandals have been evaluated—including the scandal leading to the Mollen Commission. We then move into an examination of how misconduct was manifested and how it changed in the NYPD over the next two decades.

To do this we submitted many of the misconduct-event-related variables to a series of exploratory factor analyses, which helped us reliably identify the most stable dimensions of misconduct across eras. We entered upwards of 25 misconduct variables into an initial analysis and found that nine event characteristics explained approximately 70 percent of all career-ending misconduct in the organization. These consisted of: officer arrested, general administrative violation, violence related, miscellaneous crimes, officer on duty at incident, officer co-offended with other officers, officer intoxicated at incident, official misconduct (bribery, corruption, and/or trafficking of drugs or weapons), and incident was related to drugs and/or drug testing. We then tested this factor solution on data that were disaggregated to correspond with the eras under study, finding that (as with the full data set) these nine characteristics explained between 62 percent and 74 percent of all career-ending misconduct in the organization. In any given era, approximately 25 percent of the cases could not be reliably classified because they exhibited idiosyncratic characteristics. We therefore confine the analyses that follow to the approximately 70 percent of all career-ending misconduct cases that fit into the nine event characteristics, allowing us to examine variation in misconduct patterns over the substudy periods (1975–79, 1980–84, 1985–89, 1990–93, 1994–96).

The Knapp Era

Prior to and during the Knapp era, it is fair to say the department's level of integrity was highly questionable, and corruption was highly organized. The Knapp Commission's final report indicates that:

> We found corruption to be widespread. It took various forms depending upon the activity involved, appearing at its most sophisticated among plainclothesmen assigned to enforcing gambling laws. In the five plainclothes divisions where our investigations were concentrated we found a strikingly standardized pattern of corruption. Plainclothesmen, participating in what is known in police parlance as a pad, collected regular bi-weekly or monthly payments amounting to as much as $3,500 from each of the gambling establishments in the area under their jurisdiction, and divided the take in equal shares. The monthly share per man (called the nut) ranged from $300 and $400 in midtown Manhattan to $1,500 in Harlem.[12] When supervisors were involved, they received a share and a half. A newly assigned plainclothesman was not entitled to his share for about two months, while he was checked out for reliability, but the earnings lost by the delay were made up to him in the form of two months' severance pay when he left the division.
>
> Corruption in narcotics enforcement lacked the organization of the gambling pads, but individual payments—known as scores —were commonly received and could be staggering in amount . . . the largest narcotics payoff uncovered in our investigation having been $80,000. Corruption among detectives assigned to general investigative duties also took the form of shakedown of individual targets of opportunity. Although these scores were not in the huge amounts found in narcotics, they not infrequently came to several

thousand dollars. Uniformed patrolmen assigned to street duties were not found to receive money on nearly so grand or organized a scale, but the large number of small payments they received present an equally serious if less dramatic problem. Uniformed patrolmen, particularly those assigned to radio patrol cars, participated in gambling pads more modest in size than those received by plainclothes units and received regular payments from construction sites, bars, grocery stores and other business establishments.

Of course, not all policemen are corrupt. If we are to exclude such petty infractions as free meals, an appreciable number do not engage in any corrupt activities. Yet, with extremely rare exceptions, even those who themselves engage in no corrupt activities are involved in corruption in the sense that they take no steps to prevent what they know or suspect to be going on about them.[13]

This assessment and the efforts of Patrick V. Murphy, the reform police commissioner of the time appointed by Mayor John Lindsay, produced major changes in the NYPD during the years immediately prior to 1975. The former Plainclothes Division, the gambling enforcement unit cited by the Knapp Commission, was abolished. The Organized Crime Control Bureau was created, with responsibility for gambling, prostitution, and alcohol enforcement, and for narcotics enforcement, as well. The discretion of both narcotics and vice officers was greatly limited by a general prohibition on self-initiated enforcement action. Uniformed officers were relieved of responsibility for enforcing construction codes, liquor laws, Sabbath laws (which required most businesses to remain closed on Sundays), and most narcotics laws, all of which had been identified by the Knapp Commission as sources of corruption. The Street Crime Unit, a proactive unit that sought out violent crime, was also created. Its officers comprised 1 percent of the department's personnel and made 16 percent of its violent crime arrests.

For the first time in modern history, police supervisors and commanders were held closely accountable for the behavior of their personnel. Commanders were required to identify corruption hazards in their precincts and units and to develop *integrity plans* to prevent and detect corruption. Commanders whose officers were implicated in scandal were transferred to undesirable assignments/geographies, demoted, and otherwise pressured to retire.[14] Internal Affairs was greatly enhanced in both size and responsibility. Its proactive efforts, including the field operative program, were implemented. The command discipline system was created, marking the first time that supervisors and commanders could discipline officers without imposing the punitive penalties and career-long stigma associated with Trial Room proceedings. In addition, in response to a Knapp recommendation, Governor Nelson Rockefeller appointed a special prosecutor charged only with investigating and prosecuting corruption in the New York City criminal justice system.

After a two-and-a-half-year freeze, the department began hiring vigorously in 1973,[15] enlisting more than 6,200 new officers in 23 months. These first *post-Knapp* recruits differed in several ways from those of previous generations. Formerly, the department had two titles for those who entered the department: patrolman and police woman. Patrolmen did the uniformed cops' job, but police women were not assigned to patrol duties, and they were hired in very small numbers to do specialized investigative work, matron duty, and service as youth officers. This changed with the equal opportunity legislation and litigation of the early 1970s when, for the first time, the department hired men and women on an equal basis as *police officers*. The first substantial numbers of female officers entered the department at this time.

Recruits entered to a new training curriculum, revised in accord with the recommendations of a 1969 Law Enforcement Assistance Administration study.[16] The training was far more rigorous than had been true in the past and, for the first time, served as a part of the agency's screening process. Prior to this time, appointment to the department was a de facto lifetime sinecure, and probationary officers were terminated only for the most serious misconduct. In some post-Knapp classes, however, recruit attrition was as high as 20 percent, with recruits washing out because of failures in academic, physical, or firearms and tactics training. Others were terminated as a result of poor performance in the new three-month field training program that followed academic training. The New York State Board of Regents evaluated the recruit curriculum as the equivalent of 35 undergraduate semester hours.

The department developed a *career path*, designed to make eligibility for desirable and specialized assignments contingent on successful prior service in high activity "A" precincts. This reduced the influence of the *hook system*, under which those who had connections to highly placed police or governmental officials historically had been awarded the most desirable assignments. The department introduced a performance evaluation system and an early warning system designed to identify and counsel officers whose histories suggested that they were violence-prone. For the first time, it allowed officers to take educational leaves of absence.

By at least one scholarly account, this great emphasis on professionalism changed the culture of the department dramatically. Elizabeth Reuss-Ianni studied the department, and concluded that its former monolithic cop culture had split into two.[17] The first, the *street cop culture*, adhered to the old values of loyalty to one's peers and unit, and was what remained of the department's pre-Knapp worldview. The second, the *management cop culture*, was dedicated to professional and objective standards of performance, and was practiced by the upwardly mobile young supervisors and commanders who populated headquarters and who emulated Murphy's example. This split produced a clash in which street-level officers came to regard themselves not as part of the single entity that had existed prior to Knapp, but as a minority that was criticized not only by people outside the department, but by their own bosses as well.

Thus, when the first officers in our study were being forced out of the NYPD, the department was coming out of one of the most tumultuous periods in its history. It had been engaged in major conflict with the Black Liberation Army, which ambushed and killed four of its officers and wounded several others. It had been through two major scandals, for which many of its officers still faced criminal and administrative trials; it had hired its first women patrol officers; and had seen major internal reforms at virtually every operational and support level. Then, in 1975, New York City went broke.

Post-Knapp and the Fiscal Crisis: 1975–1979

On June 30, 1975, after months of negotiating and largely begging for funds, New York City laid off its junior 5,000 police officers, virtually all of the post-Knapp cohort in whom it had invested so heavily. Indeed, the last recruit class hired prior to the layoffs entered the department in November 1974. During the next five years the NYPD did not hire a single officer; and during those years, it contracted by another 8,000 officers, mostly due to attrition, shrinking from 32,000 to 21,000 officers. Included in that 11,000-officer reduction was virtually every female officer hired after the court and legislature mandated that women be hired on an equal basis with men. In fact, more than a quarter (28%) of the 5,000 officers initially laid off were women.[18]

When a police agency loses 34 percent of its sworn workforce in just a few years' time with no concomitant reductions in city population, workload demands, or crime rates (indeed, crime was *increasing*), one might expect that police administrators would be keen to retain as many remaining officers as possible. Operating under this assumption, it stands to reason that during this time period, the organization's tolerance for misconduct might have grown to the point where only serious misconduct involving violations of criminal law would have led to officers getting *jammed up* to the point of being separated from the organization. This is not to suggest that the organization failed to sanction known violations of policies and procedures during this time period, as it probably did so. As noted previously, however, punishments for misconduct range from a reprimand to separation with many intermediate options (e.g., suspension) available to command staff personnel. Although we might expect separations to occur mostly for serious misconduct during this era, we might also expect the severity of suspensions to also increase as a way of sanctioning but still retaining officers who engaged in misbehavior. Unfortunately, we have no way of assessing the extent to which shifts in the patterns of separation were associated with concomitant shifts in patterns of suspensions or other departmental sanctions.

During this period (1975–79), 189 officers were separated for misconduct. Table 3.1 shows the characteristics of misconduct along the nine characteristics previously identified.

Table 3.1
Dominant Patterns of Organizational Misconduct in the NYPD: 1975–1979

Misconduct characteristics	Official misconduct with co-offenders (28%)	Criminal violence (22%)	Miscellaneous crimes (17%)
	Primary Dimensions of Organizational Misconduct		
Officer arrested		X	X
General administrative violation			
Violence related		X	
Miscellaneous crimes			X
Officer on-duty at incident	X		
Officer co-offended with other officers	X		
Officer intoxicated at incident			
Official misconduct (bribery, corruption, and/or trafficking of drugs or weapons)	X		
Incident was related to drugs and/or drug testing	n/a	n/a	n/a

Note: n = 189 officers

Table 3.1 shows that during the 1975–79 era, 67 percent of all career-ending misconduct could be characterized by nine event characteristics. The remaining 33 percent of the misconduct cases were idiosyncratic in nature and could not be readily "classified" along our current analytical dimensions. These data show that 28 percent of all misconduct was serious and profit-motivated (official misconduct); it was practiced by multiple co-offending officers, and it occurred largely while they were on duty. Interestingly, although this dimension of misconduct is largely criminal, it does not include "arrest" as a primary feature. These officers were likely tried in the NYPD's trial room, where (and as noted previously) the threshold for establishing guilt (largely due to different evidentiary standards) is lower than for criminal court. Thus, while officers were separated for behaviors that amounted to criminal activity, the District Attorney's Office failed to charge them criminally. It should be noted that when officers are separated for official misconduct, they typically lose their pensions. As such, if a 15+ year veteran is forced to leave the job for serious misconduct, he or she loses much more than a paycheck and current employment. In many cases, assistant district attorneys regard the loss of pension as punishment enough for "crimes" that would be difficult to prove in criminal court anyway.

The second dimension shows that 22 percent of all misconduct during this period was related to criminal violence for which the offending officer was arrested. That intoxication and on-duty status were not associated with this type suggests that the violence was likely related to off-duty violent crimes, such as robbery or domestic violence. The final dimension, which accounted for 17 percent of all career-ending misconduct, was represented by miscellaneous crimes, which typically included non-profit-motivated felonies or misdemeanors, for which the offending officer was arrested.

Post-Fiscal Crisis and the Hiring "Spree": 1980–1984

The 1980s were a period of rebuilding and growth for the NYPD. Hiring and promotions replaced layoffs and attrition, and the organization began to rapidly expand its arsenal of sworn personnel. During this period the department hired new (and rehired previously employed) police officers very quickly and, as our data collection efforts found, with minimal screening in order to bring the department back to pre-fiscal crisis strength. Indeed, as police academy class ledgers indicated, between November 1979 and July 1984, the NYPD hired 12,002 police officers. This rapid influx of officers

Table 3.2

Dominant Patterns of Organizational Misconduct in the NYPD: 1980–1984

	Primary Dimensions of Organizational Misconduct		
Misconduct characteristics	Official criminal misconduct with co-offenders (24%)	Miscellaneous crimes (20%)	Public order criminal violence (18%)
Officer arrested	X	X	X
General administrative violation			
Violence related			X
Miscellaneous crimes		X	
Officer on-duty at incident	X		
Officer co-offended with other officers	X		
Officer intoxicated at incident			X
Official misconduct (bribery, corruption, and/or trafficking of drugs or weapons)	X		
Incident was related to drugs and/or drug testing	n/a	n/a	n/a

Note: n = 247 officers

may have overwhelmed the department's capacity to conduct thorough background screenings, allowing people to join the department who would have been otherwise disqualified. It should also be noted that in 1983, the NYPD was the subject of a congressional investigation of allegations of brutality in the department. This preceded the appointment of Benjamin Ward, the department's first African American commissioner. Table 3.2 displays the most common misconduct characteristics of this era, involving a total of 247 officers. As the data in table 3.2 show, 24 percent of the organizational misconduct during this era was official on-duty criminal misconduct with co-offending officers. This dimension differed from the 1975–1979 period (shown in table 3.1) only to the extent that arrest was associated with this dimension for Period 2. These findings suggest that during the first ten years of the study period, regardless of any possible changes in the NYPD organization, traditional on-duty official misconduct, such as bribery, extortion, profit-motivated corruption, and drug/gun trafficking, committed by multiple co-offending officers represented the most observable type of police malpractice for which officers were forced to leave the job.

The patterns shifted, however, when considering the second and third dimensions identified during the 1980–84 period. The second dimension, which accounted for 20 percent of all misconduct events, represented officers getting arrested for miscellaneous crimes that were not duty-related. The third dimension, accounting for 18 percent of the misconduct cases, was related to criminal violence, intoxication, and officers getting arrested. This finding indicates that virtually one out of every five "jammed up" officers was forced to leave the job due to being arrested for public order crimes that involved violence—a marked departure from misconduct during the previous period.

Although our data do not allow us to rigorously test this argument, it stands to reason that during a period of rapid expansion, when the department hired many recruits before completing their background investigations, a substantial number of these officers would have been otherwise screened-out during the vetting process. The screening process, after all, is designed not only to identify potential integrity problems among applicants, but also to identify (and exclude) those who demonstrate a lack of maturity and good judgment. The third misconduct dimension of this period may represent a consequence of that broken screening process.

Drug Testing and the "Buddy Boys": 1985–1989

In 1985, the NYPD initiated a program to test all applicants and probationary police officers for evidence of drug use as part of the pre-employment screening process, during training at the police academy, and just prior to the expiration of the probationary period for the officers (drug tests in the NYPD vernacular are referred to as Dole tests). Generally, a positive Dole results in dismissal from the department. In 1986, the NYPD expanded the Dole program and began testing employees who were starting sensitive specialized assignments (e.g., Detective Bureau, Organized Crime Control Bureau, the Special Operations Division, and the Highway Unit). Finally, in 1989 the department introduced random drug testing of *all* in-service personnel assigned to the Organized Crime Control Bureau.[19] For these reasons, we regard the mid- to late-1980s largely as the era of drug screening in the NYPD.

This was also the era of the "Buddy Boys." The 77th Precinct encompasses a part of Brooklyn's Bedford Stuyvesant section and, in the late 1980s, was found to be home to what Sherman called a police *rotten-pocket*: a group of officers working together in a corrupt enterprise.[20] The Buddy Boys' central character was Officer Henry Winter, who had grown up in New York City's Long Island suburbs. Winter, who was assigned to steady midnight-to-eight tours of duty in uniform, apparently began his misconduct activities by delivering "street justice"—in the form of beatings—to those he believed were likely to be inadequately punished by the criminal justice system. Eventually, this treatment included burning drug suspects' money or forcing them to flush it down the toilet. Having built a reputation among his colleagues for these brazen improper tactics, Winter soon recruited some to join him in his Buddy Boys ring (which, in fact, included at least one female officer). The group expanded its activities to theft, robbery, bribery, extortion, drug dealing, and drug abuse.

McAlary's 1987 book, titled *Buddy boys: When good cops turn bad*, depicts the full range of deviant activities carried out by Winter and his colleagues. Evidence suggests that the Buddy Boys engaged in widespread drug use both off- and on-duty:

> Certainly the 77th Precinct had a drug problem. Some officers smoked marijuana in their patrol cars on the late tour and snorted cocaine in the locker room lounge. . . .
>
> We'd do a job and shoot back to Macho's Bodega . . . for a beer. We sat in the back on milk boxes, drinking bottles of beer and playing with the roaches, betting on the fastest ones. There were times we'd have eight or nine cops in the back of the store, hooting and hollering, arguing about who was going to go out to the refrigerator to get the next round of beers.[21]

The Buddy Boys eventually escalated from burning or flushing drugs (and drug money) to taking bribes to protect drug dealers, planned theft, and actual drug dealing. They routinely carried equipment with them to carry out burglaries (screwdrivers, crow bars, etc.), and they frequently talked in code over the police radio to set up times and locations for the thefts.[22] Perhaps the most disturbing accounts of Buddy Boys' illicit activities involve actual street-level drug dealing.

> It was like we were insane or something. I mean one time we hit this . . . [place] . . . on a late tour. . . . We tossed everybody. While me and Nicky were in the back searching through things, a line of customers formed. Brian started selling them coke through the slot in the door. And it was a good thing he did, too, because we came up with a small amount of money and a large amount of coke. So O'Regan made more money for us. He did it for about an hour. There was this one guy who came up to the door and wanted to sell his

sweater. It was a nice, brand-new sweater. But there was a long line so we couldn't open the door. That would have been bad for business. Brian tried to get the guy to slip the sweater under the door, but it wouldn't fit.[23]

In time, other police arrested a drug dealer who claimed that he had been buying protection from 77th Precinct officers for years. The dealer agreed to cooperate with the then-Internal Affairs Division (subsequently renamed to *Bureau*), and investigators proceeded to videotape Winter and his partner receiving payoffs from the dealer. IAD then *turned* Winter and his partner, equipping them with wire recorders as they collected evidence over the next several months against 36 other officers from the 77. Thirteen officers were indicted, one of whom committed suicide rather than surrender to authorities, and 23 were subjected to internal disciplinary procedures.[24]

The Buddy Boys scandal differed substantially from most prior corruption scandals in New York City. Although the Knapp/Serpico scandals eventually exposed widespread, but relatively low-level corruption among uniformed officers, it had its roots in long-suppressed revelations that gambling enforcement officers received regular monthly payments from the illegal gambling operators they allowed to flourish. The 1970s Special Investigations Unit scandals exposed theft, robbery, and drug trafficking by members of the NYPD's most elite drug enforcement unit.[25] The Buddy Boys were a dramatic step from these prior experiences. While many police distinguished *dirty money* from the *clean money* offered by gamblers who sought only to be left alone to ply their trades, only the SIU scandal had previously involved any organized drug corruption or other dirty money taken—by bribery, extortion, theft, or robbery. Even the SIU scandal, however, was not a clear precedent for the Buddy Boys because it involved an elite, highly specialized citywide unit, rather than a group of uniformed patrol officers assigned to a single geographic area; the Buddy Boys were local cops on the beat.

Table 3.3 shows the most common characteristics of police misconduct in the NYPD from 1985 to 1989, and it includes 552 officers. The results of the 1985–89 period show that for the first time during the study period—and despite the widely publicized Buddy Boys scandal—official misconduct was *not* the dominant form of career-ending malpractice in the NYPD. The first dimension, which accounted for 23 percent of all misconduct events, was represented by miscellaneous crimes that officers

Table 3.3

Dominant Patterns of Organizational Misconduct in the NYPD: 1985–1989

Misconduct characteristics	Primary Dimensions of Organizational Misconduct			
	Miscellaneous public order crimes (23%)	Official criminal misconduct (20%)	Drug test failures (15%)	Miscellaneous crimes (no arrest) (14%)
Officer arrested	X	X		
General administrative violation				
Violence related				
Miscellaneous crimes	X			X
Officer on-duty at incident				
Officer co-offended with other officers	X	X		
Officer intoxicated at incident	X			
Official misconduct (bribery, corruption, and/or trafficking of drugs or weapons)		X		
Incident was related to drugs and/or drug testing			X	

Note: n = 552 officers

committed together while intoxicated, and for which they were arrested. Examination of the dismissal data for this time period found that a large number of police officers who were driving together were involved in alcohol-related traffic accidents and subsequent arrest. The arrests, however, were not always limited to DWI; in many cases the officers got into fights with the drivers of the other vehicles, which made both officers subject to arrest, not just the driver. This helps explain why both co-offending and arrest are associated with this dimension, but not duty status. Indeed, this dimension shows that for the first time in the post-Knapp era, organizational misconduct was somewhat more likely to involve off-duty miscellaneous criminal offending among small groups of officers than the more traditional official misconduct. Again, the extent to which this dimension reflects a breakdown in the NYPD's screening process cannot be reliably assessed; but this dimension may represent a residual effect of hiring recruits too quickly.

The second component, which comprised 20 percent of all misconduct, was characterized by official misconduct, but was distinct from the misconduct dimensions shown in the previous tables in that it was not associated with on-duty status. It may be that most official misconduct during this era was committed while off-duty, which represents a departure from previous years. The third dimension was made up exclusively of drug screening failures and accounted for 15 percent of all misconduct. Considering that drug testing was introduced to the department in 1985, it is consistent with expectations that drug test failures would have influenced the patterns of career-ending malpractice during this era. Finally, a fourth dimension of misconduct was represented by miscellaneous crimes for which officers were not arrested.

Mollen Commission Era: 1990–1993

The Buddy Boys may have been the first in a series of episodes that unfortunately have since become commonplace in urban U.S. policing: a small group of officers assigned to some locally based special duty (in their case, steady night duty) who, usually led by some charismatic deviant, systematically brutalize, rob, and traffic in drugs. In the 1990s, a similar pattern emerged, and was investigated by both the NYPD and the independent Mollen Commission.[26] Arrests made by police in Long Island's Suffolk County showed that a group of Brooklyn officers, apparently led by Officer Michael Dowd, another charismatic suburbanite, engaged in brutality, robbery, theft, drug trafficking and abuse, and the use of their police authority to drive off rivals of the dealers who employed them.[27] Nearly simultaneously, a group of officers in Harlem's 30th Precinct—called "Nannery's Raiders"—were discovered engaging in the same sorts of activities, this time under the leadership of their sergeant. An additional group, the Morgue Boys, was found in Brooklyn's 75th Precinct, as were several officers from the 46th Precinct in the Bronx.[28] The Mollen Commission highlighted the changing nature of police misconduct:

> Today's corruption is far more criminal, violent and premeditated than traditional notions of police corruption suggest and far more invidious than corruption of a generation ago. Testimony and field investigations demonstrated that its most salient forms include groups of officers protecting and assisting drug traffickers for often sizeable profits—stealing drugs, guns and money—and often selling the stolen drugs and guns to or through criminal associates; committing burglary and robbery; conducting unlawful searches of apartments, cars and people; committing perjury and falsifying statements; and sometimes using excessive force, often in connection with corruption.[29]

Table 3.4

Dominant Patterns of Organizational Misconduct in the NYPD: 1990–1993

	Primary Dimensions of Organizational Misconduct			
Misconduct characteristics	Official criminal misconduct (24%)	On-duty offcial misconduct (20%)	Admin. rule violations (16%)	Miscellaneous crimes associated with official misconduct (14%)
Officer arrested	X			
General administrative violation			X	
Violence related				
Miscellaneous crimes				X
Officer on-duty at incident	X	X		
Officer co-offended with other officers	X			
Officer intoxicated at incident				
Official misconduct (bribery, corruption, and/or trafficking of drugs or weapons)	X	X		X
Incident was related to drugs and/or drug testing				

Note: n = 234 officers

Table 3.4 shows the dominant characteristics of police misconduct in the NYPD from 1990 to 1993 and includes a total of 234 officers. Table 3.4 shows that three of the four empirical dimensions were related to official misconduct, which represents a substantial departure from the patterns observed during the 1985–89 period. The first dimension represented the traditional form of police deviance, where officers who offended together while on-duty were arrested for official misconduct. It is interesting that, although the second dimension also included on-duty official misconduct, arrest and co-offending were not associated characteristics. The third misconduct dimension was represented solely by general administrative offenses. Among the most common administrative violations are loss of a badge or possessing a "bogus" NYPD shield.[30] The fourth dimension was again dominated by criminal activities in the form of miscellaneous crimes and official misconduct. Note that drug test failures were not a defining characteristic of any forms of misconduct during this era.

The findings from the Mollen-era analysis are notable because they show that 58 percent of all career-ending misconduct was for some form of serious profit-motivated activity, such as bribery, drug dealing, gun trafficking, etc. The extent to which public scrutiny of the department as a result of the Mollen Commission investigation distorted the actual patterns of organizational misconduct is unknown. It may be, for example, that the distribution of misconduct events remained somewhat stable over time, but that as a result of a public scandal the department devoted most of its investigative and trial room time to seeking out and punishing officers involved in official corruption. Did public order crimes largely disappear within the department during this time, or were public order offenses that were committed by officers met with punishments that stopped short of job loss? Our data cannot precisely answer that question.

Post-Mollen Era: 1994–1996

The final time period under examination spans from 1994 to 1996, the period during which Rudolph Giuliani served as Mayor of the City of New York, and the NYPD initiated its "quality of life" enforcement strategies.[31] Note that though this period includes only three complete years, 209 cases of career-ending police misconduct were identified. It was also during this period that the department again implemented several major changes to prevent and detect misconduct, as well as to hold officers and commanders accountable for improper behavior. Table 3.5 shows the defining characteristics of police misconduct during this era.

As with most of the prior analyses, data from the 1994–96 era indicate that traditional official misconduct represented the dominant pattern of career-ending malpractice. The first dimension, which accounted for 24 percent of all cases during this period, included arrest of co-offending officers for on-duty official misconduct. The second and third dimensions represented miscellaneous criminal activity during which officers were intoxicated, and were distinguishable only to the extent that arrest—which was associated with second dimension—was not associated with the third. Finally, as in Period 3, Dole failures emerged as an important characteristic of misconduct, accounting for 14 percent of all career-ending misconduct events.

It is noteworthy that during this final time period, public order criminal activity appears to have been the dominant form of organizational misconduct in the NYPD, accounting for 36 percent of all career-ending misconduct cases. This shift in the dimensions of career-ending misconduct may have been the result of decreased official, profit-motivated misbehaviors, and/or a concerted effort on the part of the Giuliani/Bratton admin-

Table 3.5

Dominant Patterns of Organizational Misconduct in the NYPD: 1994–1996

Misconduct characteristics	Primary Dimensions of Organizational Misconduct			
	Official criminal misconduct (24%)	Misc. public order crimes (21%)	Misc. public order crimes (no arrest) (15%)	Drug test failure (14%)
Officer arrested	X	X		
General administrative violation				
Violence related				
Miscellaneous crimes		X	X	
Officer on-duty at incident	X			
Officer co-offended with other officers	X			
Officer intoxicated at incident		X	X	
Official misconduct (bribery, corruption, and/or trafficking of drugs or weapons)	X			
Incident was related to drugs and/or drug testing				X

Note: n = 209 officers

istrations to more vigorously rid the department of officers who posed trouble for the organization beyond the traditional forms of misconduct.

Discussion of Misconduct Findings

Results of the organizational analysis generally show that the most stable form of career-ending misconduct in the NYPD over time has been primarily criminal and profit-motivated, committed by co-offending officers, who were usually on-duty when the events occurred. With the exception of Drug Testing and the "Buddy Boys" era (1985–89), about a quarter of all organizational misconduct over the study period matched this pattern. A few shifts in the characteristics of misconduct were noteworthy. First, the farther removed the department became from Knapp (and just on the eve of the Mollen Commission), the less official misconduct it detected. During the period 1975–79, for example, 28 percent of all career-ending misconduct in the organization was on-duty serious corruption with co-offending officers; in 1980–84, the percent of such cases fell to 24 percent; and by the 1985–89 period, official career-ending misconduct with co-offenders represented 20 percent of all misconduct events. It may be that in the years following the Serpico/Knapp scandal, the department's relatively new screening and corruption detection/prevention strategies discouraged (and even reduced) the amount of serious corruption in the organization, which could account for the observed decline. Given, however, that during the Mollen Commission era (1990–93), official misconduct in all forms accounted for 58 percent of all career-ending misconduct, the more likely scenario was that, in the years following Knapp, the department became increasingly *less* vigorous in its efforts to detect and control official misconduct. The Buddy Boys incident of the 1980s, which involved a relatively small number of officers, was probably a bellwether of the kinds of small-scale organized corruption that (1) was occurring much more systemically than the department realized, and (2) would ultimately lead to the Mollen Commission investigation.

It is probably the case that in the years immediately following Knapp (1975–79), the department was at its most vigorous in its efforts to control and detect official misconduct/corruption. As public scrutiny declined, and the department began to operate under "normal" supervision levels, it detected and sanctioned with separation increasingly less official misconduct. This does not necessarily suggest that it failed to take official misconduct seriously; it may be that official misconduct more typically received sanctions that were less punitive and final than separation from the job (particularly if there was no arrest associated with the event). It may also be the case that during times of "normal" supervision, the department sanctioned with separation more varied forms of misconduct than when it operated under intense public scrutiny. Career-ending misconduct can be a highly visible phenomenon in any police organization, particularly in the midst of a public scandal. As such, the Mollen Commission era probably distorted the actually distribution of police misconduct that was manifested in the NYPD.

Another notable shift in the patterns of career-ending misconduct occurred when drug testing was introduced into the department in 1985. During the 1985–89 and the 1994–96 periods, drug test failures accounted for 14–15 percent of all career-ending misconduct. Moreover, once drug testing was introduced, patterns of career-ending misconduct became less idiosyncratic than they had been in the past. Note that before 1985, approximately 65 percent of all career-ending misconduct followed observable patterns (based on the misconduct characteristics included in tables 3.1 and 3.2). Once drug testing became a mechanism of separation, 72–74 percent of career-ending misconduct followed observable patterns (tables 3.3–3.5). It is unlikely that drug testing led to increases in career-ending misconduct (findings presented in chapter 4 will support this assertion) so much as it did a shift in the reasons for separation. Drug testing probably became an efficient mechanism to facilitate separation for a group of officers who, without drug testing, may have been ultimately jammed up for a variety of different reasons.

Organizational Changes in Response to the Mollen Commission

The discoveries of the early 1990s produced some major changes in the NYPD's provisions for holding officers and commanders accountable for proper behavior. The former division of responsibilities between the central Internal Affairs Division and local Field Internal Affairs Units had left many cases, including the Dowd matter, undetected. This structure was eliminated. Instead, a new and unified Internal Affairs Bureau was formed, and engaged in more aggressive and proactive investigations than had been true in the past. The *field operative* program, which had been created in the 1970s and used officers and other employees to systematically and anonymously report to Internal Affairs on misconduct in their commands, had long fallen out of use, and was reinvigorated. A hotline available for employees (known as the "Pride Line") to make anonymous reports of misconduct was adopted, and the department began to scrutinize systematically officers' records in search of anomalous patterns and other risk factors that may indicate misconduct. The department examined the records of officers implicated in Mollen-era misconduct, and found that most fell into three categories when hired: they were younger than 22 years old; they had little or no education beyond the minimum high school equivalency diploma; and they had not served in the military. As a result, the entrance standards were changed to require a minimum age of 22 and a minimum of two years of college or two years of military service.

The Emergence of Zero Tolerance/Order Maintenance Policing

The scandals that the NYPD experienced during the 1980s and early 1990s occurred within an overall context of increasing crime and disorder in New York City. The NYPD's initial targeted response to the increasing crime problem came under Commissioner Lee Brown through the *Safe Streets* program, which increased the patrol force by 6,000 officers and funded a range of community crime prevention programs.[32] The tactics of the department shifted dramatically with the election of Rudy Giuliani as Mayor and his appointment of William Bratton as Commissioner of the NYPD. The Giuliani/Bratton approach involved three important strategic-level changes. First, the department adopted a Broken Windows–based strategy to target low-level social disorder and crime. As articulated in the NYPD document, *Reclaiming the Public Spaces of New York*, the department began focusing its efforts on "graffiti, aggressive panhandling, fare beating, public drunkenness, unlicensed vending, public drinking, public urination and other misdemeanor offenses."[33] Second, at the same time the NYPD shifted its attention to disorder and minor crime, it also initiated an intensive effort to curb gun violence through seizure of illegal firearms (outlined in the NYPD document, *Getting Guns off the Streets of New York*).[34] Third, both of these efforts coincided with Bratton's implementation of CompStat, a new data-driven approach that revolutionized the management and functioning of the department (see McDonald[35] for an in-depth discussion of CompStat).

As these three strategies were initiated in the mid-1990s, New York City experienced sharp declines in crime. The New York City Mayor's Office reported that, from 1993 to 1997, felony complaints dropped by 44.3 percent, including a 60.2 percent decline in homicides.[36] Although the exact cause or causes of this dramatic decrease in crime remain hotly contested, Bratton claimed responsibility through his three-pronged strategic approach —focus on low-level disorder and crime, gun interdiction, and CompStat,[37] and perceptions of CompStat's effectiveness have led to widespread adoption of the approach among big-city police departments.[38]

Although many of these changes occurred at the tail end of the period covered by *Jammed Up*, these strategic approaches have implications for the discussion of police misconduct in New York City. Specifically, by 2000 the primary tactic employed by the NYPD as part of its order maintenance philosophy was (and still is) aggressive stop, question, and frisks of pedestrians. Fagan and colleagues state that:

> By the end of the decade, stops and frisks of persons suspected of crimes had become a flashpoint for grievances by the City's minority communities. . . . In a fifteen-month period from January 1998 through March 1999, non-Hispanic Black, Hispanic black, and Hispanic White New Yorkers were three times more likely that their White counterparts to be stopped and frisked on suspicion of weapons or violent crimes.[39]

In an earlier paper, Fagan and Davies concluded that the stop and frisk activities were disproportionately focused on the "poorest neighborhoods with the highest concentrations of minority citizens, even after controlling for rates of crime and physical disorder in those places."[40] The undercurrent of tension among police and residents of the city's poorest neighborhoods had manifested itself in a number of ways, including a 75 percent increase in civil rights claims against police, and a 60 percent increase in the number of civilian complaints (from 1992 to 1996).[41] Greene argued that the increases in complaints and civil suits against police reflect the costs of the hyper-aggressive "zero tolerance" approach, and she noted that San Diego experienced similar crime declines using a community-oriented policing approach that provided "effective crime control through more efficient and humane methods."[42]

In simple terms, the NYPD's philosophical and strategic shifts during the early 1990s provide important context for understanding the tension that has persisted between the NYPD and the black community, as well as for the several flashpoint incidents that occurred during the post–*Jammed Up* time period (Louima in 1997, Diallo in 1999, and Sean Bell in 2006). In fact, during testimony before the City Council in 1997, New York City Public Advocate Mark Green stated that the torture of Abner Louima was part of a larger "pattern of police abuse, brutality, and misconduct" that the department and Mayor's office had failed to address; and that "the problem of police misconduct is disproportionately concentrated in New York City's high crime minority neighborhoods"[43]—a theme consistent with Fagan's work. We explore this theme in great detail in chapter 6.

Conclusions

The organizational and historical contexts provided in this chapter provide important context for the *Jammed Up* study, and they inform two primary conclusions. The first is that this discussion demonstrates the influence of the organizational and social environments on the detection and sanctioning of career-ending misconduct. That is, this review shows that organizational as well as city-level features and events may have shaped —and to some extent, perhaps determined—the nature and prevalence of police misconduct that is reported in the *Jammed Up* study. Given some of the shifts in the patterns of misconduct, as well as the changing social, political, and policy contexts of the NYPD over the study period, the nature and prevalence of career-ending misconduct described in later chapters may have been as much a function of organizational and historical forces as it was the actions of individual officers. This theme is explored in greater detail in chapter 6, "The Department, the City and Police

Misconduct: Looking beyond the Bad Cop." The second conclusion is that this organizational/historical review highlights both the distinctiveness of the NYPD on the one hand, and the external validity of the study findings on the other. More specifically, though the NYPD is unique in many respects, we believe the shared history among police in the United States during the study period—especially among big city police departments—highlights the degree to which this study has (1) theoretical relevance for the study of policing (and police misconduct) in general; and (2) practical relevance for police departments with regard to efforts to prevent misdeeds among their officers. This latter point is especially important, as the true value of any case study rests in the degree to which the findings travel beyond the borders of the unit (in this case, department) under study.

Finally, as we noted in chapter 1, most research on police accountability (including misconduct) tends to focus primarily on explaining, and ultimately limiting, police misconduct. The efforts of the NYPD to control corruption in the wake of Knapp and Mollen exemplify this approach. The focus, however, on limiting problematic police behaviors likely does little to encourage the kinds of behaviors that police departments (and society at large) actually desire. Indeed, and as we argue in chapter 8, practicing policing at the standard of legal minimalism does not lead to good policing. If police departments invested as much time and expertise into defining and developing standards and practices of "good" policing as they do detecting and trying to minimize "bad" policing (i.e., misconduct), they could likely accomplish more than limiting misbehaviors for intermittent periods of time.

Exploring Career-Ending Misconduct in the NYPD

Who, What, and How Often

As the title suggests, this chapter is descriptive in its scope and intent, focusing on several of the basic questions that frame the study. Specifically, we examine two broad questions related to police misconduct:

1. What was the nature and prevalence of organizational misconduct during this 22-year period that included a fairly complete cycle of scandal and reform?
2. What were the relevant personal and career history characteristics most responsible for distinguishing between officers who engaged in career-ending misconduct and officers who did not?

In simple terms: *who, what*, and *how often?* The chapter begins with our new misconduct classification scheme, which was developed through review of the misdeeds of the study officers and with the goal of addressing many of the definitional problems that have limited prior research. The remainder of the chapter is devoted to examining the prevalence of police misconduct both overall and over time (the "how often"), as well as the most common types of misdeeds (the "what," using our new classification scheme). Last, we explore the background and characteristics of study and control officers (the "who") searching for notable differences that will serve as a launching point for the multivariate analyses in the next chapter.

The Jammed Up Police Misconduct Classification Scheme

Although there is a fair amount of consensus on the key elements of the major forms of police misconduct (e.g., physical abuse of authority), there are myriad factors that make a precise definition of police misconduct elusive. These include misbehaviors that "fit" multiple definitions of misconduct (e.g., can be defined as both corruption and police crime), that are not related to the person's position as a police officer (not police crime), are administrative violations but not criminal, and misbehaviors that occur when the officer is off-duty. Several case studies illustrate these problems.

CASE STUDY
Recall Mitchell Tisdale, who was introduced in chapter 1. He was the officer who had an extramarital affair with a woman he met

at a bar while off-duty. During their encounter, a struggle over his firearm ensued, and the woman ultimately was shot to death. Tisdale disposed of his gun and failed to report the incident. Tisdale's actions subsequent to the shooting amounted to police misconduct to the extent that he was charged administratively with "failure to safeguard a firearm." This, however, is not a classic, or clear-cut, case of police misconduct because (1) Tisdale's actions that led to the shooting were not precisely related to his position as a police officer, and (2) the shooting itself was deemed to be noncriminal. Tisdale clearly violated department policy, as well as failing to take proper action as a police officer once the shooting occurred. We classify Tisdale as having committed police misconduct because of his clear intentions to evade responsibility for the shooting incident, as well as the fact that the only reason he possessed a firearm at the time of the shooting was because he was a police officer. Specifically, Tisdale fits the administrative/ failure to perform criterion, and perhaps even the obstruction of justice definition, even though he was not charged for that offense either administratively or criminally.

CASE STUDY

Recall Paul Barrett, also introduced in chapter 1. Barrett and his partner responded to investigate a possible deceased person call in a Brooklyn apartment. Upon their arrival, Barrett and his partner discovered that the resident of the apartment was indeed deceased. Before calling the city's medical examiner's office, the two officers conducted a search of the apartment, finding a stack of U.S. savings bonds. Once they cleared the call, the officers went to the bank (in plain clothes with Paul impersonating the deceased owner of the bonds) to try to cash the bonds. The two were subsequently arrested and fired from the department, but Paul was the only one convicted of a crime: conspiracy. Both officers clearly committed a profit-motivated crime; and despite the fact that Paul's partner was not convicted criminally, we nevertheless retain him in the study as a *jammed up* officer.

CASE STUDY

Finally, recall Rochelle Bearie, the divorced mother of three who, prior to entering the NYPD in 1993 as a police officer, was receiving public assistance income for herself and her three daughters. She did not inform the NYPD that she was receiving public assistance, and she failed to stop receiving public assistance income when she became a police officer. After three years of both working as an NYPD patrol officer and receiving public assistance income, her ex-husband notified the IAB, which initiated an investigation. Her case was referred to the District Attorney's Office, but she was ultimately not charged. Instead, the NYPD terminated her employment (she was still on probation) for "failure to perform." Did Officer Jackson engage in police corruption, or is this simply a case of fraud perpetrated by someone who happened to be a police officer?

In addition to our previously identified case study officers, consider the case of Officer Pete Crenshaw:

CASE STUDY
Officer Crenshaw remained at the rank of patrol officer during his 14-year career with the NYPD, though he left the Patrol Division to work for a staff unit in his tenth year of service (staff units are non-field assignments, including headquarters, the police academy, crime laboratories, custody facilities, and internal affairs). After working for a particular staff unit for several years, his commanding officer discovered that Officer Crenshaw had been forging the names of other officers on case reports in order to close out the cases without having to conduct follow-up investigations. As a result of Officer Crenshaw's actions, his unit closed numerous cases (i.e., stopped investigating them) erroneously; and because of that, most of the cases were never properly adjudicated. Officer Crenshaw was found guilty at a departmental trial for "Conduct Unbecoming an Officer" and "Wrongful Performance of Duties." Crenshaw's actions violated department policy and meet the "misuse of authority" and "personal gain" (in that he did not have to put any work into active investigations) criteria for police corruption, but the officer did not break the law.

Given the limitations highlighted in these case studies, we constructed our own classification scheme of police misconduct. Though it is informed by prior research, the classification scheme was constructed in an effort to address some of the problems outlined above, and it was expanded based on our review of the officers in this study—and their misdeeds. Our scheme includes eight different forms of police misconduct. Each is reviewed below.

1. *Profit-motivated crimes*: All offenses, other than drug trafficking and whether on-duty or off-duty, in which the end or apparent goal of officers' wrongdoing was a profit.
2. *Off-duty crimes against persons*: All assaultive behavior, except for profit-motivated robberies, by off-duty officers.
3. *Off-duty public order crimes*: All offenses, other than drug trafficking or possession, against public order, including driving while intoxicated and disorderly conduct.
4. *Drugs*: Possession and sale of drugs, and related conspiracies, as well as failing or refusing to submit to departmental drug tests.
5. *On-duty abuse*: All offenses by on-duty officers involving use of excessive force, psychological abuse, or discrimination based on citizens' membership in a class (e.g., gender, race, ethnicity, sexual preference).
6. *Obstruction of justice*: Conspiracy, perjury, official misconduct, and all offenses in which the apparent goal is obstruction or subversion of judicial proceedings.
7. *Administrative/failure to perform*: Failure to abide by departmental regulations concerning attendance, performance, obedience, reporting, and other conduct not included in other offense types.
8. *Conduct-related probationary failures*: All misconduct-related terminations of probationary officers in which misconduct in types 1–7 is not specified, and excluding simple failure in training programs.

How Often: The Prevalence of Police Misconduct in the NYPD, 1975–1996

After reviewing all relevant documentation—most notably the weekly Personnel Orders—we identified a total of 1,543 officers who were separated from the department because of misconduct (from 1975 to 1996). To determine the prevalence or frequency of career-ending misconduct in the NYPD, it is necessary to figure out how many sworn personnel were employed by the department during that time: that is, 1,543 officers were fired out of how many? During the study period, the NYPD averaged well over 30,000 uniformed officers per year, ranging from 21,500 in the late 1970s to 38,000 at the end of the study. On June 30, 1975, the department employed more than 32,000 officers, and by the end of 1996, it had hired (or absorbed from the former Housing and Transit Authority police agencies) more than 45,000 additional officers. In all, the NYPD employed about 78,000 different individuals as police officers during the study period.

Thus, the population of 1,543 officers separated for cause represents about *2 percent* of all officers employed by the NYPD from 1975 to 1996. In simple terms, career-ending misconduct in the NYPD rarely occurred during the study period, as about one officer in every 50 left the department involuntarily. This key finding should be kept in mind when considering the rest of the study findings because, whether discussing differences in annual rates of separation over time or differences between study and control officers, we are examining only a very small percentage of the NYPD's total personnel complement.

Figure 4.1 is a sequence plot showing the annual rates (per 1,000 officers) of misconduct-related separations from 1975 to 1996. Clearly, although career-ending misconduct was an uncommon event, there was notable variation in its frequency throughout the study period. Importantly, the NYPD experienced a number of organizational changes during this time that may help to explain the patterns of misconduct. For example, between 1976 and 1980 there was a consistent decline in the annual rates of career-ending misconduct. During those years, most police officers identified as corrupt during the Knapp Commission era were finally separated from service after often-lengthy investigations. It was also during this time that, because of a citywide fiscal crisis, the NYPD laid off or

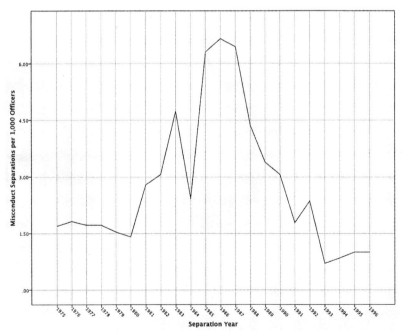

Figure 4.1. Annual Misconduct-Related Separations in the NYPD, 1975–1996

lost 11,000 officers, shrinking from 32,000 to 21,000 officers in just a few months.[1] Between 1974 and 1979, no police officers were hired into the NYPD. Organizational lore is that during this crisis period the NYPD was so short-staffed that it was extremely difficult to be separated from the department. In effect, the manpower shortage forced the department to become more tolerant of its officers' misdeeds.

During the 1980s, annual rates of misconduct began to rise, peaking in 1986 before starting to decline again. This increase coincides with the city's emergence from the fiscal crisis, when the NYPD hired new police officers very quickly and with minimal screening in order to bring the department back to pre-fiscal crisis strength.[2] Indeed, between November 1979 and July 1984, the department hired more than 12,000 police officers. The peak in 1986 is the same year of the so-called Buddy Boys misconduct scandal, when 38 officers were disciplined and/or separated all at once. In addition, in 1985 the NYPD initiated its drug testing program to screen all applicants and probationary police officers for drug use as part of the pre-employment selection process, during training at the police academy, and just prior to the expiration of the probationary period. Generally, a positive drug test resulted in automatic dismissal from the department.

Perhaps most important, however, the NYPD between 1983 and 1986 increasingly hired officers with prior arrest records. Indeed, this figure peaked in 1986, when 10 percent of all police recruits hired that year had arrest records. By 1989, only 1.7 percent of all officers hired had arrest records. The Buddy Boys misconduct scandal, drug testing, and hiring officers with arrest records in combination may explain much of the spike in career-ending misconduct that occurred during the mid-1980s. Interestingly, even as the department expanded its drug-testing program through the remainder of the 1980s and into the 1990s, annual rates of misconduct declined substantially—perhaps as a result of hiring fewer officers with prior arrest histories.

What: The Nature of Police Misconduct in the NYPD, 1975–1996

Table 4.1 shows the charge specifications against the population of separated officers, employing our misconduct classification scheme. The 1,543 separated officers generated a total of 2,465 specific charges (approximately 1.6 charges per officer). Nearly one-third of the charges involved administrative offenses—most typically for violation of departmental regulations concerning attendance, performance, obedience, and reporting. About one-fifth of the charge specifications against officers involved drugs

Table 4.1

Charge Specifications against the Study Officers: 1975–1996

Charge specifications	Percent (N)
Administrative/failure to perform	30.1 (742)
Drugs	19.0 (468)
Profit-motivated crime	15.7 (387)
Off-duty crime against persons	11.6 (286)
Obstruction of justice	10.8 (266)
Off-duty public order crimes	5.8 (144)
On-duty abuse	4.8 (119)
Conduct on probation	2.2 (53)
Total	100.0 (2,465)

Note: n = 1,543

—either sale, possession, or failure of a department drug test (or refusal to submit a specimen), and 16 percent involved profit-motivated crimes. Other less common offenses include off-duty crimes (crimes against persons, 12%; public order offenses, 6%), obstruction of justice, 11%, and conduct on probation, 2%).

On-Duty Abuse

Notably, only 119 officers ended their careers on charges that included on-duty abuse of authority (e.g., excessive force), representing 8 percent of separated officers (119 of 1,543) and one-tenth of 1 percent of officers employed during the study period (119 of 78,000). For readers familiar with media accounts of the Louima, Diallo, and Sean Bell cases (which occurred beyond the time range of the current study) and with allegations of widespread police abuse, this may seem to be an extremely small number. Three explanations may apply. The first is that, media accounts aside, the actual incidence of excessive force by New York City police is likely far smaller than many have been led to believe. There is considerable evidence in support of this contention. As Chevigny[3] and Domanick[4] suggest, the NYPD has long been noted for its attempts to control officers' discretion in use of force. The literature suggests that the department has been successful in these efforts. In 2001, the *Washington Post* ran a story examining fatal shooting rates (per 1,000 officers) among the ten largest U.S. cities during 1990–2000. The NYPD had an annual shooting rate of 0.7 per 1,000 officers, the lowest among the cities examined. Other research has suggested that, where this extreme type of police force is concerned, the NYPD has been at the bottom of the scale for the last generation.[5]

Further, Skolnick and Fyfe reported that the NYPD has been the subject of civil rights complaints to the U.S. Department of Justice much less often (again, per 1,000 officers) than any of 58 other municipal and county agencies that had been the subject of a federal study.[6]

The second explanation involves the difficulty of proving allegations of police abuse. This involves the dilemma of proving that officers, who are entitled by law and policy to great discretion in use of force, have crossed the barrier from reasonable to unreasonable force. This is a very difficult burden of proof either in criminal courts or in police administrative proceedings.[7] Consequently, findings of wrongdoing in either forum usually only occur when evidence is irrefutable. This was the case in the Rodney King incident, where the now-famous videotape contradicted the accused officers' claim that they had used only necessary and reasonable force. It was also true in the Abner Louima attack, in which the nature of the victim's injuries—a ruptured colon and bladder caused by forcible sodomy with a stick—could not be explained by any reasonable deployment of police force. In the absence of such objective evidence, however, accusations of brutality often devolve into swearing contests that cannot easily be resolved by finders of fact. Further, even if allegations of excessive force were sustained, it may be that during the study period the department tended to assign penalties that were less severe in nature than dismissal (e.g., 10-, 15-, or 30-day suspensions).

The last potential explanation for the low rate of on-duty abuse involves the degree of tolerance among colleagues regarding use of excessive force. At the start of our research—during the week immediately prior to the Louima atrocity—we conducted three focus groups, one each for patrol officers, patrol sergeants, and patrol precinct commanders. The consensus among all three groups was that, while there was virtually no tolerance among officers for profit-motivated misconduct on the part of their peers, there was a tendency for officers to be more forgiving where excessive force was concerned. All three groups told us that any officer who engaged in money corruption or drug-related misconduct could expect to be quickly reported to internal investigators. Where on-duty abuse was concerned, all three groups told us that there existed a regrettably higher degree of tolerance among the ranks. This became evident with events that began a few days later, when investigators found apparent collaboration by patrol officers to shield one or more of their colleagues from accountability in the Louima matter.[8] The response to this case included an internal investigation that won awards for its thoroughness and for penalizing those involved in concealing this episode (as well as policy changes mandating dismissal for false statements), and has no doubt affected this view among officers. Still, it should be no surprise to observers of the police that there may exist a greater degree of tolerance for excessive force, which can be treated as overzealousness, than for greed-induced money corruption. This increased tolerance certainly complicates the identification and investigation of on-duty abuse cases.

These identifications and the burden-of-proof problems with excessive force differentiate that form of deviance from profit-motivated misconduct. Since there are circumstances in which officers can reasonably employ force, the mere fact that an officer acted forcibly does not indicate wrongdoing. But there are no circumstances in which officers legitimately can accept cash or benefits other than their paychecks. Consequently, the mere proof that such an event has occurred establishes dismissible wrongdoing. Given the NYPD's historical problems with profit-motivated misconduct, this type of misdeed warrants additional consideration.

Profit-Motivated Misconduct

We present data on the nature of the profit-motivated charges against the study officers in table 4.2 using the NYPD's formal charge specification schema for such offenses. Bribe-taking, the solicitation or acceptance of money or some other benefit in return for abusing one's authority to wrongfully benefit another, is the single most frequent charge (18.6%),

Table 4.2

Profit-Motivated Charge Specifications against the Study Officers: 1975–1996

Charge specifications	Percent (N)
Bribe-taking	18.6 (72)
Grand larceny	17.1 (66)
Insurance fraud	8.6 (33)
Burglary	7.3 (28)
Petit larceny	7.3 (28)
Receiving property	3.9 (15)
Government fraud	3.1 (12)
Gratuities	2.6 (10)
Gambling	1.8 (7)
Illegal operation	1.8 (7)
Other (extortion/robbery/abusing official resources)	27.4 (106)
Total	100.0 (387)

Note: n = 1,543

followed closely by grand larceny, which is felony-level stealing (17.1%). Nearly 9 percent were charged with insurance fraud (8.6%), and 7 percent were charged with both burglary and misdemeanor-grade petit larcenies. Less common offenses include improperly appropriating property in their custody (3.9%); soliciting or receiving gratuities or accepting goods and services without paying for them (2.6%); defrauding the government (e.g., by welfare or food stamp fraud; 3.1%); operating or working for illegal gambling enterprises (1.8%); and engaging in such occupations as working in liquor-related businesses, which is forbidden to police officers by New York State law (1.8%). An additional 106 charges (27.4% of profit-motivated charges) involved profit-motivated offenses that were not specified on the NYPD's internal coding schema (e.g., extortion; abusing or misappropriating official resources; robbery). Thus, while the traditional police profit-motivated crime of bribery is the modal category among these offenses, it is clear that profit-motivated offenses not necessarily related to accused individuals' positions as police officers also occurred with some frequency (e.g., insurance fraud, petit larceny).

There is a variation in rates of on-duty abuse and profit-motivated corruption, as well as drug charges, over the study period, and these trends confirm much of the previous discussion. Clearly, the greatest variation over time occurs with drug charges, and the spikes in those offenses coincide with implementation (and expansion) of the department's drug testing program. Interestingly, the rates of profit-motivated misconduct and on-duty abuse (both much less common than drug charges) mirror one another with relatively flat rates through the 1970s and early 1980s, spikes throughout the rest of the 1980s, and a return to stable rates in the early 1990s. The earlier discussion of organizational changes helps to explain these rates (e.g., hiring of officers with prior arrest records). Notably, however, rates of both profit-motivated crime and on-duty abuse began to spike again near the end of the study period, likely a result of the misconduct scandal investigated by the Mollen Commission.

Who: Characteristics of Separated and Control Officers

A major focus of this book is to determine whether there are identifiable differences among officers in the NYPD who engaged in career-ending misconduct and those who served honorably. We had access to a wealth of information on both sets of officers, and as this section will demonstrate, there are a number of important and statistically significant differences among the separated and control officers.

Pre-Employment Personal History

Table 4.3 shows that the separated and control officers differed along a number of background, demographic, and personal history characteristics. Although the two groups were similar in terms of gender, there were several notable race/ethnicity differences. More than three-quarters of control officers were white (78.9%), compared to just 56.8 percent for the separated officers. This difference is explained almost exclusively by the greater percentage of black officers in the separated officer group (30.5% vs. 10.6% for the control group), though the modest difference in Hispanic officers is also statistically significant (11.9% vs. 9.6% for the control group). Separated officers tended to be younger than their matched peers (27.7% under the age of 22, compared to 24.4% for the control group), and they were less likely to have been born either in New York City or the state of New York (and they were more likely to reside in the city during their employment). Separated officers were twice as likely to be divorced or separated (4.3% vs. 2.1%), and they were more likely to have had children at the time of their appointment to the department (26.2% vs. 20.3%).

Consistent with prior research, the separated officer group had substantially higher rates of prior criminal involvement. Nearly one-quarter of separated officers had a prior arrest record (23.3%), compared to 13.9% of control officers. The difference in prior questionable conduct was evident across the type of offense as well. Separated officers had twice as many arrests for violent offenses (3.1% vs. 1.5%) and property offenses (7.6% vs. 3.6%), and three times as many public order arrests (14.6% vs. 5.0%). These differences were also observed in juvenile arrests, misdemeanor convictions, moving violations, and the likelihood of having immediate family members with arrest histories.

There is a presumption that individuals with prior military experience will be successful in police work, given the similarities in required personal characteristics (e.g., discipline, physical fitness), training, organizational philosophies, etc. This is often reflected in policies that grant extra credit or even absolute preference to veterans who compete for civil service jobs like policing. However, table 4.3 shows that military veteran officers were more likely than non-veterans to have been involuntarily separated from the NYPD (40.8% vs. 32.5%, respectively). With regard to branch of service, the figure shows that Navy and Air Force veterans are more frequently found among control officers, and that Marine Corps veterans are overrepresented among study officers.[9] The representation of Army veterans in both groups is virtually identical.

Table 4.3

Descriptive Comparison of Separated (Study) and Control Officers

Variable	Study group (n = 1,543)	Comparison group (n = 1,542)
Pre-Employment Personal History		
Female	15.1	13.4
White**	56.8	78.9
Black**	30.5	10.6
Hispanic*	11.9	9.6
Born in New York City*	75.8	80.3
Born elsewhere in New York State**	5.7	9.0
Born in other U.S. state**	11.3	5.3
Less than 22 years old at appointment*	27.7	24.4
Never married	64.0	66.7
Divorced/separated**	4.3	2.1
Children at appointment**	26.2	20.3
Resides outside New York City**	14.8	29.2
Prior Criminal History		
Arrested**	23.3	13.9
Violent crime arrests*	3.1	1.5
Property crime arrests**	7.6	3.6
Public order arrests**	14.6	5.0
JD/YO findings**	9.7	4.2
Misdemeanor convictions**	4.7	1.9
Moving violations*	60.8	55.2
Parking violations	28.9	30.8
Criminal/TAB summonses**	14.4	8.8
Members of immediate family arrested**	25.8	20.3
Military History		
Military service**	40.8	32.5
Among veterans only:		
Army veteran	43.6	44.7
Navy veteran**	13.7	20.9
Marine veteran**	23.5	15.2
Air Force veteran*	11.9	16.7
Private/PFC/corporal or seaman at discharge**	69.6	52.3
Sergeant/petty officer at discharge**	29.5	40.5
Officer at discharge**	0.9	7.1
Court martialed/disciplined**	21.4	14.4

*p < .05; **p < .001

There are also significant differences between the military ranks achieved by separated and control officers, and they are in the direction one might expect: separated officers generally achieved less success in the military than did their control group colleagues. For example, seven in ten of the study group veterans (69.6%) never rose above the rank of private, private first class, corporal, or seaman, compared to half (52.3%) of the control officers. Less than 1 percent of study group veterans achieved commissioned officer status in the military, while control officers accomplished this distinction eight times as frequently (7.1 percent). Perhaps not coincidentally, study group veterans were also more likely than control veterans to have been disciplined during their period of military service (21.4% vs. 14.4%).

Data on prior employment experiences also demonstrate quantifiable differences among the two groups of officers. Figure 4.2 shows that, however measured, unsatisfactory performance in prior jobs is associated

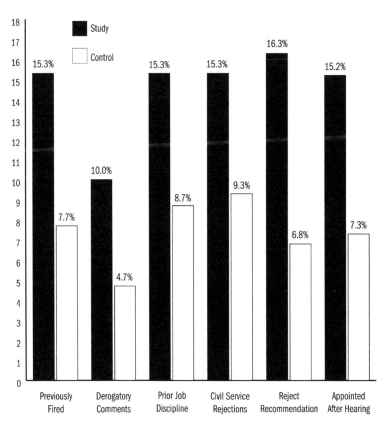

Figure 4.2. Separated and Control Officers' Prior Employment Experiences, 1975–1996

with career failure in the NYPD. Officers who previously had been fired from one or more jobs were found in the study group approximately twice as often as in the control group (15.3% vs. 7.7%), as were officers whose prior employers gave investigators derogatory information about them (10.0% vs. 4.7%). Separated officers also were more likely to have been disciplined in a prior job (15.3% vs. 8.7%), and more commonly received "do not hire" recommendations from the assigned NYPD personnel investigator (16.3% vs. 6.8%). These are all quite strong associations, producing chi square statistics significant below the 0.0001 level.

Separated and control officers also differed substantially with regard to their educational attainment. Figure 4.3 shows education level for both groups, demonstrating that officers who were separated from the department were less educated than their counterparts who served honorably.

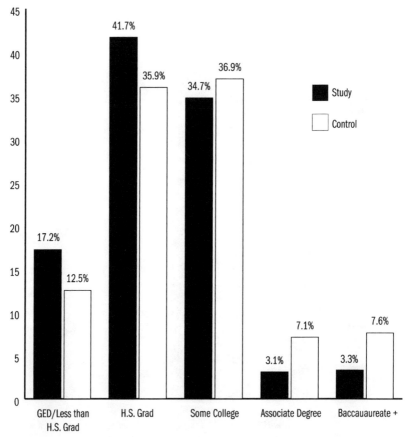

Figure 4.3. Separated and Control Officers' Educational Levels at Entry to the NYPD

Beginning at the left, the figure shows that 17.2 percent of the study officers and 12.5 percent of the control officers had a General Equivalency Diploma or had not finished high school when they became police officers (there were seven officers, all hired in the 1950s, who entered the department without having completed high school or a GED). Approximately 42 percent of the study officers and 35.9 percent of the control officers entered the department with high school diplomas and no further education. The figure's central bars show no real differences, with about 35 percent of each group having completed some college but not earning any type of degree. Substantial differences emerge in the college-degree-earning categories, with the control officers achieving Associate's or Baccalaureate degrees (7.1% and 7.6%, respectively) at more than twice the rate of study officers (3.1% and 3.3%). Certainly, the findings here ratify the NYPD's decision to require that new officers complete 60 college credits, approximately the equivalent of an associate degree, before entering the department.

Police Academy Performance

A number of studies have attempted to link performance in the police academy to various measures of later performance on the street.[10] The presumed relationship is that good performers in the academy will become good performers on the street (and vice versa for poor performers). For this study, various measures of academy performance are reported in figures 4.4 and 4.5, and in all cases, the control officers outperformed the separated officers.[11] Figure 4.4 summarizes the average performance in the academic and physical portions of academy training for both groups of officers, and seems to confirm conventional wisdom on the importance of police academy performance: the separated officers attained a mean academic average of 79.9 percent, compared to 85.8 percent for control officers. Separated officers also performed more poorly than their control counterparts on the physical aspects of academy training (mean scores of 83.4% and 88.3%, respectively). Both of these differences were statistically significant (p < .001).

Figure 4.5 shows that these trends are repeated (and statistically significant) in virtually all objective assessments of study and control officers' performance as recruits. Study officers were more likely than control officers to have reported sick with line of duty leaves (5.0% vs. 1.0%); to have reported sick with non–line of duty afflictions (30.7% vs. 19.8%); to have been late (21.7% vs. 19.5%); and to have received demerits (64.5% vs. 58.6%),

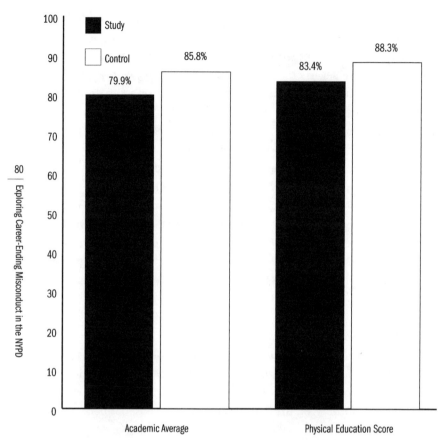

Figure 4.4. Study and Control Officers' Overal Police Academy Performance (Excluding Separated Probationers)

command disciplines (19.0% vs. 11.6%), and department charges (2.6% vs. 0.7%). Study officers were also more likely than control officers to have been held back from graduation with their class (3.9% vs. 1.2%).

Job Performance

Our original intent was to explore the relationship between career-ending misconduct and a host of measures of on-the-job performance, including citizen complaints, supervisory disciplinary actions, standard performance evaluations, line of duty civil litigation, line of duty injuries, line of duty vehicle accidents, chronically sick designations, and commendations. However, we encountered a number of problems with data collection that limited the exploration of job performance/career-ending misconduct relationships. First, performance evaluation data were spotty and inconsistent, due largely to variations in evaluation forms over time and across agencies that were merged to form the current NYPD (including the former Transit and Housing Authority police agencies). Second, the NYPD's automated systems were not nearly as developed as we originally anticipated. Thus, we found that we were unable to collect data on line of duty injuries, accidents, civil litigation, and chronic sick designations. As a result, the exploration of job performance among separated and control officers is limited to two dimensions: citizen complaints and the achievement of promotion or special assignments (presumably reserved for officers who distinguish themselves as high performers).

First, separated officers were significantly more likely to have generated citizen complaints than their counterparts who served honorably. Nearly 60

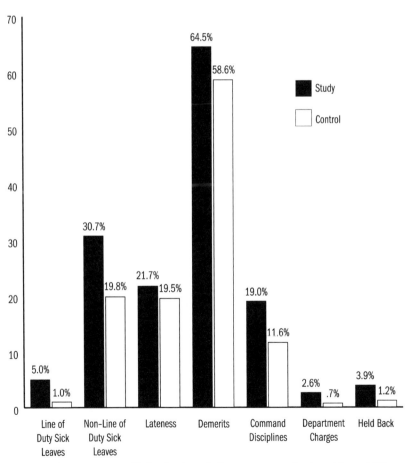

Figure 4.5. Other Measures of Police Academy Performance among Study and Control Officers

percent of separated officers (59.8%) had received at least one citizen complaint during their career with the NYPD, compared to less than half of control officers (47.9%). Overall, the study group generated an annual rate of 0.28 complaints per officer, compared to just 0.08 for control officers. When standardizing for time in the department, the differences in annual rates of complaints were still substantial, demonstrating fewer complaints for the control officers. Moreover, the group disparity grows as the complaint rate grows. For example, the study officer group was six times as likely as their control counterparts to generate an annual rate of more than one complaint per year—6.4 percent versus 0.8 percent.

Although we were unable to access key measures of officer performance such as standard supervisor evaluations or prior discipline, we do have a good proxy measure for those dimensions: advancement in the NYPD. Presumably, many of those officers who performed well at the job advanced through the ranks, either through re-assignment to specialized, administrative, or investigative units or through promotion to rank of sergeant or higher. Alternatively, low-performing officers would be much less likely to achieve these career advancements. It seems reasonable to suspect that job performance measured as career advancement (or lack thereof) would be tied to career-ending misconduct. Indeed, examination of the career histories of separated and control officers confirm these suspicions. Control officers were twice as likely as their separated counterparts to have achieved assignments in investigative (11.7% vs. 5.2%) and administrative units (13.1% vs. 3.2%), and they were nearly three times as likely to have been promoted to sergeant or above (8.2% vs. 3.2%). Clearly, among the study officers there were identifiable job performance precursors that hinted at the conduct that led to their career-ending separation.

Summary

How Often

How often do police officers engage in serious, career-ending misconduct? This appears to be a simple question. Yet, for years, a definitive answer has been elusive. This study offers clear evidence to answer this question. From 1975 to 1996, the NYPD employed approximately 78,000 officers, of which 1,543 were separated for career-ending misconduct (2%). That is, for every 100 individuals the NYPD vetted, selected, trained, equipped, and deployed to the streets of New York City, two of them engaged in serious misconduct resulting in the termination of their employment.

Our analyses of the "how often" question also uncovered some complexity to the prevalence of career-ending misconduct. Although rare, there was substantial variation in the rates of career-ending misconduct over time, and importantly, this variation appears to be explained, at least in part, by organizational factors and events. For example, the citywide fiscal crisis during the late 1970s led to the layoffs of thousands of police officers, and from 1974 to 1979 not a single new police officer joined the NYPD. We believe it is no coincidence that rates of career-ending misconduct dropped substantially during this same period. In effect, we contend that the department was forced to become more tolerant of officer misbehavior during this manpower crisis in order to maintain personnel deployment that was already stretched thin.[12] Moreover, the peak in career-ending misconduct in 1986 occurred after the department was able to return to full personnel strength and coincides both with the onset of the department's drug testing program and the increased hiring of officers with prior arrest histories. In short, although career-ending misconduct was rare, the NYPD's ability to rid itself of deviant officers was, at times, constrained by other outside (and inside) factors.

What

A logical follow-up to the "how often" question relates to the types of illicit activities that officers engage in. In simple terms, what did officers do to get fired? A wide range of activities led to officers' dismissal from the NYPD. Nearly one-third were separated for administrative violations such as attendance or obedience problems. For example, several officers were dismissed for "Failing to Respond to a Radio Run," which involved them accepting the call, but then radioing in a false disposition. Approximately one-fifth of officers were separated for drug offenses, including possession and sale, as well as failures and refusals associated with the department's drug testing program. An additional 18 percent were fired for various forms of misdeeds that occurred while the officers were off-duty.

We focused our attention on two specific forms of misconduct that are especially relevant for both the NYPD specifically and policing more generally. The first was on-duty abuse, or excessive physical force. Given media portrayals of police use of force and recent NYPD cases (Louima, Diallo, and Bell), it is perhaps surprising that just 119 officers were separated for on-duty abuse. We offered a number of explanations for this finding (e.g., the NYPD's historically infrequent use of force, and the difficulty of proving excessive force claims), but the important takeaway message is that excessive force leading to separation from the department was exceedingly rare in the NYPD. Our second point of emphasis was profit-motivated

crime, given the NYPD's longstanding problems with this form of misconduct (e.g., Knapp Commission) and problems with classifying misdeeds
traditionally thought of as "corruption." Indeed, our review of activities
classified as profit-motivated crime illustrated that much of the conduct
meets the traditional criteria associated with corruption; that it involves
use of the officer's formal authority, and that the activity is intended for
personal gain. For example, about one-fifth of profit-motivated crime involved cases of bribery—one of the classic forms of "corruption." Here are
a few examples of "classic corruption" committed by study officers:

1. Officers who attempted to bribe witnesses in an effort to protect their
   criminal enterprises (e.g., gambling, drugs, and/or prostitution rings).
2. Officers who were offered and accepted bribes in exchange for not arresting people engaged in vice activities (gambling and prostitution)
   and drug dealing.
3. Officers who demanded bribes (i.e., "shake downs") from drug dealers,
   prostitutes, gamblers, and weapons traffickers in exchange for not arresting (and in some cases, offering to protect) them.
4. Officers who attempted to bribe other officers in order to protect vice
   and drug ring enterprises with which they were associated.

Despite these examples, a substantial portion of profit-motivated crime
cases had little, if anything, to do with the individual's status as a police
officer. For example, there were numerous cases of insurance and welfare
fraud, most of which were brought to the attention of IAD by an offending
officer's disgruntled significant other.

Who

The "who" question is very simple: are officers who get fired for misconduct notably different from other officers, in terms of background and
personal characteristics, as well as training and departmental performance measures? Our analyses in this chapter uncovered a number of important distinguishing characteristics among the separated and control
officers. Compared to their counterparts who served honorably, separated
officers were:

- more likely to be minority (especially black);
- younger;
- more likely to be divorced/separated with children;

- less educated;
- more likely to have prior criminal histories;
- more likely to have poor prior employment experiences;
- more likely to experience departmental resistance toward their hiring;
- more likely to have served in the military (especially the Marines);
- more likely to have performed poorly in the Police Academy;
- more likely to have performed poorly once on the job (more citizen complaints and less advancement).

These findings are very illustrative and telling, but they do not offer a complete picture. For example, not all officers with prior poor employment experiences engaged in career-ending misconduct. And not all college-educated officers served honorably. The next chapter tests whether these bivariate relationships "hold water" when controlling for other relevent factors.

Predicting Police Misconduct

How to Recognize the Bad Cops

Police scholars and public policymakers across generations have sought to identify reliable indicators of police misconduct. The reasons for this are straightforward: officers who engage in misconduct—corruption, brutality, discrimination, and lesser forms of illegal and/or improper behavior—jeopardize the department's reputation and standing with the community; they undermine the department's performance on multiple levels (from fighting crime to protecting constitutional rights); they open up the department to costly civil litigation; and they cause harm to individual citizens. Unfortunately, researchers have offered little definitive evidence to help police departments identify who is likely to engage in misconduct—and just as important, who is not.

Research examining correlates of police misconduct, described in detail in chapter 2, has been characterized by an emphasis on both organizational/departmental factors and individual officer characteristics. Research findings on the correlates of police misconduct at the individual level have been largely mixed and often ambiguous. Some researchers, for example, have examined links between personality[1] and static[2] characteristics and police brutality; others have tested associations between personal history factors (e.g., prior employment and military experience, previous arrests, and substance abuse) and general forms of misconduct;[3] while a few have investigated the effects of education on citizen complaints.[4] As McManus[5] noted, since police officers have long been chosen from a pool of people whose characteristics and backgrounds have been largely homogenous, literature on the relationships between individual characteristics and deviance remains very limited due to a lack of variability among samples. More recent work has confirmed these observations.[6]

Research on police organizations generally has produced more reliable results, perhaps because organizational opportunity structures for misconduct are less idiosyncratic than the behaviors of individuals who might seek to exploit them. Skolnick and Fyfe[7] have argued that police agency administrators are often responsible for creating organizations that are tolerant of violence among officers as a way of maintaining street-level order and respect for authority.[8] As such, officers who work in police agencies characterized by a so-called siege mentality[9] may engage in excessive force and other forms of abuse with the implicit protection and perhaps even encouragement of departmental management. Other research has identified discrete cycles of "scandal and reform,"[10] arguing that variations over time in corruption controls and the vigor with which agencies investigate allegations of misconduct are largely responsible for variations in organizational misbehavior, primarily in the form of organized corruption.[11]

Nevertheless, the mixed results from this research, coupled with definitional inconsistencies, data access problems, and a weak theoretical foundation described in earlier chapters, has severely limited our ability to draw sound conclusions about the individual characteristics of officers that are associated with misconduct. As a result, one of the primary objectives of this study was to explore individual-level correlates of career-ending misconduct using advanced multivariate techniques (binary and multinomial logistic regression, and chi-squared automatic interaction detection, known as CHAID). The considerable size and scope of this study, in addition to unfettered access to all available police data on the study participants, represents a unique opportunity to compare and contrast the study officers to their matched counterparts who served honorably, and to identify risk and protective factors associated with career-ending misconduct. Several key differences were identified in the previous chapter; here we test those differences using multivariate analyses.

Description of Multivariate Techniques

We employed three separate multivariate techniques to determine whether the differences highlighted in chapter 4 would hold when controlling for other relevant factors. Before conducting the multivariate analyses, however, we employed a series of data reduction techniques to protect against excessive multi-collinearity, to reduce the number of variables in the models, and to identify discrete dimensions of officers' background and personal characteristics. Specifically, the authors used principal component analysis (PCA) as a data reduction technique in three categories of variables: criminal history, work history, and social conditions.

The first PCA extracted three components from the model with all criminal history variables: a *traditional criminal history* dimension composed of violent, property, and misdemeanor crimes, as well as juvenile delinquency findings; a *public order* dimension composed of public order arrests and misdemeanor convictions; and a *vehicle code violation* dimension composed of traffic and parking summons and driver's license suspensions. Two dimensions were extracted for prior work history. The first dimension reflects *employment disciplinary problems*, including number of jobs from which officer was fired, job-related disciplinary actions, and derogatory comments by prior employers. The second may be regarded as an *employment reliability* construct, composed of the number of workers' compensation claims, jobs held, and 30-day (or longer) periods of unemployment. Last, two dimensions emerged from the social conditions PCA: a *conventional family* construct composed of marital status and number of children; and a *"second start"* dimension characterized by active enrollment in school and divorce or separation. In all, these seven dimensions successfully reduced the large number of variables available for the multivariate analysis, thereby reducing potential multi-collinearity problems and simplifying the predictive models. See the appendix for a table describing these findings.

Once these dimensions of criminal and work history, and social conditions were constructed, we employed binary logistic regression in an attempt to distinguish study officers from comparison officers along the specified set of predictor variables. Logistic regression was selected because it clarifies the relationships between the outcome measure (career-ending misconduct) and each characteristic of interest while controlling for the other factors. In effect, the analysis isolates the independent impact of each characteristic on the outcome measure. The logistic regression analysis used all 3,085 cases and set the dependent variable to predict the study group (i.e., comparison officer = 0; study officer = 1).[12]

In addition, chapter 4 highlighted that study officers engaged in a wide range of illegal and improper activities that led to their separation. Given this variation, we sought to explore whether predictors may actually vary by the type of misconduct. For example, are predictors of serious criminal misconduct the same or different from predictors of administrative misconduct? To examine the extent to which the multivariate relationships were stable across dimensions of misconduct, we conducted a follow-up multinomial logistic regression analysis, specifying the following four-category dependent variable:

1. Comparison officer (n = 1,543): Not separated for misconduct.
2. Crime and serious misconduct (n = 581): Police crime, profit-motivated serious misconduct, perjury, criminal abuse of authority, other criminal events.
3. Administrative misconduct (n = 430): Serious violations of departmental rules (e.g., associating with "known" criminal offenders, moon-

lighting as bouncers at nightclubs, making false statements in reports, insubordination), violations of more general rules and procedures (e.g., failure to maintain professional standards, failure to reside within the proper geographic distance of the city, failure to take action or taking improper action).

4. Drug test failures/refusals (n = 420): Positive results on both random drug tests and drug tests that were "for cause" (e.g., for officers moving into special assignments or promotion, or officers whose behavior deviated sufficiently from "normal"). This category also includes officers who refused to take either random or for-cause drug tests (resulting in automatic dismissal).[13]

Last, we also used CHAID to identify predictors of misconduct. Like logistic regression, CHAID predicts the probability of an event occurring, but the method relies on different assumptions and properties, and uses segmentation modeling to accomplish the task. CHAID divides a population into "increasingly homogenous" segments that differ based on the dependent variable; in this case, career-ending misconduct.[14] The resulting segments are mutually exclusive and exhaustive, and as the analysis proceeds, the best predictor is selected among a particular subgroup of cases based on chi-square analysis. CHAID offers a number of advantages over traditional regression, including its ability to examine predictors for different subsets of data, and its user-friendly visual representation; and when used in combination with regression, it allows for a triangulation of findings using multiple techniques.[15]

Findings

Logistic Regression Analysis

We ran a logistic regression model to identify both risk and protective factors for career-ending misconduct. The model was internally reliable with high predictive utility, as it correctly classified 86.5 percent of the cases (with Cox and Snell R^2 and Nagelkerke R^2 values of .55 and .73, respectively). We have included the full results of the analysis in the appendix (table A.2) for the interested reader. While controlling for all other covariates, the strongest risk factors for misconduct were black officer, an average of one or more complaints per year of service, and working in inspector precincts at time of incident leading to separation. Specifically, black officers were 3.27 times more likely than white officers to be dismissed for job-related misconduct (see odds ratio column in appendix, table A.2); officers receiving an average of one or more complaints per year were 3.03 times more likely to be dismissed for misconduct compared to officers who received between zero and one complaint per year; and officers assigned to inspector precincts were 2.48 times more likely than officers assigned to staff units to be dismissed for occupational misconduct. This last finding is likely a result of differential exposure and opportunity associated with patrol assignments. Officers working patrol in busy sectors have more opportunity to engage in misconduct than officers assigned to administrative and staff units.[16] Greater rates of misconduct were also found for officers working in deputy inspector precincts (2.26 times higher), captain precincts (2.02 times higher), and police academy/field training units (1.83 times higher).

Other significant risk factors for police misconduct include the following: Latino officers were 2.0 times more likely than white officers to be dismissed; officers with prior criminal histories were 1.22 times more likely to be dismissed than officers with no prior criminal history; and more specifically, officers with public order prior offenses in their past were 1.78 times more likely to be dismissed (than officers with no priors). Last, problems in both dimensions of prior employment put officers at greater risk of experiencing career-ending termination. Officers with prior employment disciplinary problems and officers with prior employment reliability problems were 1.37 times and 1.16 times more likely to be dismissed, respectively, compared to officers with no prior employment issues.

To provide some context for these observed risk factors, recall Mitchell Tisdale, introduced in chapter 1. This was the officer who attempted to evade responsibility for the fact that his gun killed the woman in the hotel room. As previously reported, Tisdale came to the NYPD with three juvenile delinquency convictions; he had experienced disciplinary trouble in two of his previous jobs; and he received two citizen complaints as a police officer leading up to the incident in the hotel room. Most contemporary police chiefs would likely conclude that Tisdale's separation from the NYPD for misconduct should be no surprise: he engaged in misbehaviors before getting hired, he engaged in misbehaviors once on the job, and he was finally jammed up for a fairly serious breach of official protocols (indeed, his actions might have been criminal, had a DA pursued the case). An interesting question to ponder, though one that we cannot answer, is: If the NYPD had sustained the two citizen complaints and fired Tisdale before the hotel room shooting, would he have been carrying a gun with him on the night his female companion shot herself? (Recall he was carrying his duty pistol.)

As noted, the logistic regression model also identified several factors that appeared to protect officers against police misconduct. The strongest of these were increased years on the job, having an Associate's or a Bachelor's degree at time of appointment, and increased age at appointment. For example, officers with an Associate's degree were 3.5 times less likely than officers with a high school education to experience career-ending misconduct.[17] Officers with a Bachelor's degree were 2.2 times less likely than their high-school-educated colleagues to be dismissed for misconduct. In addition, officers whose fathers had served as NYPD officers were significantly less likely (albeit, not substantially) than other officers to be dismissed for misconduct; and not surprisingly, officers who achieved a supervisory rank (i.e., got promoted) were much less likely than line officers to be dismissed for misconduct (1.89 times, or 89% less likely).

It is noteworthy that, although the logistic model identified a large set of robust correlates of misconduct, not every officer forced to leave the job scored high (if at all) on the important risk factors. For example, while Mitchell Tisdale represents a template for predicting career-ending misconduct, Paul Barrett appears to have become jammed up against all odds. Recall that Barrett came from a stable family, had no arrests prior to coming to the NYPD; and indeed, he served in the police cadet corps through high school, which, presumably would have given the department increased opportunities to vet him for the job. Moreover, Barrett had no disciplinary or reliability problems in his jobs prior to entering the police academy, and he was promoted to detective in his tenth year of service.

It was in that eleventh year of service when Paul Barrett and his partner stole the U.S. savings bonds from the deceased person's apartment and tried to cash them. It is quite possible that Barrett had been engaging in profit-motivated misconduct throughout his career without ever having been caught. It is also possible that once he made detective, an assignment that offers a great deal of professional autonomy and little administrative supervision, he began engaging in misconduct on the basis of opportunities that he never had while working patrol. Whatever his offending patterns, he serves largely as a false negative when it comes to predicting police misconduct on the basis of known risk and protective factors. In chapter 7 we consider the extent to which several well-known criminological theories might also apply to police misconduct, which might help to explain cases such as Paul Barrett.

Finally, in addition to identifying risk and protective factors, we also identified factors statistically *un*associated with career-ending misconduct. Among these were military service, officer sex, prior police service, and background investigator recommendation. The regression model also included a variable indicating the mayor at time of officer's separation, in an effort to control for the effects of social and political climates in New York City, but this variable was also non-significant. Finally, assignment to a Proactive Investigation Unit was not associated with career-ending misconduct. In sum, when controlling for other factors, the strongest predictors of career-ending misconduct were:

- officer was black or Hispanic;
- citizen complaints;
- working in inspector precincts;
- having a criminal history;
- having prior employment problems.

The protective factors against career-ending misconduct include:

- increased years on the job;
- having an Associate's or Bachelor's degree at time of appointment;
- increased age at appointment;
- officers whose fathers had served in the NYPD;
- achieving a supervisory rank.

Multinomial Logistic Regression Analysis

In an effort to determine whether the predictors identified above might vary by type of misconduct, we created a more specific misconduct dependent variable that included one reference category (comparison officers) and three substantive categories: crime/serious misconduct, administrative violations, drug test failures/refusals. A multinomial logistic regression model was then estimated to observe any possible significant differences among types of career-ending misconduct. The model diagnostics show a high degree of internal reliability (83.3 percent of the total cases were correctly classified. See appendix, table A.3 for the full results).

The findings largely confirm those from the previous analyses, with a few important exceptions. As with the binary logistic model, the multinomial model shows that previous arrests, previous employment problems (disciplinary troubles and unreliability), citizen complaints, working in a street-level assignment (i.e., a patrol precinct), and being a non-white officer were risk factors for criminal misconduct. Having a Bachelor's degree and making rank were protective factors. These findings largely held for administrative violations, except that race was not significantly (or substantively) related to administrative violations. In addition, education and making rank were not protective factors for administrative violations.

For drug failures, disciplinary problems at prior jobs (but not unreliability), citizen complaints, patrol assignments (but not drug enforcement assignments), and prior arrests were significant, as well as race: both black and Hispanic officers were more likely, respectively, to be dismissed or otherwise separated for drug test failures/refusals as compared to white officers. Again, these findings largely confirm those for the criminal/serious misconduct outcome. In addition, a Bachelor's degree (but no other levels of education) was a significant protective factor against drug test failures/refusals.

Across all categories of misconduct, problematic work histories, criminal justice contacts, and duty assignments where officers most likely interacted with the public on a regular basis were important risk factors. For the types of misconduct that were largely outside the department's control—i.e., criminal misconduct (which generally gets referred to the District Attorney), and drug test failures (for which the department leaves itself virtually no discretion—drug test failures automatically lead to dismissal), black and Latino officers were more likely to be separated for them. For administrative violations, where the department can largely choose how to investigate and respond, race was not a factor.

CHAID Analysis

The third set of analyses we employed, called CHAID, allows us to examine predictors of misconduct in a different way. We have included the tables here in the chapter to simplify and guide the discussion of findings. The start of the segmentation tree begins with the "root node" (or node 0) reflecting all 3,085 cases and a base misconduct rate of 49.98 percent (i.e., half of the sample engaged in career-ending misconduct). Using chi square, the first split is made based on officer race, resulting in three additional cells for white/Asian officers, black officers, and Hispanic officers. The split was made based on their rates of misconduct: 41.95 percent for white/Asian officers (n = 2,131), 74.44 percent for black officers (n = 626); and 55.49 percent for Hispanic officers (n = 328). As indicated in the earlier analyses, officer race is clearly a very strong predictor of career-ending misconduct. The initial split allows us to create three separate CHAID trees by officer race, and permits comparison of risk and protective factors among white/Asian, black, and Hispanic officers.

The first CHAID tree includes all 328 Hispanic officers only. The first split for Hispanic officers is made based on whether the NYPD background investigator (BI) made a recommendation against hiring the officer. There are 84 Hispanic officers who had such a recommendation, and 86.9 percent of them experienced career-ending misconduct. In the other cell (BI recommended hiring), we see the remaining 244 Hispanic officers, of which 44.67 percent experienced career-ending misconduct. In simple terms, the background investigator recommendation for or against hiring produces a 40 percent swing in misconduct rates among Hispanic officers, and isolates a group of Hispanic officers with a very high dismissal rate (n = 84). Additional splits are made off of the larger cell of officers who had "hire" recommendations. The first split is made off of this cell according to the "second start" dimension (enrolled in school, separated/divorced; see PCA discussion earlier). Note that the characteristics of lower cells on the CHAID tree are cumulative—that is, you interpret the results by reading back up the tree. So at this level, Hispanic officers who had their investigator recommend hiring *and* who experienced a second start (n = 81; with a misconduct rate of 29.63%) posted much lower misconduct rates than those who had their investigator recommend hiring but who did not have a second start (n = 163 with a misconduct rate of 52.15%). A final split is made off of the "no second start" cell based on education level, with college education serving as a protective factor. All of these officers had recommendations to hire from their background investigator, and they had no second start. But those with college education (at least some) were significantly less likely to be dismissed for misconduct (41.67% compared to 63.29% for those with a high school diploma or less).

There are four categories of Hispanic officers identified in the analysis, including their group characteristics, misconduct rate (from 86.9% to 29.6%), and size (table 5.1). For example, at the top we see the high-risk group of Hispanic officers who had their background investigator recommend against hiring (86.9% separated); compared to just 29.6 percent of Hispanic officers who had a positive hiring recommendation and who experienced a second start during their employment.

The second CHAID tree represents the 626 black officers only. The root node indicates that three-quarters of the black officers in the study experienced career-ending misconduct (74.4%). The initial split is made based on the public order criminal history dimension—that is, whether the officers had public order arrests or misdemeanor convictions prior to joining the NYPD (see earlier PCA discussion). Among the 197 black officers who did have this type of prior criminal history, 93.4 percent experienced career-ending misconduct. Of the remaining 429 black officers, 65.7 percent were dismissed for misconduct. Additional splits are made off of this cell based on getting a promotion (protective factor), the second start dimension (protective factor), the employment reliability dimension (risk factor), and gender (female, protective factor)—each separating a group of black officers with either low or high rates of misconduct. Table 5.1 (bottom) shows the six identified categories of black officers, including their characteristics, misconduct rates, and cell size. The group of black officers with the lowest misconduct rate—just 39.3 percent (recall the 74.4% base rate)—are those with no public order prior criminal history who were promoted (group #6; n = 56). Two groups of black officers posted misconduct rates of just over 50 percent—still low given the group base rate: females with no public order criminal history, who were not promoted and had no second start, but had good prior employment reliability (42 officers with a misconduct rate of 52.4%); officers with no public order criminal history and no promotion, but who experienced a second start (117 officers with

Table 5.1

Summary of CHAID Analysis End Groups: Hispanic and Black Officers

Hispanic officer characteristics	Separated (%)	N
1. Investigator against hiring	86.9	84
2. Investigator for hiring; no second start; high school diploma	63.3	79
3. Investigator for hiring; no second start; college education	41.7	84
4. Investigator for hiring; second start	29.6	81
Total	55.5	328

Black officer characteristics	Separated (%)	N
1. Public order priors	93.4	197
2. No public order priors; no promotion; no second start; unreliable prior employment	87.9	91
3. No public order priors; no promotion; no second start; reliable prior employment; male	75.6	123
4. No public order priors; no promotion; second start	55.6	117
5. No public order priors; no promotion; no second start; reliable prior employment; female	52.4	42
6. No public order priors; received promotion	39.3	56
Total	74.4	626

a misconduct rate of 55.6%). At the other end we see two high-risk groups of black officers: 197 officers who had a prior public order criminal history (93.4% separated); and 91 who had no public order criminal history, no promotion, no second start, but were unreliable in prior employment (87.9% separated).

The third CHAID analysis is for the remaining 2,131 white officers, with a base misconduct rate of 41.95 percent. The initial split for white officers is made based on whether the officer experienced a change in marital status during his/her time on the job, with getting married serving as a very strong protective factor: 656 white officers got married and only 23.17 percent experienced career-ending misconduct. The other 1,475 white officers had no change in marital status or got divorced, and they posted a misconduct rate twice as high as their counterparts who got married (50.31%). Among the officers who got married, additional splits are made based on public order criminal history (risk factor), background investigator recommended against hiring (risk factor), and college education (protective factor). Among the 1,475 officers who did not get married, the next split is made based on officer rank at time of separation, with promotion serving as a protective factor: among the 248 white officers who did not get married but were promoted, just 26.21 percent experienced career-ending misconduct. The other categories of rank had much higher misconduct rates (probationary officers, 60.76%, and patrol officers, 51.98%). Additional splits are made off of these rank categories based on public order criminal history (risk factor), juvenile criminal history (risk factor), background investigator recommended against hiring (risk factor), was married at appointment (protective factor), less than 22 years old at appointment (risk factor), and had driver's license suspended in the past (risk factor).

Table 5.2 summarizes the 15 identified categories of white officers, with career-ending misconduct rates ranging from 3.5 percent (for 85 officers who got married, had no public order criminal history, BI recommended hiring, and who had a college degree) to 90.4 percent (for 114 officers who did not get married, the BI recommended against hiring, and who were still probationary officers when they left the department). Generally speaking, the 15 groups can be separated into low-, medium-, and high-risk categories (keep in mind the 41.9% base rate). Groups 11–15 have low rates of career-ending misconduct—from 3.5 percent to 25.6 percent—and are characterized by several protective factors: getting married during time on the job, being married at appointment, college education, and getting promoted. Alternatively, groups 1–5 have high rates of misconduct

Table 5.2

Summary of CHAID Analysis End Groups: White Officers

White Officer Characteristics	Separated (%)	N
1. No marital change/divorce; probationary officer; BI recommended against hiring	90.4	114
2. No marital change/divorce; patrol officer; no juvenile history; no public order history; less than 22 years old at appointment; license suspended	75.6	41
3. No marital change/divorce; patrol officer; juvenile history	75.0	96
4. No marital change/divorce; patrol officer; no juvenile history; public order history	70.5	61
5. No marital change/divorce; probationary officer; BI recommended hiring; not married at appointment	59.4	246
6. Got married; public order history	50.8	67
7. No marital change/divorce; patrol officer; no juvenile history; no public order history; less than 22 years old at appointment; driver's license not suspended	50.5	214
8. No marital change/divorce; promoted; public order history	45.9	74
9. Got married; no public order history; BI recommended against hiring	44.4	45
10. No change in marital/divorce; patrol officer; no juvenile history; no public order history; older than 22 at appointment	41.2	369
11. No change in marital/divorce; probationary officer; BI recommended hiring; married at appointment	25.6	86
12. Got married; no public order history; BI recommended hiring; high school education only (or less)	24.7	267
13. No marital change/divorce; promoted; no public order history	17.8	174
14. Got married; no public order history; BI recommended hiring; some college (no degree)	15.1	192
15. Got married; no public order history; BI recommended hiring; college degree	3.5	85
Total	41.9	2,131

—from 90.4 percent to 59.4 percent—and are characterized by several risk factors: background investigator recommended against hiring, juvenile or public order criminal history, driver's license suspended in the past, and under 22 years old at appointment.[18] Groups 6–10 have misconduct rates near the group average (41.9%) and have a mix of risk and protective factors. For example, group 8 consists of 74 officers who did not get married and had public order criminal histories, but who also got promoted (misconduct rate of 45.9%).

In sum, though officer race served as the initial split—with minority officers experiencing higher misconduct rates than white officers—the rest of the CHAID analysis shows substantial consistency in risk and protective factors across officer race. That is, the characteristics that served as risk factors for black and Hispanic officers—such as prior criminal history and background investigator recommended against hiring—also tended to serve as risk factors for white officers. The same can also be said for protective factors, such as college education, the second start dimension, and promotion. We explore the implications of these findings in greater detail below.

In this chapter, we sought to test whether the differences identified between study and comparison officers in chapter 4 held when controlling for other factors via multivariate techniques. There were a number of significant, identifiable differences between study and comparison officers that serve as risk and protective factors for police misconduct, and importantly, there was substantial consistency in both (1) predictors across forms of misconduct—with a few notable exceptions, and (2) across multivariate techniques.

Risk Factors of Misconduct

The most intriguing finding involves race and police misconduct. Although results showed that black officers were three times more likely to experience career-ending separation for serious misconduct and drug test failures than white officers, and officer race served as the initial split for CHAID, closer inspection of the data highlights several other dimensions to the race/misconduct relationship. Early on in the study period, all non-white officers (black, Hispanic, and Asian) were significantly more likely than white officers to be involuntarily separated for misconduct. Over the years studied, this disparity faded for Hispanic and Asian officers so that their separation rates became virtually indistinguishable from the separation rate for white officers. Over the same period, the black officers' rate decreased, but remained much higher than those for other groups. Taken together, these trends suggest that as the NYPD has become more diverse, it has become better behaved. This is strong evidence in support of efforts to make police agencies closely representative of the populations they serve.

Yet the persistence of the finding for black officers remains troubling. There are many possible, and not mutually exclusive, explanations for this race finding. Martin[19] studied the entry of women into the Washington, DC Metropolitan Police Department, observing that they proceeded through a stage that Everett C. Hughes[20] described as "tokenism." During this stage, members of new and growing groups are closely monitored by peers and supervisors in dominant groups, and are treated with suspicion and a high degree of skepticism about their ability to perform. During this period, each token is treated as a representative of his or her group, and minor acts of misconduct may be seen as symptoms of more serious problems. Under such close scrutiny, accounts of misconduct or substandard performance by individual tokens become "organizational lore," and are attributed to the entire group represented by the token. As token groups grow, however, dominants become more accustomed to, and less suspicious of, the presence and performance of tokens. With additional growth, the new group loses its token status, gains organizational power and prestige, and begins to exert real influence on both the formal and informal cultures of the organization. At the same time, the solidarity of the dominant group breaks down, as the new groups assimilate into it.

The data suggest that these processes have been at work in the NYPD. Hispanic and Asian officers, as well as women, have grown significantly in NYPD ranks over the last generation and have advanced rapidly through the ranks into positions of influence. The representation of Hispanics as a percentage of the NYPD grew by 75.4 percent between 1986 and 1996. Similarly, Asians increased by 127.5 percent and women increased by 65.2 percent. Black representation increased by only 28.8 percent (almost entirely as a result of the merger of the more heavily black Housing and Transit Police Departments into the NYPD), while white representation decreased by 13.4 percent. In addition, the number of Hispanic supervisory and command personnel increased by 68.5 percent (from 257 to 433) between 1990 (the first year for which such data are available) and 1996, while Asian supervisors and commanders increased by 293.8 percent (16 to 63) and women supervisors and commanders increased by 111.4 percent (from 229 to 484). Black supervisors increased by only 18.9 percent (from 333 to 396) during the same period.

By these measures, therefore, Hispanic, Asian, and women officers appear to have become well-integrated into the NYPD during the period under study. Their increased representation in the department may have allowed them to shed their status as tokens, and their movement up the ranks may have increased their influence over the department's culture and processes while also reducing their exposure to the risks of discipline faced by those at the department's lowest level. These processes of integration during the period studied may have left black officers as the department's "out-group," with separation rates unlike those of the other racial groups or females.

Although we cannot fully rule out the possibility of a race effect in individual cases, it appears unlikely that this disparity is the result of any quantifiable discrimination in the disposition of cases. Recall that the multinomial logistic model found that, while black and Hispanic officers were more likely than whites to be separated for serious/criminal misconduct and drug test failures/refusals, they were no more likely than whites to be separated for administrative misconduct. For criminal or other serious misconduct, as well as for drug test failures or refusing to take drug tests, the NYPD has little discretion over how to respond: As per departmental policy (and in some cases, state law), such officers are generally dismissed from employment. The department has the *most* discretion over how to respond to administrative rule violations. If organizational responses to misconduct were racially biased, we would expect those biases to show in the area of administrative dismissals/separations—i.e., black officers would show high rates of dismissal for administrative violations. As the multinomial findings show, however, race was not significantly (or substantially) associated with administrative misconduct.

Still, in this context as in others, race may be a proxy for some unmeasured factors, such as an urban experience, and/or vigorous resistance to being charged. For example, Fyfe[21] found that, although black officers were more likely than white officers to be subjects of departmental discipline, they were also more likely than white officers to force a departmental trial in the adjudication of their disciplinary cases. Officers who forced departmental trials—regardless of racial background—were significantly more likely than officers who pled guilty (charges and specifications being equal) to be dismissed upon a guilty case disposition. Thus, some percentage of black officers' greater likelihood of "engaging" in career-ending misconduct in the present study may be an artifact of the way they often proceed through the disciplinary process.

Several other pre-employment factors emerged as significant predictors of misconduct, including prior criminal history, documented problems in prior jobs, and red flags in the background investigation (leading to recommendations against hiring). Prior research has also documented these risk factors.[22] Thus, the results from this study suggest that departments' resource commitment to front-end screening is well founded. By screening out those with prior arrests and prior employment problems, and by following background investigator recommendations, departments can significantly reduce the likelihood of hiring future "bad cops."

Protective Factors of Police Misconduct

Among protective factors, the findings highlight the importance of promotion, education, and training. Evidence supporting college education requirements for police has been mixed, but results here clearly show that officers with Associate's or Bachelor's degrees were less likely to be separated for misconduct (i.e., criminal and drug failures) as compared to less educated officers. Moreover, the education findings—as well as the finding linking citizen complaints to misconduct—have implications for the use of early intervention or warning systems, as poor performance in these measures can be included as factors that serve as potential red flags.[23] Walker also suggests that early intervention systems can "serve to identify and reward good performance,"[24] and education and early complaint history could serve as indicators in that capacity as well.

Also, a number of "social" characteristics emerged as significant risk or protective factors, including young age at appointment (risk), being married at time of appointment (protective), getting married while on the job (protective), and experiencing second start variables (e.g., going back to school; protective). These variables have important implications as well, particularly for efforts to apply criminological theory to the study of police officer misconduct. In chapter 7 we explore these issues in greater detail by examining the findings in the context of several prevailing theories of criminology, including strain, life course, social learning, and self-control.

Factors Unrelated to Police Misconduct

The analyses presented in this chapter also showed that a number of factors were unrelated to police misconduct, including officer sex, military service, and prior police service. Perhaps the most interesting of these non-significant findings involves assignment to Proactive Investigation. Many police scholars, dating back to August Vollmer, have argued that assignments in narcotics (historically) and street crimes units (more recently) are problematic due to the aggressive nature of such assignments, the deployment strategies of departments that utilize these assignments (especially street crimes units), and the degree to which officers (particularly in narcotics) must form close professional relationships with informants, drug dealers, and users under circumstances where supervision and accountability potential are very low.

There are a number of possible explanations for the non-significance of this variable. First, it may be that the misconduct of officers assigned to these units is more likely to go undetected or unreported because of the illegal activities of those who are victimized (e.g., drug dealers typically do not file complaints against officers who steal cash or drugs). Moreover, the misconduct may have been reported, but complaints were less likely to be sustained because of the credibility of the victims. Finally, the officers assigned to the aggressive but elite narcotics and street crimes units may have represented the best collection of officers serving in the NYPD over the study period. It may be that the extra layer of screening, the fact that candidates often must first establish track records of excellence in other assignments, and the competition to gain entrance to such coveted assignments, creates a sampling bias that favors the best qualified officers. In fact, we cannot rule out any of these possible explanations.

Reconciling Individual and Organizational Risk

Although this chapter focused exclusively on risk and protective factors of career-ending misconduct among individual officers, it is important to note that such correlates are not devoid of context. The rates of career-ending misconduct varied considerably in the NYPD over the study period; and although our data do not allow us to conduct rigorous tests that might definitively explain such variations, we discussed those variations within historic and organizational contexts, offering some explanations for why the patterns may have changed over time. We now consider the interactions that might exist between individual correlates of police misconduct and organizational policies that might exacerbate the effects of those correlates. As the findings in this chapter have shown, when NYPD officers came to the job with arrest records and prior employment problems, they were at much higher risk of engaging in career-ending misconduct than were other officers. Although the meaning and etiological bases of these findings are discussed in greater detail in chapter 7 ("Can Criminology Help Us Understand Police Misconduct?"), at their most basic level, these findings confirm what many criminologists already know: The best predictors of *future* antisocial behaviors are *prior* antisocial behaviors.

As we reported in chapter 4, the average annual rate of career-ending misconduct in the NYPD was approximately 2 per 1000 officers. As figure 4.1 in chapter 4 demonstrated, however, this was a moving average: At the end of the Knapp era, when the NYPD laid off or by attrition lost 11,000 police officers, the annual rates of career-ending misconduct declined substantially. In the early 1980s, once the city emerged from the fiscal crisis and the NYPD was again allowed to hire, it brought on the thousands of new and returning sworn personnel very quickly and (as our data showed) with minimal screening in many cases. During these initial years of the hiring spree, the rates of career-ending misconduct increased considerably, such that by the mid- to late 1980s the annual rate of career-ending misconduct was 5.2 officers per 1,000 (up from about 1.2 officers per 1,000 in 1976). During the hiring spree, which lasted from about 1980 through 1985, fully 10 percent of all persons hired as police officers into the NYPD had moderate to serious criminal histories.

Colin Ahearne, introduced in chapter 1, serves as the archetype of what went wrong during the hiring spree. Ahearne grew up around drug dealers, participated in the drug trade himself, and by the time he was hired into the NYPD, he had already been arrested twice for possession of drugs. Moreover, while he was working as an NYPD officer, he maintained his close ties with "known drug dealers." During the data collection process for the original *Bad Cops* study, when the first author of this volume initially located Ahearne's personnel file, he discovered that most of the file was incomplete. In fact, as with many other *jammed up* officers of this era, we obtained most of our pre-employment information about Ahearne from court documents that were the result of the misconduct that led to his separation from the department. It seems clear that had background investigators completed Ahearne's pre-employment screening before hiring him, he never would have worn the uniform of the NYPD. Indeed, concentrating officers with known risk factors of misconduct (e.g., criminal histories) into a police organization seems problematic for a least two reasons. First, they are at high risk of engaging in misconduct on their own; and second, their antisocial behaviors (or tendencies) may be "contagious" to other officers who may be at risk (but perhaps without the overt risk factors) of engaging in misconduct if they are somehow socialized to do so. It seems clear that police department recruitment and screening strategies can contribute to, or protect against, the systemic manifestation of organizational misconduct.

Conclusion

The findings here confirm much of the conventional wisdom about the police. Young officers who entered the police service with no post-secondary education, records of prior criminality and prior poor employment, who did not advance in the police organization, who worked in busy patrol assignments, and who accumulated histories of complaints were more likely than others to have ended their careers in involuntary separation. Conversely, relatively well-educated officers with minimal or no criminal histories, perhaps including a family history in a police organization, who were married or got married while on the job, and who advanced through departmental ranks, were much less likely to engage in career-ending misconduct.

Perhaps the most valuable policy implications of the findings from this chapter relate to departmental screening processes. Due to the low visibility of police work, the unique opportunities for misconduct presented to police officers, and the conflict that often exists between the police and the public in certain communities, it seems clear that police departments should continue to invest heavily in pre-employment screening processes that exclude people who have demonstrated records of criminal involvement and employee disciplinary problems. Moreover, the present findings also suggest the importance of screening *in* or identifying potential police officers whose presence in police organizations may have the effect of making them better behaved. In this regard, racial/ethnic diversity and post-secondary educational requirements stand out as important factors related to lower rates of career-ending misconduct.

The Department, the City, and Police Misconduct

Looking beyond the Bad Cop

By the time this book is published, over 14 years will have elapsed from the point at which our misconduct data ended in 1996. Since that time, both the department and the city have experienced major events and changes, such as a substantial crime drop,[1] the attacks of September 11, and the increased emphasis on "zero-tolerance" policing strategies.[2] In addition, the department was the subject of at least three high-profile abuse scandals—those involving Abner Louima, Amadou Diallo, and Patrick Dorismond—which considerably challenged the legitimacy of the NYPD among members of its public.[3] This passage of time and the intervening events allow us now to reflect on the meaning of the present findings and to place them in the context of how the city and department have continued to evolve. The present chapter, therefore, has three goals. First, it summarizes several studies of policing and police misconduct at the precinct level that the first author published between 2002 and 2006 for the purposes of highlighting the importance of "place" and "time" when examining police misconduct and other behaviors. Next, it attempts to contextualize those findings by interpreting them in relation to the changing ecological structure of the city during the study period. Finally, it proposes that if we are to move beyond defining acceptable policing practices as the absence (or control) of police misconduct, then it is time to supplement typical examinations of the "bad" cop with those that try to define and encourage "good" policing. In this sense, the present chapter begins to argue that "good" and "bad" policing are not at opposite ends of the same continuum. Rather, they are two distinct constructs that probably should be measured along different continuums.

CHAPTER SIX

Reviewing Macro-Level Findings

After leaving the NYPD as a researcher in 1999, the first author published a series of academic articles examining different dimensions of policing and police misconduct from the view of patrol precincts. Collectively, such examinations demonstrate how the social ecology of police officers' working environments can influence patterns of policing and police misconduct, as well as organizational decisions about deployment and so-called aggressive policing practices. Additionally, given that all of these examinations were longitudinal, they allow us to draw conclusions about the importance of considering not just *where* the policing took place, but also *when* it took place.

In the first of these papers, titled "The Social Ecology of Police Misconduct," Kane[4] combined the NYPD data with U.S. Census Bureau data to examine the extent to which the structural antecedents of social disorganization and racial conflict predicted patterns of police misconduct within and between police precincts from 1975 to 1996. The study found that structural disadvantage,[5] population mobility,[6] and changes in percent Latino population were associated with misconduct within precincts over time. These findings indicated that systemic resource deprivation, barriers to upward mobility, and political marginalization (all indicated by structural disadvantage), as well as continuously disrupted local social networks (indicated by population mobility), likely made it difficult for residents to invoke the conventional mechanisms of police accountability in response to incidents of officer misconduct. That increases in percent Latino predicted increased misconduct (even while changes in percent black population did not) also suggested something about the unwillingness and/or inability of largely Latino communities to report and/ or effectively protect against police misconduct. In addition, all of these macro-indicators suggest an overall opportunity structure for police misconduct that likely did not exist in more economically and socially stable communities.

In the public health arena, researchers have identified a phenomenon known as the "double jeopardy" hypothesis.[7] According to the hypothesis, when the structural features of *place* create systemic opportunities for disease pathologies to develop and sustain, and when the same structural features make it difficult or impossible for community residents to harness external government and/or health resources to respond to the disease, the community is victimized twice—partly due to opportunities and partly due to a lack of political clout to combat the opportunities. To a great extent, Kane's[8] study represents an application of the double jeopardy hypothesis to the social ecology of police misconduct with one important addition. First, structural disadvantage likely created opportunity structures for police misconduct, and at the same time made it difficult or impossible for community members to effectively hold the police accountable for misconduct. Next, these were the same communities that experienced the highest crime rates in the city over the study period, which theoretically suggests a need for the increased deployment of crime control resources to these communities. Thus, and as Kane[9] notes, "the very communities likely in need of the most protection *by* the police due to conditions favoring deviance also may be in need of the greatest protection *from* the police due to conditions favoring deviance" (emphasis added).

While Kane's[10] examination identified structural predictors of police misconduct, a follow-up study—which also used the NYPD data and covered the years 1975–1996—placed misconduct on the other side of the causal chain and demonstrated the consequences of misconduct in structurally disadvantaged police precincts. In this paper, titled, "Compromised Police Legitimacy as a Predictor of Violent Crime in Structurally Disadvantaged Communities," Kane[11] integrated the social disorganization, procedural justice, and "Code of the Street"[12] perspectives to test the extent to which incidences of police misconduct predicted increases in violent crime across three community contexts: those that were structurally stable, those that were highly structurally disadvantaged, and those that were extremely structurally disadvantaged.[13]

Kane[14] built on the work of researchers who have argued that as structural disadvantage increases in communities, perceptions of both social and legal marginalization also tend to increase,[15] perceptions of police misconduct increase,[16] and feelings of fairness and procedural justice often *decrease*.[17] For these reasons, Kane[18] theorized that incidents of police misconduct (and overly aggressive arrest practices) should have differential effects on patterns of police legitimacy across different community contexts. Specifically, Kane hypothesized that in communities characterized by high and/or extreme levels of structural disadvantage, police misconduct would lead to increases in violent crime to the extent that the misconduct led residents to stop reporting crimes and giving police information about crimes that were in the making.

Consistent with expectations, Kane[19] found that in communities characterized by low disadvantage (i.e., structurally stable), incidents of police misconduct had no significant effect on patterns of violent crime. In communities characterized by "high disadvantage," police misconduct had a significant and moderate positive effect on violent crime; and in communities characterized by "extreme disadvantage," police misconduct had a significant and strong effect on violence. Indeed, in extremely disadvantaged communities, incidents of police misconduct were the strongest predictor of violent crimes. Kane's study supports other urban sociological inquiries that have demonstrated that communities characterized by racially concentrated economic resource deprivation—and the consequent social isolation of such places—respond differently than others to added environmental stressors or pressures.[20] That is, the effects of police misconduct were amplified in communities characterized by extreme structural disadvantage.

Collectively, Kane's 2002 and 2005 studies[21] demonstrate the importance of considering both the causes and consequences of police misconduct, especially in resource-deprived communities. In particular, by moving police misconduct to the right side of the equation (i.e., as an independent variable), Kane[22] begins to show some of the unintended consequences of "bad" policing. It is one thing, for example, to demonstrate that the structural features of communities can predict variations in police misconduct (as did Kane[23]); it is quite another to show that incidents of misconduct can actually lead to the very behaviors that police departments are presumably working to prevent—i.e., violent crime. Indeed, Kane[24] highlights an implicit purpose of the present chapter: to move beyond police misconduct as the standard for "bad" policing.

For example, in addition to testing the effects of police misconduct, Kane[25] also tested the extent to which "overly" aggressive policing predicted increases in violent crime in structurally disadvantaged communities. Testing the theory that too many arrests in politically marginalized communities could lead to increased violent crime due to compromised police legitimacy, Kane[26] created a measure of "police responsiveness" that captured both "under-" and "over-" policing. To do this, Kane calculated the mean number of violent crime arrests per officer in structurally stable communities, and used this as the baseline against which to compare levels of arrests in disadvantaged communities (adjusting for violent crime complaints). Thus, the values of the "police responsiveness" variable were not simply the actual numbers of arrests in police precincts. They were deviations from the mean of violent crime arrests in the least disadvantaged communities.

As Kane[27] reports, 71 percent of the low disadvantaged communities were "adequately" policed; 53 percent of the highly disadvantaged communities were adequately policed; and only 17 percent of the extremely disadvantaged communities were adequately policed. Moreover, none of the extremely disadvantaged communities were under-policed. Kane reports that in both "highly" and "extremely" disadvantaged communities, over-policing predicted increases in violent crime to virtually the same extent as police misconduct. It is difficult to overstate the importance of this finding: while controlling for police misconduct, patterns of over-policing led to increased violent crime; while controlling for over-policing, misconduct predicted increases in violent crime. Thus, for substantive purposes, over-policing and police misconduct likely measure two dimensions of the same construct—"bad" policing—and they appear to lead to the same problematic outcomes in structurally disadvantaged communities.

In the next study that used the NYPD macro-level data, titled "On the Limits of Social Control: Structural Deterrence and the Policing of 'Suppressible' Crimes," Kane[28] tested the extent to which violent crime arrests within and across police precincts might reduce subsequent violent crime.[29] Kane borrowed from the social psychological literature on environmental hazards to argue that within police precincts, officer arrests might represent local hazards (or risk events), which may disrupt the offending patterns in ways that could reduce crime. Kane also tested the extent to which this macro-deterrence argument was salient for both rational (e.g., burglary and robbery) and "heat of the moment" (e.g., aggravated assault) crimes. Consistent with theoretical expectations, Kane[30] found that increased arrest levels led to decreased rates of robbery and burglary but not aggravated assault. Moreover, the effects of arrest on burglary and robbery were curvilinear: as arrests increased, burglary and robbery decreased, but only to a point. Once a threshold of arrests was met, burglary and robbery both began to increase again, demonstrating the conditional effects of police coercion on crime rates.

A final study that used the NYPD data was Kane's (2003) work, "Social Control in the Metropolis: A Community-Level Examination of the Minority Group-Threat Hypothesis." This study might be considered substantively different from the others reviewed here because it did not examine variations in within-precinct behaviors, such as crime and misconduct, so much as it examined organizational behaviors conceived at the department level. Specifically, Kane[31] tested the extent to which changes in the minority populations of police precincts from 1975 to 1996 predicted changes in police deployment patterns in precincts over the same time period. Grounded in the conflict perspective, Kane[32] argued that as communities increased in their Latino and/or African American populations, the police department might respond by deploying either *more* or *fewer* officers to those communities, depending on whether the increases were viewed as "threatening" to the incumbent population.

Interestingly, Kane found that variations in the African American population over time had no significant effect on patterns of police deployment, while variations in the Latino population exerted moderate influence over deployment. Note that these findings held even when controlling for previous deployment, crime rates, and structural disadvantage. Findings for the Latino population, however, were nuanced: increases in Latino representation led to the deployment of more police officers, but only if the communities remained below a threshold of 25 percent Latino. Once communities became 25 percent or more Latino, the relationship between Latino representation and police deployment turned negative. Thus, for the Latino population in New York City, Kane[33] found support for the minority group threat hypothesis in communities that remained below 25 percent Latino. In communities that breached the 25 percent Latino threshold, Kane's findings found support for a variation of Liska and Chamlin's "benign neglect" hypothesis, which assumes that communities characterized by increasingly non-white residential populations often get less police attention than primarily white communities.[34]

It is interesting that both Kane's 2002 and 2003 studies[35] found that changes in the African American population had no significant effects on the outcomes of interest (i.e., police misconduct and deployment), while changes in the Latino population explained variations in both outcomes. To the extent that changes in the Latino population over time represented some indicator of both ethnic conflict (in terms of misconduct potential) and ethnic threat (in terms of police deployment), we might conclude that such variations meant something different than variations in the African American population in New York City. As Jackson[36] has noted, different minority/ethnic groups often trigger different threat responses at different periods of time even when studied in the same place. To better understand Kane's findings, it may be instructive to examine changes in the spatial distributions of the African American and Latino populations across and within police precincts over the study period.

Figures 6.1 and 6.2 are maps that show the spatial distribution of the African American population across police precincts of New York City for 1970 and 1980. The maps were created with ArcMap 9.2, and the categories were based on the Jenk's classification system, which minimizes within-group value ranges while maximizing distances between breaks in categories. As the data in figure 6.1 show, 15 (19.7%) police precincts contained between zero and 9.1 percent black population in 1970, and 29 (30.2%) precincts contained no more than 18 percent black population. Exactly half (38) of the police precincts contained between 18 and 37 percent black population in 1970, indicating that African Americans were reasonably well distributed across police precincts at this decennial

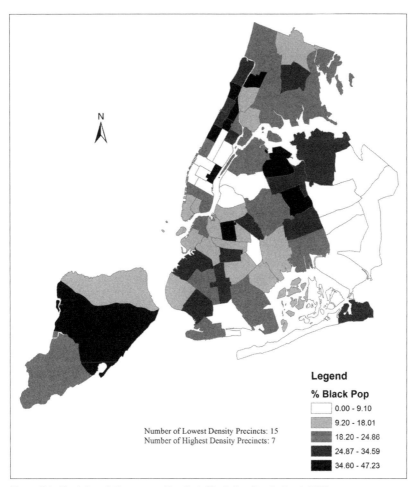

Figure 6.1. Black Population across New York City Police Precincts at 1970

measurement point. It is important to note that no police precinct was more than two-thirds African American in 1970 (seven precincts had from 37.39 to 59.27 percent black population).

By 1980, the spatial distribution of African Americans changed fairly dramatically across New York City. As the data in figure 6.2 show, by 1980, 23 police precincts contained fewer than 7 percent African American residents. Moreover, and whereas no police precincts in 1970 contained more than 59 percent African American residents, by 1980, 12 precincts contained between 55.5 and 94.8 percent African American residents. The evidence from these two temporal points is clear: between 1970 and 1980, the police precincts in which almost no (i.e., up to 8%) African Americans

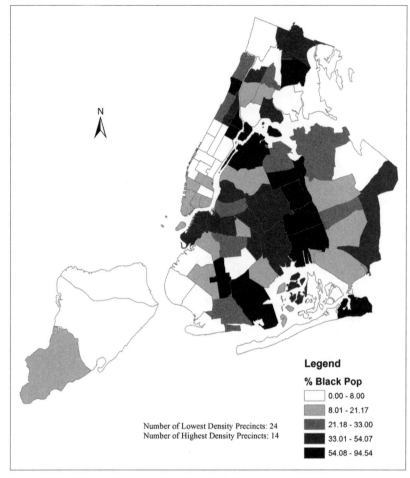

Figure 6.2. Black Population across New York City Police Precincts at 1980

lived almost tripled in number, while those at the highest end of the concentration distribution doubled. Even without estimating any formal tests of dissimilarity, figures 6.1 and 6.2 show that the black population between 1970 and 1980 across New York City police precincts became increasingly residentially segregated—even while census data (i.e., SF3 at 1970 and 1980) show that the city as a whole *lost* black residents over that time period. Data for 1990 (figure not shown) show virtually equivalent distributions as those from 1980. Clearly, the most rapid transition for the African American population during the study period occurred between 1970 and 1980, which is consistent with what researchers have found across U.S. metropolitan areas more generally during the same time period.[37]

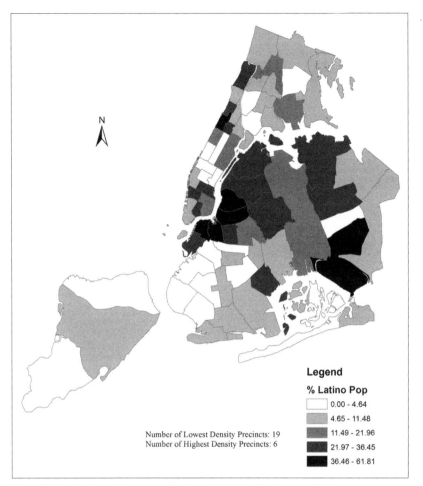

Number of Lowest Density Precincts: 19
Number of Highest Density Precincts: 6

Legend

% Latino Pop

	0.00 - 4.64
	4.65 - 11.48
	11.49 - 21.96
	21.97 - 36.45
	36.46 - 61.81

Figure 6.3. Latino Population across New York City Police Precincts at 1970

Figures 6.3 and 6.4 are maps that show the spatial distributions of the Latino population across police precincts of New York City from 1970 to 1980. As the data in figure 6.3 show, 19 police precincts contained between zero and approximately 5 percent Latino residents in 1970. Only six police precincts contained the highest concentration, ranging from roughly 36 to 62 percent Latino population. It is noteworthy that 45 (59.2%) police precincts in 1970 contained no more than 11.5 percent Latino population; and among the other precincts, Latinos were reasonably well represented. By 1980, 22 (28.95%) police precincts contained between zero and 9.21 percent Latino population. The remaining 54 precincts contained between 9.21 percent and 72.5 percent Latino population. Between 1970 and 1980,

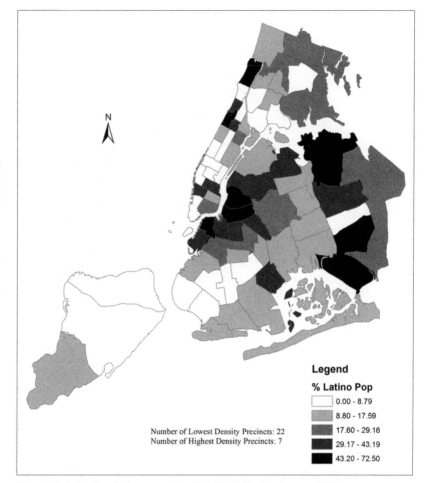

Figure 6.4. Latino Population across New York City Police Precincts at 1980

most police precincts in New York City gained in Latino representation, while the city as a whole saw a substantial increase in Latino residents. Moreover, New York City as a whole continued to increase substantially in its population of Latino residents from 1980 to 1990, though the spatial distribution of Latinos did not change substantively between those two time periods.

Overall, the data in figures 6.1 through 6.4, as well as census data from the SF3 files more generally, show two major results: (1) whereas the spatial distribution of Latino residents across New York City police precincts remained fairly consistent over time, the spatial distribution of African Americans became increasingly concentrated in a smaller number of precincts; and (2) these observed distributions and redistributions occurred while New York City (overall) lost black residents from 1970 to 1990, and gained substantially in Latino residents. A salient question for present purposes is, *how might these population shifts have influenced policing and police misconduct over the study period?*

Recall that Kane's 2002 and 2003 studies[38] found that, while controlling for other relevant factors, increased Latino representation in police precincts predicted increases in police misconduct and (at least to a point) increases in police deployment. Moreover, recall that changes in percent African American population were not associated with either outcome. It may be that over the study period, and from a "conflict" perspective, as the African American population shrank in total numbers and became increasingly concentrated into a smaller number of spatial areas, they may have been seen as "under control" by the power elites of New York City. It may also be the case that, despite the declining overall representation and the increased concentration into a smaller number of precincts, the African American population may have gained enough political clout over the study period to resist potential threat responses by those who historically held power in New York City.

Conversely, it may be that the rapid increase of Latino residents into New York City between 1970 and 1990 may have triggered threat responses by those who controlled formal social control resources and who may have felt encroached upon by a new and increasingly visible "subordinate" group. Under such circumstances, Latino residents would have relatively little political clout to alter deployment patterns; and, as noted previously, they might have found it difficult to hold police officers accountable for misconduct that occurred in their communities.

The results of Kane's precinct-level examinations accomplished at least three ends.[39] First, they demonstrate the importance of considering the "place" when examining patterns of both police misconduct and coercion. Second, they identify some of the social costs of "legitimate" policing behaviors (e.g., arrests). Although the majority of this book thus far has focused on bad policing in terms of officers getting "jammed up" for misconduct, Kane's macro-level work illustrates the justification for expanding the discussion of bad policing so that it includes legal applications of coercion that may have deleterious consequences. For example, in 1999, four NYPD plainclothes officers fired 41 shots at Amadou Diallo (hitting him 19 times and killing him) in a case of mistaken identity. This case may be viewed as part of the overall social cost of aggressive policing strategies. In

2000, Patrick Dorismond was shot and killed by an undercover NYPD narcotics officer in an altercation that began when one of the officers tried to buy drugs from Dorismond (drugs that Dorismond did not have)—representing another example of the social costs of aggressive policing.

Finally, it is important to consider not only *where* research takes place, but also *when* it takes place. All of Kane's macro-level studies argued that when conducting social ecological research on policing, longitudinal designs are important so that they may capture the influence of change itself on policing outcomes. As Sampson[40] argued, community-level studies (generally) should be guided by a "dynamic contextualism," which considers specific events to be a function of where they occur temporally and spatially. Sampson wrote:

> [B]ecause society changes, people in different cohorts age in different ways . . . Aging and social change do not always work in tandem, however, giving rise to the principle of asynchrony. In particular, because society is composed of successive cohorts of individuals who are themselves aging in new ways, they continually force their predecessors into and out of roles in the social structure.[41]

Sampson's observations are particularly salient to Kane's research because changes in precinct-level composition, political culture, public policy, and enforcement orientations may have influenced police misconduct and other outcomes over the study period. Had the present study been conducted at a different time period, findings about race, ethnicity, and police misconduct may have been very different, as different groups may have posed different levels of threat to New York City power elites at different temporal periods.

Moving Beyond "Bad" Cops

This book largely has been concerned with "bad" policing. Although important, there are major limitations both conceptually and in terms of policy and practice with focusing almost exclusively on police misconduct: while such a study might inform applications of criminological theory to police deviance (see chapter 7), and might have implications for police accountability processes, it does very little to actually improve police practices and strategies. Indeed, and as indicated earlier, we argue here that "bad" policing and "good" policing are two separate constructs that are likely measured along two different continuums.

For example, our research has shown that officers who receive citizen complaints are more likely than others to engage in career-ending misconduct. Our research has also shown that the officers who work in patrol precincts as compared to those who work "indoors" are more likely to engage in career-ending misconduct. These findings, however, can be somewhat misleading. Let us suppose that there are two police officers of equivalent qualifications and life history profiles who are assigned to the same anti-crime unit. Officer A makes three arrests per week for serious crimes, is generally well regarded by the community he serves; but he receives a few citizen complaints related to arrests he has made over the course of any given one-year period. Suppose the complaints are lodged by people he has arrested, and/or by bystanders in the street interested in "jamming up" the officer. Even if we can assume that the complaints are dismissed or adjudicated as unfounded, Officer A likely will be identified by an Early Warning System as potentially problematic, and he would likely be subjected to elevated scrutiny by the disciplinary command staff.

In contrast to Officer A, suppose that Officer B makes just four arrests per month, is virtually unknown to the residents of the community he polices, and receives no citizen complaints over any given one-year period. Moreover, let us assume that because Officer B is virtually unknown to the residents in his beat area, he develops no informants and receives no information about crimes in the making or other potential criminal enterprises. By most police department standards, Officer B may be practicing "good" policing: he stays just productive enough (in terms of arrest activity) to satisfy his line supervisor, while staying under the radar of the disciplinary command staff. But is Officer B practicing "good" policing, or is he practicing what Klockars[42] called "legal minimalism"—i.e., doing just enough work to maintain decent scores on performance evaluations but not enough work to risk getting into trouble?

The relationship, however, between aggressive policing, good policing, and police misconduct can be difficult to understand. As Kane[43] has shown, too much "aggressive" policing can backfire, particularly in the most vulnerable communities;[44] but at the same time, too little policing can undermine police legitimacy. Moreover, both aggressive and restrained policing can be viewed as either "good" or "bad" policing, depending on the contexts in which they are examined.

Historically, community policing programs were designed as police-community partnerships, which de-emphasized arrests as a primary policing function. Recently, however, so-called broken-windows policing strategies have been increasingly integrated with community policing efforts and are almost exclusively based on the assumption that more arrests mean less crime (see chapter 3 for a discussion of this style of policing in New York City). This trend highlights the gap that seems to exist between the costs and benefits of police tactics and strategies. To the extent that the most vulnerable communities respond to arrest-based policing strategies by showing increases in the very crimes that police are trying to prevent, then surely current crime reduction assumptions are at least somewhat misunderstood. This is not to say that the police have no role in structurally disadvantaged communities. Most likely, the police have an *important* role in such places, but they may be failing to recognize their own potentials. A number of years ago, the first author worked on a study of crime and community policing in the public housing projects of North Philadelphia.[45] During structured interviews, the research team asked community residents about their perceptions of crime and policing in their neighborhood. The most common response given by public housing residents was, "We need more protection, but we don't want the police." The implication was clear: when it came to policing, more of the same was not welcomed.

A Risky Enterprise

The role of the police and the nature of police work virtually assure that the profession is a risky enterprise. It is risky from a personal safety standpoint, and it is risky from a liability standpoint. "Aggressive" police officers are often those who strive to protect life in the community while vigorously seeking out opportunities to arrest those engaging in alleged criminal activities. Such officers place themselves at risk both in terms of personal safety and liability. Importantly, liability does not have to be measured only in terms of civil litigation. It also can be measured in terms of organizational inconvenience: aggressive police officers who work in settings characterized by high disorder and high crime might make lots of arrests, but they also might receive higher than average numbers of citizen complaints. The latter may cause such officers to be viewed as inconvenient to the organization because of the number of disciplinary reviews they trigger and because of the public scrutiny they may bring to the department. At the same time, however, aggressive police officers also may be the ones who have the trust of the community. They may be the officers who maintain several informants; and they may gain a great deal of information about crimes in the making that might be prevented. Officers practicing legal minimalism probably do not become organizational inconveniences, but they also do virtually nothing to further the goals of either the organization or "the job." In simple terms, legal minimalists are not bad cops who get "jammed up," but they certainly are not good cops either. In chapter 8 we will explore these issues further and introduce a conceptual model that helps begin the process of defining good policing, which is not necessarily linked to the reduction of police misconduct. The next chapter, however, returns to a discussion of causes, and seeks to apply criminological theory to the question of why officers engage in deviant behavior.

Explaining Bad Behavior

Can Criminology Help Us Understand Police Misconduct?

With Jonathon A. Cooper and Tasha Kunzi

Now we switch gears and return to the larger issue of trying to explain the causes of police misconduct.[1] This question brings us back to some important issues raised earlier. The first involves efforts to understand police misconduct from a criminological perspective. The utility of criminological theories for informing criminal justice policy and practice has received a good deal of attention recently. For example, Klofas, Hipple, and McGarrell,[2] in their discussion of the success of Project Safe Neighborhood projects, explained how theories of crime can be utilized to better understand problem-oriented solutions to crime problems. Similarly, Barlow and Decker edited a volume explicitly integrating criminological theories in public policy.[3] To date, however, there have been surprisingly few applications of criminological theory to the study of police misconduct.

The second issue involves the limitations of prevailing definitions of police misconduct. One of the issues that has limited conventional definitions—and the one most relevant for this discussion—involves the difficulty in differentiating between forms of police misconduct that are administrative deviance but not criminal (e.g., failure to take a drug test or moonlighting), and forms that are inherently criminal (i.e., the act would be considered a crime regardless of whether it was committed by a police officer or a citizen—such as burglary). For our purposes here, we set aside this distinction and argue that police misconduct, whether criminal or not, represents deviant behavior; that is, behavior that deviates from expected standards of behavior within the police department. As such, misconduct may be explained by theories of deviant behavior. Importantly, there are several criminological theories that are interested not only in explaining criminal activity, but also in understanding deviant behavior in all its variety.

In this chapter we seek to address both of these issues by focusing on the deviant nature of police misconduct and exploring the applicability of criminological theory to the problem. First, however, we review the limited research that has sought to explain police misconduct from a theoretical perspective, most notably the rotten apple perspective, noble cause, and Kappeler et al.'s anthropological framework. These theoretical perspectives tend to focus on the individual officer (e.g., psychological) or are organizational in nature. Then, with this prior work as context, we introduce four widely accepted criminological theories—strain, social learning, self-control, and life course[4]—and consider each as a framework for understanding police misconduct. For each theory, we offer a brief discussion of its basic assumptions, as well as how it can be useful for the study of police misconduct. We then use each theory as a context within which to interpret the primary findings from the *Jammed Up* study. Each section concludes with a discussion of "next steps" for the continued and better use of the theory in future police misconduct research. As a word of caution, the reader should bear in mind that this is not a specific test of any of the aforementioned theories. Rather, it is an exploratory venture to raise questions and facilitate discussion about the utility of the theories for understanding misdeeds committed by police officers. Given the paucity in prior efforts to draw on criminological theory and the potential for expanding our understanding of police misconduct, we think it is a worthy exploratory endeavor.

Prior Research Using Theoretical Frameworks to Understand Police Misconduct

With the exception of a few recent studies, most identified research on police misconduct has been conducted in the absence of rigorous theoretical frameworks.[5] This may be in part due to the aforementioned difficulty of fully and clearly defining police misconduct. Although a substantial portion of police misconduct represents administrative non-conformity (similar to non-conformity in other occupational settings) and fits well with organizational theories, a great deal of police misconduct is illegal and may be explained by traditional criminological or justice theories. Regardless, there have been few efforts to apply theoretical frameworks to the problem of police misconduct.

The Rotten Apple Theory

The rotten apple theory has traditionally been posited by police chiefs when an officer or group of officers engages in police misconduct. The rotten apple theory holds that the officers were involved in their deviant behavior on their own without the knowledge or support of their co-workers and superiors. Continuing the analogy, those officers represent a few bad or "rotten" apples in the barrel, and once they are removed, the problem is fixed—the rest of the apples and the barrel are fine. This theory offers the simplest and easiest-to-fix interpretation of police misconduct, which likely explains its attractiveness for police chiefs: by simply removing the "rotten apples" the problem is solved, and the organization is spared any real responsibility or scrutiny for the problem.

The Knapp Commission took the rotten apple theory to task in its final report, arguing that it had, in many ways, prevented significant reforms from being implemented to address police misconduct. In the commission's view, the rotten apple theory had re-inforced the code of silence and prevented motivated police managers from starting reforms to correct the problem.[6] Others have argued that the rotten apple theory fails to explain why some departments have long histories of police misconduct, or why it has become so pervasive in other departments.[7] Also, the theory does not explain why an honest officer becomes corrupt. Back to the analogy, if there is nothing wrong with the barrel or the rest of the apples in the barrel, the theory would suggest that the apple was rotten beforehand. That is, the problem officer was susceptible to misconduct, or entered policing specifically to engage in misconduct, and the department's selection process failed to screen him/her out. Yet, research on police recruits indicates that they are not morally inferior and, in fact, that they most often enter policing for altruistic and practical reasons.[8]

In addition, there are many cases of police misconduct over the past two decades which seem to defy the rotten apple explanation. As we know, the Knapp Commission found corruption in the NYPD to be "widespread . . . with a strikingly standardized pattern."[9] Throughout the 1980s and 1990s, the Washington, DC Metropolitan Police Department (DCMPD) suffered through a host of scandals involving corruption, mismanagement, deception, political cover-ups, and abuse of authority.[10] In their discussion of the Rodney King beating, Skolnick and Fyfe persuasively argued:

> The dominance of this philosophy—in Chief Gates' terms, the "LAPD mentality"—suggests that King's beating could scarcely have been an isolated incident. More than 20 LAPD officers witnessed King's beating, which continued for nearly two minutes. Those who administered it assumed that their fellow officers would not report the misconduct and were prepared to lie on their behalf. In this respect, police brutality is like police corruption— there may be some rotten apples, but usually the barrel itself is rotten. Two cops can go berserk, but twenty cops embody a subculture of policing.[11]

Yet, there have been recent cases which seem to support the rotten apple theory. Delattre argued that the Miami River Cops—involved in drugs and corruption in the 1980s—were rotten apples because there was no evidence of systemic corruption in the rest of the police department.[12] And in New York, the Mollen Commission concluded that the corruption was limited to a handful of officers only.[13]

Other Applications of Theory to the Examination of Police Misconduct

Recently, there have been a few efforts to apply criminological theory to the study of police misconduct, typically using scenario-based vignettes and officer self-report as a methodology. Chapell and Piquero used social learning theory to explore variation in attitudes toward misconduct between officers who received complaints and those who did not in a sample of Philadelphia police officers.[14] The researchers operationalized misconduct in scenario-based vignettes as theft (illegal), excessive use of force (likely illegal), and accepting gifts and free meals from members of the public (administratively impermissible, but not illegal). All of the officers in the sample viewed accepting gifts as normative and unrelated to misconduct. Officers who self-reported that they had been the subject of a citizen complaint were more likely to perceive excessive force as less serious than their counterparts who had not received citizen complaints.[15]

Hickman and colleagues applied Tittle's control balance theory to a sample of Philadelphia police officers, and found that officers who experienced control deficits (they were subjected to more control than they exercised) were more likely to indicate in hypothetical scenarios that they would report the misconduct of their colleagues (than those with control surpluses—who exercised more control than they were subject to).[16] In a cross-national study of police agencies, Klockars and co-authors explored relationships among officer assessments of the seriousness of transgressions, the level of discipline warranted, and the willingness to report the misconduct of their peers.[17] The study found that the seriousness of the misconduct in hypothetical scenarios was strongly predictive of both the willingness to report the transgression to superiors and the level of discipline they deemed appropriate. Hickman, Piquero, and Greene reported similar findings in their study of Philadelphia police.[18] Pogarksy and Piquero assessed the impact of key elements of deterrence theory (certainty, severity, and celerity) on officer perceptions of engaging in misconduct in hypothetical scenarios and found that "deterrence considerations appear to figure prominently in police misconduct decisions," though certainty and celerity of punishment were more influential than severity.[19]

In one of the few theoretically driven studies to date using official police data, Harris recently examined a cohort of police officers using the life course perspective.[20] Harris focuses on less serious forms of misconduct (not career-ending) and finds that most misdeeds occur early on in officers' careers—though for some, the deviance persists through their entire careers. This study is explored in greater detail in the life course section of this chapter. Other examples of theoretically derived research include applications of opportunity theory,[21] the so-called authoritarian personality,[22] and the police subculture perspective.[23] Research has also linked the ecological indicators of social disorganization and racial conflict to patterns of police misconduct, arguing that communities characterized by social network and cultural attenuation are those in which (1) police are most likely to take advantage of misconduct opportunities, and (2) residents are least likely to have access to the conventional mechanisms of accountability.[24] Additionally, several police scholars have tied the prevalence of police misconduct to organizational factors, such as variation in the vigor with which agencies pursue deviance[25] and informal culture.[26]

The Noble Cause

Several scholars, most notably Delattre[27] and Crank and Caldero,[28] have sought to explain police misconduct through the lens of the "noble cause." The noble cause explanation centers on a means-ends debate of policing, with noble cause representing the ends or goals of the profession. Crank and Caldero[29] define noble cause as

> a profound moral commitment to make the world a safe place to live. Put simply, it is getting bad guys off the street. Police believe that they're on the side of angels and their purpose in life is getting rid of bad guys. They are trained and armed to protect the innocent and think about that goal in terms of "keeping the scum off the streets." It is not simply a verbal commitment, recited at graduation at the local Peace Officer Standards and Training (POST) academy. Nor is it something police have to learn. It's something to which they are morally committed.

Crank and Caldero argue that noble cause misconduct emerges from this ends-oriented focus on policing. The ends of policing are so noble—law, order, protecting the innocent, getting bad guys off the streets—that the means of how those ends are achieved become less important. Several other scholars have made important contributions to our understanding of police misconduct by adopting and articulating the means-ends dilemma of policing. Klockars[30] draws on the film, *Dirty Harry*, to demonstrate the use of dirty means to achieve a noble or good end—what he calls the *Dirty Harry problem.* In the movie, Dirty Harry tortures a killer to extract information (and a confession) on the whereabouts of a kidnapped girl—a dirty mean to achieve a noble end. Klockars argues that the Dirty Harry problem is at the core of the police role, in large part because key operating assumptions within the police culture predispose officers to think they are dealing with guilty people, regardless of the evidence. And if the individual is perceived as guilty, then the use of dirty means to achieve a noble and good end becomes acceptable.[31] That is, police no longer are defined by or enforce the law; instead, the law becomes a tool they use to enforce their morality.[32]

> If the police act on their moral predispositions in pursuit of good ends, then whatever they do must be itself good. . . . If they accept a free dinner in order to safeguard a restaurant, it is because society owes them. And if they mistreat suspects, it is because they are the law, and suspects get what they deserve. Noble-case corruption thus becomes a gateway for material-reward corruption. Where noble-cause corruption flourishes, material-reward corruption cannot be far behind.[33]

Structural Explanations: Kappeler et al.'s Anthropological Framework

In perhaps the most extensive theoretical framework developed to date, Kappeler and colleagues proposed a "police worldview" explanation of police deviance. The crux of this framework is that police are part of an occupational subculture with a worldview that teaches them to distinguish between insiders and outsiders (us vs. them). This worldview is developed and maintained by a number of factors, including strong cultural themes (emphasizing bravery, autonomy, secrecy), an acculturation process that teaches those themes, and adherence to an elaborate set of rules or postulates that govern the subculture.[34] Moreover, there are several key opportunity and organizational structural elements that facilitate the commission of deviant acts.[35]

Opportunity Structures

The police hold unique power because of their authority, and "the special legal privileges accorded the police provide unprecedented opportunities to engage in deviance without arousing suspicion."[36] These powers include the authority to stop, question, search, and use force. Moreover, the ambiguity of the law allows for situational application and permits officers to use the law to meet their own personal objectives, which may involve misconduct.[37] Second, public opinion polls have consistently found that most Americans are satisfied with the police, view them as honest and free from corruption, and that these attitudes have been very stable over time. Kappeler et al. argue that this perception makes detecting police deviance much more difficult because citizens "assume" police will be deviance-free.[38]

The last three opportunity structures are isolation, discretion, and lack of supervision. Police officers, especially in suburban and rural areas, spend most of their shift alone. Also, many citizen encounters with police occur in isolation, reducing the likelihood that the encounter will be witnessed by others. At the same time, police officers exercise extraordinary discretion when carrying out their duties. Their broad discretion allows police officers to choose the time, location, and citizens that they will engage. As a result, officers interested in illegitimate activities can select times, locations, and victims (i.e., those engaged in crime or who are vulnerable) that reduce the chances their deviant behavior will be reported or observed by others.[39] Last, police officers generally work with no direct supervision.[40] Poor supervision serves a number of interests for the supervisor and the department, including reduction of personal conflicts with officers, insulation from deviant activities (deniability), and protection of the supervisors' own questionable activities.[41] Clearly, the lack of adequate supervision increases opportunities for misconduct.

Organizational Structures

Most law enforcement agencies today are highly departmentalized, with multiple areas of specialization: homicide, sex crimes, narcotics, etc. Specialized units are at greater risk of engaging in deviant behavior because of greater autonomy, more discretion, greater access to resources with less accountability, and greater exposure to opportunities for corruption (i.e., more interaction with individuals actively seeking to avoid police involvement).[42] In addition, opportunities for advancement in a police department—whether it has ten officers or 10,000—is limited; yet, the only way to get a significant pay increase is through promotion.[43] Promotions typically come at irregular intervals and are often postponed because of budgetary constraints. The lack of opportunity for promotion clearly limits officers' ability to improve their salary and position in the organization. Officers who are frustrated with their career path or unhappy with their pay may be tempted to seek illegitimate means to add to their salary. "When the means to achieve social and economic goals are structurally blocked, as they are in most police organizations, the potential for police deviance and corruption increases."[44]

The existence of a distinct subculture among the police is well-established. Early work by Westley defined some of the key elements of the police subculture, including an emphasis on secrecy, group solidarity, and reliance of violence.[45] Skolnick argued that the police develop a working personality shaped by the danger and authority of their work, and because of the potential for danger, they develop a "perceptual shorthand" to identify those who may represent a threat (the symbolic assailant).[46] The distinct "us versus them" mentality is a common theme among the classic works on police subculture. Van Maanen, for example, noted that police placed citizens into one of three categories: know nothings (law-abiding citizens who "know nothing" about policing), suspicious persons (likely criminals), and assholes (those who challenge police officers' authority).[47] More recently, Skolnick and Fyfe maintained that the "cops as soldiers" philosophy has served to deepen the divide among police and citizens, and that it contributes to police misconduct.[48] That is, frustration and anger over "not winning the war" builds up in officers over time. For some officers, these emotions can boil over and lead to abusive behavior toward the "enemy"—typically the inner city black male.[49]

In sum, this prior theoretical work, though limited, offers a good starting point for the rest of the chapter. With this discussion as a backdrop, we now turn to a more thorough consideration of four traditional criminological theories as frameworks for understanding police misconduct. These include general strain, social learning, low self-control, and the life course perspective.

General Strain

What the Theory Says
Strain theory began with the works of Durkheim.[50] Later, Merton[51] would write a seminal article called "Social Structure and Anomie" in which he

used Durkheim's statements to create a theory of deviance and offending. In this article, Merton outlined a theory of deviant behavior based on goals and the means to achieve those goals. The idea was that society and its culture set goals for its members while, at the same time, fostering a system that limits certain groups or individuals from achieving these goals. In such a state, those individuals may react by continuing to value those goals, but rejecting the means to achieve them. In Merton's terms, these individuals are innovators. Although Merton suggested that societal goals can refer to anything held up by a culture to be desirable, he focused on wealth. In this sense, innovators want wealth, but do not follow the prescribed norms to acquire it. Instead, they may resort to criminal activity to acquire wealth.

Anomie was very popular among criminologists and policymakers until the 1960s. However, after several studies demonstrated weak empirical support for the theory, it fell out of favor among social scientists and policymakers alike.[52] Despite this, various versions of strain theory[53] eventually dovetailed into two contemporary theoretical camps: institutional anomie (not discussed as it applies to large levels of analysis, such as cities and nations, as opposed to individual police officers)[54] and general strain theory (GST).[55] GST integrates other forms of strain beyond that caused by cultural goals and the inability to achieve such goals. Its principle author is Robert Agnew.

Agnew[56] discussed three forms of strain: (1) the inability to achieve a valued goal; (2) the loss of something a person values; and (3) the presence/introduction of something a person does not like. According to Agnew,[57] certain types of strain are more conducive to offending than others. Specifically, strain that is seen as unjust, high in magnitude, or accompanied by the presence of low self-control is more predictive of offending behavior. GST further states that the relationship between strain and crime is mediated by emotion. Broadly speaking, this emotion is negative affect (such as feeling badly). Simply stated, strain, perceived or real, makes a person feel bad, and they may engage in deviant behavior to alleviate such strain. The offending behavior is seen as a way of *coping* with the bad feelings that come along with the strain experience. Since Agnew's[58] initial reformulation, strain theory has again received scientific attention. Using better measures of strain, contemporary strain theorists have found promising support for its link to criminal offending.[59]

Applying the Theory to the Study of Police Misconduct

There are numerous sources of strain for a police officer. Some of these include: the role conflict between using coercive force while trying to protect the rights of others,[60] constantly being exposed to the worst side of humanity or, at the very least, to those who are generally unhappy to see you,[61] frustration with other agencies in the criminal justice system (e.g., District Attorneys who won't prosecute cases), and poor police-community relations.[62] In the late 1970s, Manning[63] stated that a police officer's job is nearly impossible: "To much of the public, the police are seen as alertly ready to respond to citizen demands, as crime-fighters, as an efficient, bureaucratic, highly organized force that keeps society from falling into chaos" (p. 13). Not much has changed for law enforcement agencies since then.[64] The impossible mandate comes from the officer's own sense of duty,[65] but also results from how police officers are evaluated. Since the inception of the Uniform Crime Reports, police have been judged according to numerical standards. This has included, among other things, arrest rates and crime rates, as well as calls for service and response time. Skolnick and Fyfe[66] called this the numbers game. Regardless of how it has been measured, the focus has been on producing quantifiable results. For police officers, there is a disconnect between aspirations and outcomes that creates a strain. Police officers, having little control over crime, can never produce enough numbers to satisfy a frightened public fueled by media and political images of violence and victimization, nor to satisfy supervisors and the brass. This creates anxiety, disenchantment, jadedness, and other negative affect within the police officer's psyche, especially because officers recognize that good policing will, in many cases, *not* produce a number. Skolnick and Fyfe, for example, said:

> Good cops always seem to identify the causes of problems and to come up with the least troublesome ways of solving them. Good cops think ahead and always leave a way out of any tough situation. Good cops rarely have to resort to the law to solve minor order maintenance problems like drunks and noisy kids on the street. Good cops spend their time finding out about the people and places on their beats instead of lurking at speed traps or near badly marked stop signs.[67]

As a result, police may, then, cope with the negative affect associated with this strain through illegitimate policing practices. One instance, related directly to the population described in this book, is the episode of the Buddy Boys of the NYPD during the 1980s:

Henry Winter, for example, tried to justify his robbery of drug dealers by saying that he got tired of arresting drug dealers, only to see them back on the street the next day. Brian O'Regan also suggested that he robbed drug dealers merely to punish them. To both officers, the inefficient, ineffective, and awkward criminal justice system was the real culprit; since the system was a failure, officers had to resort to their own means of dealing with the drug problem.[68]

Strain can also be understood as stress. Policing has traditionally been considered a stressful occupation.[69] Sources of stress in policing include individual-level factors (such as "Being responsible for protecting other people"), work environment factors (such as "The potential role conflict between law enforcement and serving the public"), organizational factors (such as "Policies and procedures that officers do not support"), and external environmental factors (such as "Frustration with the criminal justice system").[70] Although there is some disagreement over how much policing is objectively a stressful occupation versus being perceived as stressful by police officers,[71] the effects of stress on police officers are nevertheless very real.[72] Stress requires some sort of coping method in order to avoid unfortunate consequences. These consequences include burn-out,[73] cynicism,[74] depression, poor health, and behavioral problems.[75] The result of stress, understood as a source of strain, may also include misconduct as predicted by GST.

Using GST as a framework for understanding police misconduct is not without its limitations. For example, research has consistently suggested that not everyone copes with strain in criminal or even negative ways.[76] Figuring out which forms of strain in which circumstances lead to offending has been a challenge for strain researchers. This challenge has been compounded by findings that suggest there are certain individual characteristics that may also influence the strain–crime connection.[77] These factors complicate the use of a strain framework to study police misconduct. Although policing as a public service profession is similar to other public sector jobs, it is unique in a number of respects, such as demands on their time and the right to use coercive force. This introduces a number of strains unanticipated by GST. Also, although the debate continues regarding why the policing subculture exists (that is, are police officers socialized, selected, or some combination of the two[78]), its presence not only introduces more unique strains to police officers not present to the general public, but also introduces a number of personal characteristics that may mediate how officers cope with strain. These are challenges of which future researchers will need to be aware.

General Strain Theory and the Jammed Up Study

Applying GST to the current study provides a number of opportunities for understanding police misconduct, as there are several variables pertinent to the strain framework. These variables can be divided into two categories: those dealing directly with sources of strain, and those dealing with ways to cope with strain. In terms of variables associated with sources of strain, one possible variable is being supervised. The study found that those who held supervisory positions were less likely to be dismissed for misconduct. Being supervised may present sources of strain to an officer in the form of expectations that they cannot achieve and that are out of their control to decide. Or, it may be that the failure to be promoted creates strain. This is especially salient when the low salary associated with being a New York police patrol officer may itself present strains when coupled with having a family.

Consider, for example, Ricky Tolson, one of our "characters" introduced in chapter 1. Tolson worked his entire 15-year career in Midtown–Manhattan South, mostly as a patrol officer; but after 10 years, he moved to narcotics. At that point he hooked up with a small group of officers and began stealing drugs from drug dealers and selling them on the open market. One can speculate that financial strain may have characterized Tolson's entire career, and that when he found himself working a highly discretionary, largely unsupervised assignment, laden with virtually limitless opportunities for corruption, he began to "innovate," in Merton's early terminology. It may also be that Tolson experienced strain from both his own financial situation and his perceived inadequacies of the criminal justice system—particularly if he believed that drug dealers often committed their crimes repeatedly and with very few official consequences.

Similarly, a person's race/ethnicity within the organizational context could also be understood as a source of strain: "Policing . . . tends to be dominated by employees who are both white and male; thus it seems reasonable to assume that both minority and female police officers might demonstrate lower levels of job satisfaction than their white male counterparts, who set the tone for an agency's organizational culture. Research findings on these issues are inconsistent, however."[79] Using GST may go a long way in understanding the study's findings that black and Latino officers were more likely to be dismissed for misconduct than their white counterparts. What is more, it may be the case that minority officers are observed more closely than their white counterparts and subsequently punished more seriously. This *tokenism*[80] can also be understood as a source of strain unique to minority officers.

Other variables in the study are associated with ways of coping with strain. For example, it seems reasonable to assume that having more education may provide officers with healthier coping mechanisms. Attaining a college degree requires time-management skills, the ability to receive criticism, and provides opportunities to learn how to work with others. Previous research has found that, in terms of satisfaction, having an education appears to be related to lower levels of job satisfaction.[81] This study's findings suggest the opposite: officers with college education appeared to be less likely to be dismissed for misconduct. Similarly, being older at age of appointment and years on the job were also associated with not being dismissed for misconduct. In other words: experience and maturity may provide for better coping skills to handle the strains and stresses associated with police work. Perhaps most interesting is the finding that having a father who is or was an NYPD officer was associated with not being separated from the department. This finding begs a number of interpretations. From the viewpoint of GST, it could mean that such officers are better equipped to cope with strain because of paternal mentoring. Also, this same officer may already have a network of supportive police officers who also know or knew his father, and this network may act as a coping mechanism against harmful strain. Similarly, as the CHAID analysis revealed, getting married while on the job and the second start dimension (that is, getting married, going back to school, or getting divorced) both emerged as protective factors. Some of these events may be seen as reducing strain (for example, divorce) while others may be seen as ways to cope better with strain (for example, getting married). Going back to school can also be understood as a coping mechanism insofar as it provides officers another outlet in their life, thus providing them an identity outside of their profession.

Next Steps for General Strain Theory and Police Misconduct

Because policing is such a stressful profession, and located uniquely between the citizenry and the government, it is a fruitful venue for exploring the theoretical prowess of GST. Researchers should pinpoint specific and unique sources of strain for police officers. As discussed above, Agnew[82] outlined three sources of strain: (1) the inability to achieve a valued goal; (2) the loss of something a person values; and (3) the presence/introduction of something a person does not like. There are elements of policing that fit well within each of these domains. For example, with regard to the inability to achieve a valued goal, it is a commonly vented frustration among police officers that their efforts are under-appreciated by citizens, the media, and the brass. Or, in terms of the loss of something a person values, the stress that policing may put on an officer's personal life may result in loss of friendship networks or even divorce. Loss of a close partner due to a fatal encounter may also create strain. Finally, the presence or introduction of something a person does not like could be represented by the daily interaction with citizens who are not interested in the officer's "services," or the repeated exposure to the worst of humanity. These specific areas, as well as others not discussed here, should be explored and extended to see *if* and *in what ways* they relate to police misconduct.

To explore these and other variables, researchers could make use of data that already exist within agency databases and combine them with personal interviews. Law enforcement agencies, especially those that maintain early intervention systems,[83] collect a host of data relative to incidents and sometimes to specific officers.[84] These data are important, but limited insofar as (a) they rely on incidents that have been brought to the agency's overall attention through arrest reports or complaint forms, and (b) they lack psychological batteries[85] which are at the heart of GST. This means that, as currently collected, agency data are unable to determine the totality of what is going on, nor is it able to tap into the core constructs of GST. Personal interviews could be used to fill in these gaps. Also, researchers could take a cue from clinicians and medical researchers and explore GST and police misconduct through specific case studies: by having in-depth interviews and life histories of officers who either engaged in misconduct or did not engage in misconduct, we may be able to tease out what sorts of strains officers are under, the manner in which they cope with these strains, and how those strains are tied to misconduct.

Social Learning Theory

What the Theory Says

Social learning theory was originally developed by Akers and Burgess[86] to explain why certain people commit acts that deviate from the norms of society. Social learning theory posits that individuals experience a learning process that produces both conforming and deviant behavior. Akers presented four essential processes that serve as avenues of social learning. These are: differential association, definitions, differential reinforcement, and modeling/imitation. According to Akers, the balance of these four processes serves to determine whether an individual is going to be more likely to engage in conforming or deviant behavior.

DIFFERENTIAL ASSOCIATION

Differential association is one's direct interaction and association with groups of individuals who participate in a certain type of behavior or adhere to a set of norms, attitudes, and values consistent with such behavior. There are two different types of differential association groups—primary and secondary. Primary groups (which include associations with family and friends) have the most influence over an individual, while secondary groups are more distant and may include such things as the media or the Internet. The strength of the group's influence is determined by its priority (i.e., the associations that began earlier), duration (i.e., the associations that occupy a large amount of the individual's time), frequency (i.e., there is a large amount of interaction with the group), and intensity (i.e., the individual values the importance of the relationship with the group). In short, differential association exposes an individual to a social context in which all additional mechanisms of social learning theory function.[87]

DEFINITIONS

Definitions refer to an individual's beliefs and attitudes that serve to define an act as right or wrong.[88] More specifically, definitions are "one's own orientations, rationalizations, justifications, excuses, and other attitudes that define the commission of an act as relatively more right or wrong, good or bad, desirable or undesirable, justified or unjustified, and appropriate or inappropriate."[89] Definitions can be learned through interactions with differential association groups, as well as through exposure to societal norms and values. The more an individual has internalized these definitions determines whether they are going to be able to justify the commission of a criminal act (i.e., neutralization), or refrain from such deviant temptations. In short, when an individual subscribes to definitions more favorable of deviant behavior, they are more likely to engage in deviance.

DIFFERENTIAL REINFORCEMENT

Differential reinforcement refers to an individual mentally weighing the potential benefits and consequences of a given action in order to determine whether he/she should or should not commit an offense. In addition, the individual will reflect upon the actual rewards and/or consequences they received for similar actions in the past. In essence, the greater the probability and value of a reward is for a given crime, in comparison to any potential punishment, the more likely the individual is to commit the offense.

MODELING/IMITATION

Finally, modeling/imitation occurs when an individual observes a particular behavior, either directly or indirectly (e.g., in the media), and accordingly decides to engage in a similar behavior. An individual's likelihood of imitating a given behavior is determined by the model's characteristics, the actual behavior observed, as well as the observed rewards/punishments of the behavior.

Of social learning theory's four main processes (i.e., differential association, definitions, reinforcement, modeling/imitation), the most influential is differential association. The reasoning behind this is twofold. First, Akers asserted that the majority of favorable and unfavorable definitions toward deviance are developed through close interactions with peers. Second, differential association refers to the people whom an individual has the most contact with (i.e., peer associations). In other words, an individual: (1) learns favorable and unfavorable definitions toward deviance from their peers; (2) acts according to such definitions; and (3) experiences positive or negative reinforcement (or punishment) following their definition-driven behavior. The role of one's peers is not only to provide favorable and unfavorable definitions of deviance, but also to provide a model of how one should behave.

Applying the Theory to the Study of Police Misconduct

Differential Association

In policing, the primary differential association group is the peer group of fellow officers from whom an individual officer learns definitions.

Additionally, research suggests that police officers receive the most intense pressure not from the community they serve, but from their peers.[90] The peer pressure phenomenon has been well-defined in the police literature through identification of a "police subculture" (see chapter 2 for a thorough discussion of the police subculture as it relates to police misconduct; as well as discussion of Chappell and Piquero's application of social learning theory to police misconduct). In essence, the police subculture facilitates deviant behavior by "transmitting the beliefs, values, definitions, and 'manners of expression' that depart from acceptable behavior," but meet the values of the deviant subculture.[91] Moreover, the police subculture permits officers to justify deviant behavior, further promoting officer misconduct.[92] The police subculture and peer pressure are further strengthened through the desire for support and approval from fellow officers who understand the feelings of social isolation that often accompany the occupation of policing.[93] The support and approval granted by other officers often serves to intensify peer influence and control, and thus, intensifies the acceptance of deviance and misconduct. Not surprisingly, this cycle continues to perpetuate itself as the feelings of social isolation trigger officers to want to spend more time with co-workers in an attempt to increase feelings of acceptance.[94] Additionally, research suggests that the influence of the police subculture is so strong that it causes individuals to adopt the definitions of their department no matter how strongly they originally opposed them. Thus, these newly acquired definitions cause officers to begin viewing the world through "cognitive lenses" that are often distorted.[95] For example, Savitz noted that as recruits transitioned from the academy to the workforce, their attitudes concerning deviance became much more permissive, as their exposure to the police culture dramatically increased.[96] More specifically, as time progressed, the officers began favoring lesser amounts of punishment for police misconduct, particularly in the areas of theft and accepting bribes.

Definitions

According to Akers, if an individual feels strongly *against* a particular act, then they will be less likely to engage in it. In the policing subculture, however, research has suggested that individuals will engage in deviance even if their previous definitions were unfavorable toward such behaviors. Because of the "definitions" aspect of social learning theory and how it differs in the policing subculture, it has been argued that specific definitions of police deviance and misconduct need to be developed.[97] Additionally, researchers have stressed the importance of research designed to identify the process by which these definitions are created within a police department. Specifically, there is a need for more studies concerning the multi-stage development of police corruption, normative order, as well as general rules and practices implemented by police departments.[98]

Differential Reinforcement

Similar to differential association, reinforcement can play a significant role in perpetuating a police officer's deviant behavior. In fact, a police officer's desire for peer approval and acceptance can be so strong that he/she may engage in deviant behaviors in order to maintain good standing within their department.[99] Additionally, it has been theorized that reinforcements received from members of the police subculture have more of an influence on deviant behavior than the officers' definitions toward deviance alone.[100]

According to social learning theory, proper functioning of differential reinforcement relies on the continuation of peer associations.[101] Furthermore, if one's association with delinquent peers is discontinued, then reinforcement will subside, resulting in the abatement of their deviant behavior. In the policing subculture, however, it is sometimes difficult for an officer to distinguish deviant co-workers from those who are not deviant (let alone separate himself/herself from them).[102] In other cases, officers may refuse to acknowledge that their actions are deviant. For example, many officers refuse to consider the acceptance of free meals and services as a form of deviance. Thus, these officers rarely anticipate any penalties for accepting such meals and services. Examples such as these serve to support the claim that the police subculture encourages officer misconduct.

Much research has been conducted on the development and impact of the police subculture. This research is relevant in terms of social learning theory, as many researchers have attempted to link the deviant subculture of the police to peer associations within the department. These tests have found that when a new police officer is introduced to the subculture, they will be exposed to "models of behavior that will influence his or her own attitudes and behavior."[103] Furthermore, results of these studies suggested that over time, officers accept and internalize the deviant definitions shared by their fellow officers. This is due to the fact that they are exposed to their fellow officers at a higher rate than other individuals in their lives (i.e., frequency).

There are a few limitations to using social learning theory as an explanation of officer misconduct. For example, the theory suggests that misconduct will occur in officer groups and/or it will be widespread throughout the department. There are many instances, however, where misconduct does indeed involve "just a few rotten apples." Alternatively, it fails to explain why some officers do *not* engage in misconduct when they are surrounded by colleagues who do. Moreover, oftentimes officers who engage in misconduct possess a number of individual characteristics, such as being married or getting promoted, that should have protected them from engaging in risky behavior. Or officers possess individual-level risk factors—such as having a prior criminal record—but they do not engage in misconduct.

Social Learning Theory and the Jammed Up Study

Recall again Ricky Tolson from chapter 1 and from our discussion of strain theory. Prior to engaging in profit-motivated misconduct, Tolson had no obvious risk factors for crime or misconduct (with the possible exception of being young, i.e., 21, when appointed to the job): he had no criminal history, no apparent troubles in previous jobs, and virtually no problems while serving with the NYPD. Moreover, if the department suspected Tolson of having integrity problems, it is unlikely that police administrators would have allowed him to transfer into such a sensitive assignment as narcotics. Thus, it is possible that once entering his new unit, Tolson was overwhelmed by definitions that favored misconduct, and/or by a subculture of differential reinforcement that placed great value on the solidarity that often comes from engaging in group- level deviance. Tolson's case is also interesting because it suggests the ways in which two or more criminological theories might be integrated to explain police misconduct. As previously considered, Tolson may have operated under considerable financial strain during his career, but it was not until he met the "right" people under the proper circumstances that he had both the opportunities to engage in misconduct and the peer affirmations necessary to reinforce such behaviors.

Social learning theory also may be applicable to the current study for other reasons. For example, the study's key finding demonstrated that an officer's race is one of the strongest predictors of whether he/she will engage in career-ending misconduct. Specifically, it was discovered that black and Hispanic officers were much more likely to engage in misconduct than white officers (74.44% for black officers and

55.49% for Hispanic officers, as compared to 41.95% for white officers). While this finding is somewhat controversial and we offer a number of potential explanations for it, we also cannot rule out the possibility that there may be cultural social learning processes taking place within one's race that can increase the risk of engaging in deviant behavior in the workplace. In other words, it is possible that black and Hispanic officers came from backgrounds where deviant definitions were more accepted, and these definitions have translated into more tolerant views of police misconduct. Given the current study's limitations, we cannot comment definitively, one way or the other, on this potential social learning explanation.

The current study also found that officers with fathers who worked for the NYPD were less likely to engage in misconduct. This finding is consistent with social learning theory, given the four main learning processes. For example, it is reasonable to assume that officers who were raised by a police officer were (1) closely associated with their fathers; (2) conditioned to respect the police; and (3) taught definitions favorable of the policing profession. Thus, they desired to model their father's behavior and enter the policing profession as well.

Another finding in chapter 5 revealed that higher levels of education were related to lower rates of police misconduct. Specifically, it was found that officers who pursued degrees beyond high school (e.g., Associate's degree, Bachelor's degree) were much less likely to experience career-ending misconduct. Findings such as these pose the question of whether being closely associated with peers in an educational environment causes individuals to learn definitions less favorable toward deviant behavior. Furthermore, it was discovered that officers who experienced a "second start" (e.g., going back to school, getting separated/divorced, etc.) were less likely to experience career-ending misconduct. This suggests that conventional, life-changing events can socialize an officer in such a way that is less favorable toward misconduct.

Results from chapter 5 also suggested that the number of years on the job was negatively associated with misconduct. This finding is interesting, as prior research has suggested that over time, officers accept and internalize the deviant definitions shared by their fellow officers. It is possible, then, that as an officer's tenure on the police force progresses, he/she begins to associate with officers who hold definitions that are less favorable toward deviance. In addition to number of years on the job, it was found that promotion to a higher departmental rank resulted in less incidents of career-ending misconduct.

Finally, results from chapter 5 demonstrated how getting married can be a strong protective factor for police officers in terms of occupational misconduct (especially for white officers). This finding suggests that the association to conventional others, such as a husband or a wife, can result in the increased exposure of definitions less favorable of deviance. More importantly, it is also possible that marriage can weaken the strength of the police subculture, as officers will begin to spend less time associating with their fellow officers, and more time with significant others outside of the police department. In other words, marriage has the potential to influence the duration, frequency, and intensity components of the police differential association group.

Next Steps for Social Learning Theory and Police Misconduct

Social learning theory is quite capable of providing insights on the causes and correlates of officer misconduct. Thus, it is important that researchers continue to analyze officer conduct from a social learning standpoint. In terms of the police subculture, social learning theorists would certainly argue that there is a learning process within the department in which officers are socialized to commit deviant acts (or alternatively, to avoid committing such acts). Furthermore, under a social learning paradigm, the police subculture also is responsible for teaching officers about the bulk of the deviant acts they come to accept as an inherent aspect of their job (e.g., the acceptance of free meals and services). With that in mind, it is important that future research is focused on the police subculture, as it teaches officers to perceive situations, events, and individuals in a distorted way that is unique to the policing profession.[104]

There are a number of additional issues that should be explored in future research to study the utility of social learning theory. The first is officer race. In the *Jammed Up* study, black and Hispanic officers were much more likely to engage in misconduct than white officers. However, we also noted that, over time, levels of officer misconduct decreased as the department became more diverse. The impact of racial and gender diversity on the social learning processes of the police subculture are unknown and should be explored. Additionally, the *Jammed Up* study suggests that increased schooling can reduce the likelihood of career-ending misconduct. This includes officers who decide to go back to school while working for the department (i.e., the "second start" dimension). As a result, it may be possible for police departments to potentially reduce misconduct by encouraging officers to enroll or re-enroll in college. Last, the impact of important events in the non-professional aspects of officers' lives—such as getting married or divorced—on the power of social learning processes remains unclear and should be examined in future research.

Low Self-Control

What the Theory Says

In 1990, Gottfredson and Hirschi developed what they considered to be a general theory of crime, proposing that one's level of self-control can be used to understand why certain individuals engage in criminal behaviors and others do not. According to Gottfredson and Hirschi, low self-control is an "enduring predisposition" that increases the chances that individuals will engage in crime when presented with suitable opportunities. They further elaborated that self-control is composed of six components—impulsivity, risk seeking, a volatile temper, a tendency to be self-centered, a preference for simple tasks, and a preference for physical rather than mental tasks.[105] According to the authors, higher levels of self-control provide individuals with the restraint necessary to avoid engaging in criminal behavior. Lower levels of self-control, however, make it difficult for an individual to resist the appeal of criminal opportunities. Importantly, the theory posits that self-control, or the lack of self-control, is established early (i.e., by ages 10–12) and remains relatively stable across the life course and throughout varying situations.[106] In other words, major life events, such as marriage and employment, should have little effect on one's early-established level of self-control.

In essence, Gottfredson and Hirschi's theory stated that criminal behavior results from a combination of opportunity and the "tendency to avoid acts whose long-term costs exceed their momentary advantages."[107] Individuals who engage in criminal acts also tend to participate in analogous behaviors that provide immediate gratification, such as substance abuse, gambling, smoking, speeding, and risky sexual behaviors.[108] According to self-control theory, criminals do not specialize in one particular kind of crime, nor do they plan their criminal behavior very far in advance—they simply respond to whatever feasible criminal opportunities they encounter in a given situation.

Since its conception in 1990, Gottfredson and Hirschi's self-control theory has received a good deal of theoretical attention and empirical support.[109] Furthermore, a recent meta-analysis of the empirical literature examining Gottfredson and Hirschi's self-control theory found that a low level of self-control is consistently related—both positively and significantly—to criminal and analogous activity.[110] As a result of its empirical support and popularity, self-control theory is likely to remain prominent in future criminological research.

Despite the strong empirical support for self-control theory, there is still debate over how it should be measured. According to Gottfredson and Hirschi, it should be measured behaviorally, but many other researchers argue that it is best understood through attitudinal measures.[111] Gottfredson and Hirschi tend to prefer behavioral measures of self-control because they assert that an individual's level of self-control can actually influence the manner in which they respond to attitudinal-based questions.[112] Still, in 1993, Grasmick and his colleagues developed one of the first attitudinal measures of self-control. In doing so, they constructed a 24-item scale composed of questions related to the six components originally outlined in Gottfredson and Hirschi's theory (i.e., impulsivity, risk seeking, volatile temper, physical tasks, simple tasks, and self-centeredness). The Grasmick et al. scale has been widely supported by empirical research, and as a result, has become one of the most frequently used attitudinal measures of self-control.

Interestingly, studies using attitudinal measures as well as those using behavioral measures have demonstrated strong relationships between self-control and criminal behavior.[113] In fact, in Pratt and Cullen's meta-analysis of self-control and crime, the authors found that behavioral and attitudinal measures of self-control were both sufficient predictors of criminal behavior.

Applying the Theory to the Study of Police Misconduct

As previously stated, low self-control is conceived by Gottfredson and Hirschi as a predisposition that increases the probability that individuals will engage in crime when presented with suitable criminal opportunities. In fact, many researchers argue that the "opportunity" component of self-control theory is more important in the explanation of criminal behavior than one's level of self-control alone.[114] With that in mind, it is easy to understand how low self-control might be useful for explaining police misconduct. The very nature of police work results in officers being confronted with opportunities to engage in deviance on a daily basis. These opportunities include the use or sale of seized drugs, protection of illegal activity, accepting gifts and meals from the public, neglect of duty, excessive force, and brutality.

One of the more frequently encountered opportunities for deviance that police officers are faced with is opportunistic theft.[115] That is, when officers are placed in a situation where they are given a unique opportunity to steal an item, and act accordingly. For example, an officer confiscates money or drugs from an offender and fails to turn the contraband in to the department. Or an officer is called to the scene of a burglary and decides to steal something, knowing that the burglar will be blamed. Consistent with self-control theory, it is clear that such opportunistic theft results from a combination of opportunity and an officer's perception that the act's momentary advantages exceed its long-term cost.

Recently, several researchers have advanced an alternative conceptualization of self-control theory, calling it "self-control strength." Self-control strength refers to the idea that self-control is a resource that can be depleted as an individual repeatedly exercises it.[116] Moreover, these studies suggest that once an individual's pre-existing amount of self-control strength becomes depleted, it takes a significant amount of time to restore itself.[117]

In one recent test of self-control strength, results suggested that individuals who experience more self-control demands while at work are more vulnerable to experience self-control depletion, and are thus more likely to engage in acts of deviance while at work.[118] This finding is very pertinent in the policing profession, as it suggests that officers who *do* exercise restraint when presented with feasible opportunities of deviance might eventually experience a weakening of their self-control, and thus, succumb to the temptations of criminality. Furthermore, an additional study suggested that an individual becomes more vulnerable to self-control depletion in situations of high arousal and fatigue, which police officers tend to experience more frequently than those in other occupations.[119] One cannot help but wonder whether aspects of the occupation cause police officers to become more vulnerable to self-control depletion.

Despite self-control theory's popularity and support throughout criminal justice literature, there are still a few limitations of using self-control theory to explain police misconduct. For example, Gottfredson and Hirschi have argued that individuals with strong social bonds, such as stable employment and attachment to peers, are less likely to engage in criminality. With that in mind, it might be difficult to apply the theory to police misconduct because police officers *do* tend to have strong employment and peer bonds. Furthermore, contrary to one of self-control's key theoretical assumptions, existing research suggests that certain social bonds (e.g., marriage)—even when formed later in adulthood—can steer former offenders onto a pathway of law-abiding behavior.[120] Findings such as these conflict with Gottfredson and Hirschi's argument that major life events, such as marriage and employment, should have little effect on one's early-established level of self-control.

Self-Control Theory and the Jammed Up Study

Self-control theory can be applied to the current study in a number of ways. For example, officers with higher levels of education at their time of appointment were less likely to engage in misconduct. This makes sense when one considers the six elements of self-control, which include a preference for simple and physical tasks, rather than mental tasks. Getting an education requires a lot of mental effort—effort that individuals with low self-control are frequently unable to put forth—so it seems rather intuitive that officers with low self-control might have lower levels of education.

The relationship between low self-control and misconduct can also be observed by looking at an officer's prior employment history. One of the key findings from chapter 5 is that officers who received disciplinary sanctions in their previous job were more likely to engage in career-ending misconduct. Considering the theory's volatile temper component, it is reasonable to assume that those with low self-control might experience disciplinary problems during the course of employment, both in previous jobs and while with the police department. The risk-taking and impulsivity components of self-control may also play a role in this, as these individuals might use the autonomous nature of policing to their advantage and look for new, exciting ways to satisfy their need for risky deviant behavior. Furthermore, it was discovered that officers who received a promotion to a higher departmental rank were less likely to experience career-ending misconduct (only 26.21% of officers who were promoted engaged in career-ending misconduct, according to the CHAID analyses). This makes sense, as it can be theorized that officers with low self-control, prior disciplinary problems, and poor employment histories would be unlikely candidates for promotion in the first place.

Chapter 5 also revealed that officers with a prior criminal history (especially those with a juvenile criminal history) were more likely to engage in career-ending misconduct. In fact, among the 197 black officers who had public order arrests or misdemeanor convictions prior to joining the NYPD, 93.4 percent experienced career-ending misconduct (see CHAID findings). This finding raises the possibility that these officers never developed a sufficient level of self-control as adolescents, and that their low level of self-control has continued to influence their actions into adulthood. The study's results also revealed that having a formerly suspended driver's license was also a risk factor in predicting officer misconduct. When one considers the reasons an individual's driver's license might be suspended (e.g., reckless driving, alcohol or drug-related offense, etc.), it is not difficult to envision the potential for a low self-control explanation.

Recall that at some point in chapter 5 we noted that several of our primary findings regarding the correlates of police misconduct among individual officers conformed to the expectations that many criminologists already hold: The best predictors of *future* antisocial behaviors are *prior* antisocial behaviors. It should be of little surprise, then, that officers such as Colin Ahearne engage in career-ending misconduct. We introduced Ahearne in chapter 1 as the officer who was hired in the early 1980s just when the NYPD emerged from its fiscal crisis and hiring freeze era. He came to the job with a fairly extensive (that is, for police recruits) arrest history, and according to department records, maintained his associations with "known drug dealers" after being hired by the NYPD. For Ahearne, perhaps the question should not be, *"Why did he engage in police misconduct?"* but rather, *"How is it that it took 10 years before he got caught?"* Whether trying to explain criminal offending in general or police misconduct in particular, Colin Ahearne appears to be a classic example of control theory. The primary differences between Colin Ahearne and Ricky Tolson were that, while the latter may have "learned" the value and craft of misconduct once on the job, the former came to the job having already been socialized in the drug trade.

Next Steps for Self-Control Theory and Police Misconduct

Currently, the relationship between self-control theory and police misconduct has been under-researched. Due to self-control theory's potential to provide a helpful explanation of police deviance, there is much to be gained from examining this relationship more thoroughly. Moreover, in light of the emerging empirical research on the concepts of self-control strength and self-control depletion, it would be interesting to consider whether the policing occupation puts one at a higher risk of self-control depletion. For example, it might be useful to examine whether police officers who experience increased levels of anxiety, arousal, and fatigue while at work are also more likely to experience a lowering of their self-control level, and thus, experience an increased likelihood of engaging in police misconduct.

Indicators of low self-control could also be used to determine which officers are at a higher risk of experiencing career-ending misconduct. As discussed in chapter 5, an NYPD background investigator's recommendation for or against an officer's hiring was frequently a good predictor of whether the officer was going to engage in misconduct. In fact, of the 84 Hispanic officers for whom the background investigator made a recommendation against hiring, 86.9 percent of them experienced career-ending misconduct (as compared to 44.67% of those who were recommended for hire). This raises the question of whether an increased awareness of the indicators of low self-control could assist the background investigators in making more reliable recommendations for hiring officers.[121]

Life Course Criminology

What the Theory Says

Most criminological theories make statements about individuals or groups of individuals at particular time periods (like adolescence) or in certain locations (like in poor neighborhoods). These theories are interested in the differences in behavior between individuals. Life course criminology, on the other hand, is more interested in the differences in behavior of a single individual. It tries to answer such questions as "Why does a person start offending?" "Why does that same person stop offending?" and "How does an individual's offending behavior *today* relate to their offending behavior *tomorrow*?" In other words, life course criminology considers the offending behavior of a single individual over time while taking into account that individual's unique life circumstances *at any given time period*.[122]

At any given time period is part of what makes life course criminology so unique: it accepts that an individual's context changes throughout his/her life. These changes are called *transitions*, and represent short periods of a person's life, such as starting a new job or getting married, that may have a dramatic impact on his/her current *trajectory*. A trajectory represents a person's current direction in life, for example holding a job, or going to school. Transitions that change a person's trajectory are called *turning points*. An example of a turning point would be getting a job that keeps an adolescent out of trouble after school. Understanding how trajectories form and impact a person's offending behavior, along with understanding when transitions become turning points, is the goal of life course criminologists.[123]

Three of the most popular life course criminological theories include the dual-taxonomy approach,[124] the age-graded approach,[125] and the interactional approach.[126] The dual-taxonomy theory points out that while most adolescents engage in some form of delinquent behavior, the majority will eventually desist. Those who do not desist typically began offending very early in adolescence, and will continue well into adulthood.[127] The age-graded approach, on the other hand, is more interested in why some people do not offend seriously at all or cease offending, rather than explaining why a person committed a crime. The theory states that informal social control is the key: the more pressure, obligation, and influence a person feels to not engage in offending behavior, the more likely they will not engage in criminal acts. For the age-graded perspective, important changes happen during a person's life that have direct relevance for levels of informal social control. For example: informal social control from parents and teachers drops precipitously when an 18-year-old moves out and starts attending college.[128] Finally, the interactional approach combines elements of strain, social learning, life course, and other criminological theories to present a comprehensive explanation for the offending behavior of lower-class males. This theory suggests that each individual possesses a level of antisocial potential. A person's antisocial potential is realized under specific circumstances, which change with age, environment, and previous experiences.[129]

Each of these approaches attempts to explain the following ideas associated with career criminal behavior:

- *Onset*: This occurs at the point in a person's life when they first commit a delinquent or criminal act.
- *Desistance*: This happens when an individual ceases to engage in criminal behavior.
- *Duration*: This is a measurement of time between an individual's onset and their desistance.

- *Frequency*: This is a measurement of how actively or regularly a person engages in criminal behavior within a given period of time.
- *Participation*: This is a global measurement of criminal offenders within a certain population at any given time. It sets a baseline to understand career criminals (those with high frequency) as opposed to those who have broken the law a few times (those with very low frequency).[130]

Each of these theories, while still in the development stage, has nevertheless been supported by several studies. They are inherently difficult to research, given the need for study participation over long periods of time, but several longitudinal studies have demonstrated very promising results.[131]

Applying the Theory to the Study of Police Misconduct

Recently, one researcher applied life course criminology to the study of police misconduct. Christopher J. Harris's book, called *Pathways of Police Misconduct*, examined two groups of officers from a large northeastern police agency.[132] Officers comprising the first group entered the police force between 1987 and 1990—Harris called this group the late 1980s group. The late 1990s group entered the police force between 1991 and 1994. For all officers in the study, data were collected up to 2001. Harris's study is unique because it represents the first (and as yet only) longitudinal study of police misconduct employing the life course criminology paradigm.

In his book, Harris highlighted a number of challenges in studying police behavior under the life course framework. Two specific problems will be discussed here. First, in many studies of criminal behavior, the life course criminology theory is tested using data from police departments, courts, and correctional institutions. The problem with data from these sources is that they miss an unknown number of offenders who did not get caught. For life course research, this problem is exaggerated because of the possibility that as life course persistent offenders continue to offend, they may get better at avoiding detection. This problem carries over to the study of police misconduct: whether using citizen complaints or internal complaints (which is what Harris does), studying police misconduct is wholly contingent upon police officers getting caught breaking the rules. Because the police subculture is dominated by a code of silence that often prevents wrong behavior from coming to light,[133] this may be even more difficult for police researchers.

The second problem is with the ideas of onset and desistance.[134] This is related to the first problem, because if a researcher is using arrest data, for example, to determine when an offender begins his/her criminal career, that researcher may be missing the mark. The same applies for desistance. However, it is also the case that, over long periods of time, offenders may start up and stop offending two or three times, according to specific life trajectories and turning points. What's more, an offender who is incarcerated has by default desisted in criminal behavior (in most cases). Similarly for police officers: their misconduct onset may be masked until a citizen or fellow officer complains. More important, dismissal from the agency is a default desistance. This makes it difficult to use the life course theory in understanding police misconduct because it limits the researcher's chances at seeing the individual's "life-as-a-police-officer" play out. One possible solution to this is to focus on less serious forms of misconduct that may result in official action just shy of dismissal, which is what Harris has done. Overall, Harris found that while most police misconduct occurs early in a career, there are a nontrivial number of officers who persist in misconduct throughout their whole career. Although Harris's study is not without methodological weaknesses, this finding alone is enough to warrant more attention to the life course paradigm in the study of police misconduct.

Life Course Theory and the Jammed Up Study

Because the study discussed in this book details police misconduct over a 20-year period for more than 3,000 officers, life course criminology is a very appropriate theoretical framework. The current study can be understood as presenting a whole suite of factors that may influence why some officers engage in misconduct leading to dismissal and why some do not. Many of these variables are events, and can be understood within the framework of life course criminology. For example: receiving a promotion, earning a college degree, maturing in the job (measured as "Years on the job"), getting married or divorced, and disciplinary outcomes were all variables found to be significantly predictive of whether an officer engaged in career-ending misconduct. Using the life course framework allows for an understanding of how each of these events acts as turning points for certain officers, either pushing them to continue engaging in misconduct, or protecting against future misconduct.

The comprehensiveness of information for each officer gleaned through the data collection process allows for a rich depiction of "life" trajectories, transitions, and turning points. This may shed light on the phenomenon that most officers, if they do engage in misconduct, do so primarily at the front end of their careers. Further, it will shift the focus from comparing different officers to understanding individual officer behavior. For example, the current study suggests that the mandatory drug testing policy implemented in the late 1980s is one potential explanation for patterns in NYPD dismissal rates. That is, the policy change is an explanation for why some officers were dismissed while other officers were not. Applying the life course criminology framework would allow researchers to understand why one officer engaged in misconduct before the mandatory drug testing, and why they did not do so afterward; or, if they merely changed *modus operandi.*

The longitudinal nature of the research time frame combined with the richness and detail of the data certainly create an ideal situation for exploring police misconduct using the life course paradigm. Added to these strengths is the fact that the study contains multiple measurements of police misconduct. This may help cope with the artificial desistance problem discussed above: rather than focusing on misconduct so egregious that officials' hands are tied as to the ultimate outcome of dismissal, researchers can hone in on those low-level misconduct problems for which officials have some level of discretion in determining what to do about the officer. This would allow researchers to enjoy a longer study time frame than what might otherwise be allowed.

Next Steps for Life Course Theory and Police Misconduct

There are two keys to studying life course theory as it applies to police misconduct: pinpointing events associated with the theory, and doing so within a longitudinal framework. In terms of pinpointing theoretical events, researchers first need to outline what constitutes a trajectory for a policing career. That is, are there normal career paths for police officers, such as paths that lead some officers to seek out administrative positions, while others remain patrol officers? Is there such a thing as a path to police misconduct? More important, what are the distinguishing features of these trajectories? In a similar vein, researchers need to account for and define specific turning points. Recall that turning points are those events that have the capacity to shift an individual from one trajectory to another. Are there such linchpin moments in an officer's career that have sway over where they are headed professionally? Finally, fully understanding the connections between what an officer does early on and how it plays out in a sequence of events of the course of a career is vital to understanding misconduct through life course theory.

The second key is acquiring longitudinal data. This is no easy task, and remains the bane of most social science researchers. Agencies that employ some sort of early intervention system[135] may be best positioned to hold the necessary data. But for reasons discussed throughout this section, such systems are limited in the depth and breadth of data available. This issue is made more difficult because, done properly, life course criminology as applied to police misconduct should consider variables both before and after an officer's career: what pushed the officer to become a police officer? What did they do after their career? This will provide a more comprehensive understanding of whether police misconduct is something idiosyncratic to the profession, or if it is the manifestation of an underlying propensity toward misbehavior.[136] Gathering this data will be the biggest challenge for those interested in this line of research. Still, longitudinal research is a mainstay of both the social and psychological researchers, and prior studies can serve as a guide for future endeavors focused on policing.

To sum it up, life course criminology is focused on what events in an individual's life pull them away from offending behavior, or push them toward it. This theoretical framework has the potential to be meaningfully applied to the study of police misconduct because, just as offenders experience important events throughout their lives, officers also experience life-changing events throughout their careers. As a case in point, life course criminology helps to paint a fascinating picture of the trajectories of the 3,085 officers in the *Jammed Up* study, including the misconduct trajectories of more than 1,500 NYPD officers.

Conclusions

This exploratory venture sought to address a gap in police research by employing theoretical frameworks to examine officer misconduct. After a review of the prevailing theoretical frameworks, including rotten apple, noble cause, Kappeler et al.'s anthropological framework, and a handful of preliminary efforts using criminological theories, we consider misconduct through the lens of four widely accepted criminological theories. Given that the *Jammed Up* study was not designed as a test of any particular theory, there are limits to what we can say about each, and we leave it to the reader to determine which theory offers the most (or least) promise. We do think that additional investigation of each theory is warranted, however. For example, the application of life course theory to a police officer's career—with trajectories and turning points—is very intriguing. Consideration of stress as a source of strain also raises interesting possibilities. Moreover, although we noted at the beginning of the chapter that there is a distinction between non-criminal (or administrative) and criminal misconduct, we set aside that difference because several of the theories described here offer insights into both types of misdeeds, under a more general rubric of deviant behavior. Social learning theory, for example, highlights the adoption of deviant norms through the police subculture, which can include both criminal misconduct (e.g., theft) and administrative deviance such as accepting free meals and moonlighting. Self-control theory may also be applicable in this regard. In the end, efforts to reduce police misconduct will be increasingly successful when they are informed by a more complete understanding of the causes of the phenomena. We think that this chapter offers much food for thought in that regard, and we hope it initiates a dialogue over the utility of criminological theory for explaining police misbehavior.

What We Know about Being Jammed Up, and Transitioning to a Discourse on Good Policing

The present volume represents the culmination of one of the largest and most comprehensive studies of police misconduct ever conducted in the United States. With the help of roughly 20 NYPD employees (who worked on the study after hours at Police Headquarters), and with unprecedented access granted by the command staff of the NYPD, the research team collected data on both individual police officers and the organization over a 50-year time period.[1] The research process itself, coupled with results of multiple quantitative analyses, allow us to draw several conclusions about the causes, consequences, and meaning of career-ending police misconduct. The present chapter summarizes the major findings and reflects on the process of gathering data, defining police misconduct through the use of departmental records, and the meaning of being *jammed up*. In addition, building on observations made in chapter 6 and elsewhere in the book, we conclude by offering a model based on Fyfe's body of research that might facilitate "good" policing, which we hope will allow police scholars to move away from defining good policing as simply the absence or the control of police misconduct.

CHAPTER EIGHT

Summary of Major Findings

As previously noted, the most interesting, complicated, and vexing finding was related to race, ethnicity, and police misconduct. Recall that the study found that while controlling for a large number of individual-level factors, African American police officers were more than three times more likely than white officers to be separated from the department for misconduct, while Hispanic officers were twice as likely as white officers to be separated for misconduct. It is interesting that over the course of the study, misconduct disparities between white and Hispanic officers decreased to the point where their rates of career-ending misconduct became virtually indistinguishable by 1996. Over the same time period, the NYPD became increasingly integrated along racial, ethnic, and gender dimensions. It may be that with the increased diversity in the organization, the traditional "white male" cultural domination that likely existed in the NYPD—as in many (if not most) American police departments—may have been tempered over time to the point that women and Hispanic officers came to be contributors to the culture rather than being expected to adopt it. Over that same time period, however, although the disparities between

African American and white officers decreased, black officers remained at least twice as likely as white officers to be separated for misconduct.

The race and ethnicity findings, however, are nuanced. The multivariate examinations showed that while controlling for a long list of theoretical covariates, the misconduct disparities between white and non-white officers were largely driven by involvement in serious misconduct and drug use. These are the types of misconduct for which the department is left with little discretion as to how to respond, particularly when it comes to criminal matters. There were no significant differences between white and non-white officers in terms of administrative misconduct—i.e., the type for which the department has a great deal of discretion when it comes to responding to the misconduct—suggesting parity in terms of identifying, investigating, and adjudicating administrative rule violations across racial and ethnic dimensions. This is not to suggest, however, that the NYPD has no culpability over the production of career-ending misconduct patterns by race and ethnicity. If the police department over this time period hired African American and Hispanic officers into the police officer ranks but generally failed to promote them into the supervisory ranks, then this may have left the impression that non-white officers were somehow less capable than white officers; and this perception may have led to increased scrutiny of African American and Hispanic officers over the white officers. Moreover, the longer one remains a line officer, the longer one is exposed to opportunities for misconduct. If white and non-white officers are promoted at differential rates, then their exposures to risky settings also vary by race/ethnicity. Recall, for example, that the strongest factor that protected African American officers from career-ending misconduct was getting promoted to a supervisory rank.

It may also be the case that African American and Hispanic officers tended to be assigned disproportionately to "risky" police precincts—i.e., those characterized by social disorganization and police-citizen conflict.[2] Under such circumstances, and consistent with the communities and crime literature, we would expect that officers assigned to risky environments would be more likely to engage in career misconduct than those assigned to more socially/economically stable precincts. Perhaps more than other findings, those for race, ethnicity, and misconduct produced a few more questions than they answered, indicating a substantial limitation of the present methodology. Although the matched case design is methodologically reliable (assuming good quality data), allowing researchers to address multiple research questions with great efficiency across a large sample, it nevertheless compromises some context for the sake of validity. To more thoroughly investigate and understand the meaning of race and ethnicity as "predictors" of career-ending misconduct, future studies should use qualitative designs (e.g., ethnography) to better address this very complex relationship.

The study also found that problematic personal histories predicted career-ending police misconduct. To a great extent, these findings were consistent with "common sense" explanations of deviance: *The best predictors of behavioral problems at time 2 were behavioral problems at time 1.* For example, disciplinary and reliability problems in previous jobs predicted police misconduct for all officers, and so did prior criminal involvement. The latter findings were particularly salient for African American officers, whose probability for misconduct was amplified by prior public order arrests (recall the CHAID analyses in chapter 5). Moreover, once an officer was on the job, a strong predictor of career-ending misconduct was the mean number of complaints the officer had per year. Indeed, yearly complaints were the second strongest predictor of police misconduct for the entire sample, eclipsed only by "African American" officer.

In addition to examining the predictors of police misconduct, the study also identified several factors that appeared to protect officers from engaging in career-ending misconduct. For example, for the entire sample, a college education exerted a strong protective effect against career-ending misconduct. Interestingly, obtaining an Associates' degree had the strongest protective effect, followed closely by a Bachelors' degree. Although postgraduate work was also inversely associated with misconduct, its effect was not statistically significant. As noted previously, the relationship between college and police misconduct is a difficult one to interpret. Although predictive in this study, it is possible that the relationship is spurious—i.e., that both earning a college degree and not getting *jammed up* are caused by a third, unmeasured factor. It may be, for example, that some form of internalized personal commitment and/or a value system that the study did not measure may have led some officers to both earn a college degree and become relatively successful in their careers (or at the very least, to not become *jammed up*).

The fact that education and age at appointment were inversely associated with the misconduct outcome suggests something about the role of maturity in protecting officers (and perhaps organizations) from career-ending misconduct. Like the risk factors, the protective factors were nuanced and conditioned primarily by officer race. Among Hispanic officers, for example, the probability of engaging in career-ending misconduct decreased substantially when the background investigators recommended hiring the officer at the conclusion of the job application process. Among the entire sample, background investigator recommendations were not statistically significant predictors of misconduct. For reasons that are difficult to explain, these "clinical" assessments of job fitness seemed salient only for Hispanic and white officers, again suggesting the need for a more contextualized methodology to study this issue in the future.

For African American officers, the two strongest protective factors were reliability in prior jobs, and (as noted above) getting promoted to a supervisory rank. When African American officers had no prior public order offenses *and* they were promoted into supervisory ranks, their likelihood of engaging in career-ending misconduct dropped by almost 40 percent. For white officers (like Hispanic officers), background investigator approval was a fairly robust factor that protected against career-ending misconduct. In addition, and unlike non-white officers, both being married at appointment and getting married at some point while on the job substantially decreased the probability of engaging in career-ending misconduct. To some extent, this finding supports the life course criminology perspective, which finds that marriage often decreases the risk of engaging in crime, particularly for males.[3]

The identification of risk and protective factors at the individual officer level is particularly interesting when considered within the context of the larger organization over time. As noted previously, the misconduct study was roughly anchored by two major public scandals; it included time periods where the department laid off thousands of police officers with almost one stroke of the pen, hired nobody for several years, and then hired back thousands of officers almost faster than it could train them. It certainly hired many officers faster than it was able to complete background investigations on them, which largely accounts for the great sample heterogeneity: Many applicants who became police officers in the early 1980s never would have been hired had the department taken the time to have completed background investigations on them.

For example, recall that the individual-level findings showed that prior arrests were a strong predictor of career-ending misconduct, and that in 1986, 10 percent of all officers hired into the NYPD had arrest records. Over the next 12 months, the rate of organizational misconduct went from approximately 3 per 1,000 officers to over 5 per 1,000 officers. Although our research methodology does not permit us to make rigorous causal inferences about the link between individual arrests and organizational misconduct, we nevertheless conclude that the hiring and screening practices of the NYPD may have substantially influenced rates of career-ending misconduct observed at the organizational level. Although most police departments in the modern era likely do not hire police officers with extensive criminal histories, police departments can likely do themselves a favor by hiring "mature" candidates (in terms of age), those with a postsecondary education, and those with few if no prior arrests. Such hiring practices may help to keep rates of organizational misconduct low, while potentially ensuring a higher level of professionalism among officers.

Because of the size of the NYPD and the vastness more generally of New York City, it may be natural to question the extent to which findings from the present study can generalize to other police organizations[4]—the average of which employs no more than 20 sworn officers. We argue here that it is precisely the size and magnitude of both the city and its police department that may inform both policies and practices of other departments across the country. With the exception perhaps of the police departments in the cities of Chicago, Los Angeles, and Philadelphia, no other city in the country could possibly generate the number of cases required to conduct a reliable statistical analysis of career-ending misconduct than did the NYPD. Moreover, because the time period studied included such great variation in terms of hiring practices, from a temporal standpoint, the study's methodology almost represents a natural time-series experiment. Thus, any police department in the United States that will hire, lay off, and/or rehire officers, that will develop recruitment protocols and minimum job standards for employment, and that will seek to understand the importance of organizational diversity as it relates to misconduct, should benefit from the findings reported in this volume.

Why the Definition of Jammed Up Matters

It is important to emphasize that both the individual-level and organizational findings related to risk and protective factors of police misconduct are wholly contingent upon how misconduct is defined. When the research team first set out to conduct a study of police misconduct in the NYPD, it presumed (perhaps naïvely) that the largest police department in the country would have maintained extensive records on who had been separated for misconduct and when. Moreover, the research team also expected to define misconduct in terms of officers who had been dismissed or terminated from employment—largely following the methodology of the Uniform Crime Reports (UCR), which define "crime" in terms of criminal complaint. We quickly learned that neither was the case: The department did not know how many officers had been terminated or dismissed, let alone separated from employment over the time period studied; and it did not maintain separation records in a centralized database.[5] As it turned out, the absence of centralized records demonstrated the need for the research team to expand its definition of police misconduct. Using departmental designations of "terminated" or "dismissed" would have compromised construct validity.

Contrary to at least one recent criticism of the original *Bad Cops* study,[6] the research team did not limit its outcome measure to "corruption," or "deviance"; and it did not allow the NYPD to inform us of who had engaged in misconduct.[7] In fact, by studying career-ending misconduct, our findings say almost as much about the organization as they do about the individuals who engaged in the misconduct. As noted in previous chapters, when collecting the data for the original *Bad Cops* study, the research team (i.e., the first author of this volume) reviewed personnel orders issued by the NYPD over the 22-year study period. From that review, we identified every police officer who left the job as the result of allegations of misconduct, whether the officer was fired, allowed to retire, resigned without the permission of the police commissioner, or resigned with the permission of the police commissioner. This methodology allowed us to include cases that we likely would have excluded had we focused solely on officers who were terminated or dismissed. The methodology also allowed insights into the value system of the organization.

Drawing on Weber, Gulick, and Urwick,[8] Manning observes that government bureaus are "organized pockets of secrecy," and that "it is well known that organizational records are a confirmation of decisions made by more personal means."[9] Although Manning meant this as a criticism of the current study, we regard his observation as confirmation of our methodological approach. To a great extent, police (and other formal) organizations are in part decision-making entities; and, like police officers on the street who have to decide when to arrest a suspect, police organizations must decide how to investigate and respond to potential incidents of officer misconduct. As with the police officer decision-making literature,[10] which generally shows that the more serious the incident, the less discretion officers use when deciding to invoke formal authority (e.g., arrests, deadly force), the present study finds a similar pattern at the organizational level. For serious cases of police misconduct, when there was solid evidence that officers had broken the law or violated major administrative policies, the NYPD generally exercised little discretion when deciding on dispositions: if found culpable, the offending officer(s) were released from employment either through termination or dismissal. Thus, any study of police misconduct that were to rely on dismissals and terminations very likely would produce information about the most serious and most important types of police misconduct (similar to studies of crime that rely on UCR or the National Incident-Based Reporting System [NIBRS] data).

The present study, however, did not rely simply on dismissals and terminations for its definition of police misconduct. The research team made many "clinical" assessments about who should be included as study officers based on the circumstances of the separation. For example, if review of the personnel orders showed that an officer had been placed on administrative leave or suspension, and then subsequent personnel orders showed that the officer had "resigned with the permission of the police commissioner," then the research team located that officer's personnel file for review. In many cases, the initial review indicated that, although the officer appeared to have resigned under neutral circumstances, further examination showed that the officer had been accused of a major crime but was allowed to leave voluntarily because he/she gave evidence against other officers. Another common suspicious finding made during the records review process was when an officer had been dismissed or terminated for relatively minor or vague policy infractions—e.g., "conduct unbecoming an officer," "out of uniform," or other so-called white socks violations. When the research team encountered these types of separations, it always located the relevant officer's personnel file for further review. In many cases, we found that when an officer had been dismissed for a relatively minor event, that officer usually had been the subject of prior investigations for serious misconduct, had multiple citizen complaints that had been adjudicated as unsustained, or was somehow viewed as a problem within the organization (e.g., had been the subject of multiple command disciplines).

Using this methodology allowed us to conclude that getting *jammed up* means a combination of two factors: (1) the officer engaged in serious behavioral problems, which led to separation; and (2) because the officer's behavior violated rules that conflicted with the proper functioning of the organization, the department decided that the officer was a problem and not a good fit in the agency. This designation of "problem" officer led the organization to investigate and finally separate the officer. As such, regardless of the final disposition (e.g., termination or dismissal), the true meaning of *jammed up* resides in the circumstances surrounding the events that led to the separation. Perhaps above all else, police organizations strive to maintain discipline, adherence to the chain of command, and control over the information they present to their audiences (i.e., the public). One of the most basic and perhaps effective methods for maintaining that control is to identify and rid themselves of "problem" officers. Unlike the criminal justice system, which relies on very high standards for establishing criminal guilt, police departments have both the resources and the expertise to investigate and hold accountable officers identified as problems. In recognizing this organizational decision-making process, the present methodology purposely worked within the department's own record-keeping framework to identify officers who engaged in career-ending misconduct.

Bridging the Gap between Bad Cops and Good Policing

It would be inaccurate to characterize the current study as one that attempted to distinguish good cops from bad cops.[11] Rather, and as noted, this was a study that attempted to distinguish officers who engaged in career misconduct from other officers. The distinction is subtle but crucial: the sampling strategy first identified officers who had been separated for career-ending misconduct and then randomly matched them to a group of officers who had not been separated for career-ending misconduct. The comparison sample was in no way stratified to select "good" cops for the purposes of comparing them to "bad" cops. As a result, the most the study can do is distinguish officers who engaged in career-ending misconduct from any other average officer. Moreover, although the primary focus of the present volume was to define career-ending police misconduct in a meaningful way, and then to identify risk factors for career-ending misconduct, it also sought to initiate a larger discussion of bad policing—which certainly incorporates misconduct—but also includes using and perhaps misusing legal forms of police coercion. In simple terms, bad policing is more than just criminal and administrative misdeeds. Importantly, this expanded conception of bad policing lays the groundwork for introducing the equally important, though different, discussion of what constitutes good policing.

To this end, the review in chapter 6 largely moved away from studying individual officers (which had been the primary focus of the volume to that point), to studying patterns of misconduct and aggressive policing in the contexts of *where* that policing took place. In that chapter we showed that, although NYPD enforcement strategies may have produced crime rate reductions, the benefits of those reductions were counterbalanced by the costs: crime rate reductions (at the precinct level) were often short-lived or salient for only certain types of crimes;[12] enforcement strategies that may have worked in some communities seemed to have had deleterious effects in others;[13] and evidence shows that the department sometimes used the ethnic composition of places as one determinant of police deployment.[14]

While chapter 6 serves as a summary of the first author's prior work and places this study in its proper ecological context, it also serves as the anchor for our transition from bad policing to good policing. In many ways, this makes chapter 6 the most important chapter in the book because it lays a foundation for our conception of good and bad policing as two distinct phenomena—each worthy of inquiry independent of the other. Importantly, this shift in focus to good policing brings us back to the work of James Fyfe, the original architect of the *Bad Cops* study. Like many classically oriented scholars of the police, Fyfe devoted most of his professional life to thinking (and writing) about police accountability less in terms of the absence (or reduction) of misconduct and more in terms of the production of "good" policing. Fyfe argued that the best way for the police to develop a "good" policing standard was to adopt a protection of life mandate. Fyfe argued that all police policy and strategy orientations should derive from a "protection of life" paradigm.[15]

Current Accountability Standards Do Not Necessarily Encourage Good Policing

In discussions of (and even in our classes on) police accountability, we often focus on redressing and/or preventing misconduct—i.e., police behaviors that violate administrative and/or legal standards like those described throughout this book. Perhaps the most obvious of these is profit-motivated misconduct, such as when officers steal drugs from drug dealers and then sell them, or when officers protect gambling or prostitution enterprises in exchange for money or other forms of currency. Certainly, it is important both to detect and respond to such forms of police malpractice—because that is what they are: malpractice, in the legal sense of the term, i.e., as an intentional harm done by a person violating well-understood rules of his or her profession.

Similarly, abuse of police authority when we can accurately identify it (e.g., physical and verbal abuse) seems equally important to redress and prevent; and because by definition official misconduct and abuse of authority are wrong, sanctioning such behaviors is generally non-controversial and expected. For this we have the conventional mechanisms of police accountability: trial courts (both civil and criminal), appellate courts, and police department disciplinary review processes. In addition to these mechanisms, there are the police administrators who often implement internal policies in response to mounting social and legal pressures to conform to emerging legal standards. Virtually all these accountability models are driven by bodies external to the police, which are then theoretically integrated into the organization from a top-down approach; and although we generally know that we do not want corrupt or overly violent police officers, we often do not know exactly what we do want in our police. As Grant and Grant[16] have aptly noted, police department hiring practices are generally designed to screen out undesirable applicants, which is substantively different from trying to screen in desirable applicants. In that context and at the aggregate level, it is not uncommon for police departments to use accountability mechanisms to limit misconduct or excessive force. At the same time, however, these accountability mechanisms do little to improve the overall quality of policing.

Toward the Protection of Life and Good Policing

Although the general right to use coercive authority resides at the core of public policing, coercion used primarily to satisfy law enforcement ends often sets the stage for abuse scandals[17] and compromised police legitimacy;[18] and it ignores Peter Manning's argument that the primary job of the police is to "look after people,"[19] an argument analogous to a protection of life mandate. Looking after people means that the police sometimes arrest drug dealers for the intrinsic reasons of protecting children from harm, protecting the community from potential violence, and in some cases, protecting substance abusers from themselves. Looking after people, however, does not mean that the police use drug arrests in certain communities to simply gather information on other criminal activity—in effect to perpetuate the production of (felony) arrest statistics.[20] This is not looking after people or protecting life, and it is not "good" policing. It is using coercion in order to justify the use of more coercion.

Police can point to the numbers to prove they are doing something important; but it is arguable whether, in terms of costs versus benefits, such aggressive tactics produce good overall. Their crime reduction effects are contested, and the resentment they engender can discourage entire communities from cooperating with police when criminal investigations could indeed prevent crime. In short, setting aside public incidents of police misconduct—which are clear examples of "bad" policing—aggressive policing in targeted communities, even when called "community policing," might not be good policing because it does not protect life in the long run.

There are several ways by which Fyfe's protection of life philosophy and good policing principles might be integrated. When the public demands that the police bring coercion to bear on a social problem (e.g., responding to domestic abusers, clearing skateboarders from public areas), the message should be filtered through a "protection of life" organizational culture that places equal value on the victims, communities, and the offenders; and the police administration should seek the input of highly skilled officers in the development of strategies and practices designed to respond to the problem with the interests of all parties (offender, victim, community) in mind. One way by which the protection of life organizational culture may effectively filter down through the bureaucratic layers of the agency is via the field training officers (FTOs). Toch[21] argued that for the purposes of controlling police violence, field training officers were instrumental in bridging the gap for new officers between the messages they received in the training academy and the messages they received from their peers once on the street. Toch argued that FTOs serve a crucial organizational role because, among other functions, they help probationary police officers practice their recently acquired skills in live settings while under highly structured supervision. During this formative period in a police officer's career, FTOs can help new officers interpret street encounters in ways that allow them to learn and practice good policing through the metaphorical lenses of a protection of life mandate. Once they complete their field training programs, police officers may continue to practice good policing and the protection of life in both patrol and specialized settings.

To the extent that the organization fosters an integrated protection of life and good policing paradigm both through transmitting a consistent protection of life value system from top to bottom and reinforcing that message by altering performance evaluation criteria in ways that encourage constructive police decision making (which may not always involve enforcement outcomes), then the organization may develop a cycle where the "protection of life" value system is conveyed during the training academy and reinforced by the organization through the field training program and field appraisal processes. Ultimately, the organization

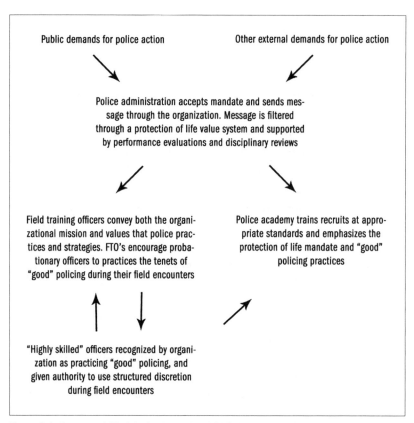

Figure 8.1. Conceptual Model of a Protection of Life Paradigm Informed by "Good" Policing Strategies

may identify "highly skilled" officers (who also may serve as FTOs), whose "good policing" activities are recognized by the organization and fed back into training academy curricula so that the organization may continually learn from the practices of good police officers.

Figure 8.1 offers a proposed model that shows a process by which the public and other external forces largely shape the police mandate (recall the previous discussion of the sources of the police mandate), which the police administration transmits through the organization. For present purposes, the model shows that the police administration communicates the agency's protection of life mission directly to the police academy and to field training officers. The police academy trains recruits at the appropriate professional standards while emphasizing "good policing" and the protection of life. The FTOs integrate the mission and strategies when training probationary police officers. Notice that a critical component of the model is that officers recognized among their peers as highly skilled have opportunities to work with the academy and FTOs, creating a "feedback loop" that will help develop standards of good policing throughout the organization.

Eventually, the good policing practices inform both the academy and field training programs, representing primarily a "bottom-up" approach to developing good policing standards. The model is perhaps overly simplified in that it ignores communication channels between the administration and specialized units, all of which likely have a stake in "good" policing and the protection of life. The model presented in figure 8.1 is meant to initiate a discussion of how the top-down role definition approach might reconcile with a bottom-up "good policing" paradigm that is guided by a protection of life organizational value system.

It is important to note two caveats. First, as is commonly acknowledged, American policing is bureaucratically structured as a quasi-military institution; and in the military, authority flows from the top down. It is typical for field-grade and general officers to develop battle plans while giving company-grade officers and enlisted personnel (i.e., those at the lowest levels of their rank structures) both incomplete information and little discretion as to how to execute the battle plans.[22] As Skolnick and Fyfe[23] observe, however, this is the exact opposite of how police organizations operate: in policing, the people at the lowest level of the bureaucracy (e.g., patrol officers) have the most knowledge of street-level conditions; they have the greatest autonomy because of the unsupervised nature of their work; and they provide crucial information to the highest levels of the organization. Thus, for these and other reasons (described below), the paramilitary structure of policing seems largely incompatible with the concepts of the "highly skilled" officer and of structured discretion for patrol officers, which represent fundamental elements of the integrated good policing and protection of life mandate.

As a second caveat, it should be noted that in order for an organization to perpetuate a system such as described in figure 8.1, it must develop (and perhaps alter) incentive and disincentive programs to encourage good policing while discouraging bad policing. Performance evaluation practices must be consistent throughout the organization to reward police practices that are consistent with the protection of life mandate; and although it remains important to respond to and redress allegations of police misconduct, organizations must move beyond the traditional approaches to police accountability by also examining patterns of police authority that are poorly distributed across people and places (e.g., deployment practices that place residents of certain communities at disproportionate risk of arrest/apprehension due to extra-legal factors, such as racial composition).

An integrated protection of life and good policing approach could accomplish several things. First, it would allow the line officers to become recognized by the organization as "specialists" in a given area (e.g., working with juveniles, de-escalating domestic violence events), and it would allow them to help inform the style of policing in their organization. This bottom-up approach would likely achieve increased compliance to policy, as officers might take "ownership" in the development of strategies and practices. Next, the integrated protection of life philosophy would assign value to officer decisions that do not necessarily end in arrest. Indeed, such an approach would likely make transparent decisions that police officers were already making, but that may have violated departmental policy. To some extent, this integrated program may be viewed as a form of problem-oriented policing informed by Davis's arguments favoring "structured discretion."[24]

In terms of daily practices, an integrated protection of life and good policing approach would certainly include law enforcement as a major police function. It would also emphasize the development of "little" practices that encourage civility in police officers and would remind them that they are generally visitors to, and not residents of, the communities they serve. During coercive transactions with the public, the protection of life mandate would make room for officers to say "please," "thank you," and "I'm sorry" where appropriate. The protection of life mandate would allow officers to think of crime more as a public health matter than as the result of defective people making deviant choices. In short, it would remind police officers to respect and value people who are contacted by police while at their worst, people who are not thinking clearly, even people who pose some threat to the public order and public safety.

Conclusions

This chapter sought to accomplish two objectives. First, it began with a review of key findings from perhaps the largest study of police misconduct ever conducted. The findings here confirm conventional wisdom in a number of ways, particularly with regard to the screening processes departments use to exclude those who are ill-suited for the job. Going back to the officers introduced at the beginning of chapter 1, Mitchell Tisdale had several "red flags" in his past that this study highlighted as predictive of his eventual termination from the department. But we also argue that the examination of police misconduct is highly complex, and a focus solely on individual-level characteristics presents an incomplete picture. The career-ending separation of Paul Barrett (also from chapter 1) —who had no red flags in his past, who was married, and who had been promoted— highlights this important point. In simple terms, this study has answered some old questions about the causes and correlates of police misconduct, but in the process, it has also raised additional, perhaps more vexing questions. Much more work needs to be done with regard to bad policing, and we think this book offers some key insights on how that work should progress.

Second, this chapter sought to transition away from bad policing to initiate a dialogue on good policing. To that end, we introduced a model of good policing, grounded in Fyfe's protection of life principle. To some readers this transition may seem awkward or stilted—or the good policing dialogue may seem "out of place" in a book that focuses primarily on police misconduct. This is exactly our point and perhaps the most important takeaway message from *Jammed Up*. Good policing and bad policing do not fit together like pieces of a puzzle. They are not extremes on the same continuum. Good policing is not the absence of police misconduct. In fact, they represent two completely separate puzzles; and while they may share some pieces, they are indeed two different constructs and must be examined as such. We believe that discussions of good policing have been stunted by failure to deconstruct this good/bad conception, and we offer this as a foundational principle to guide future inquiry into police behavior and performance. Finally, we do not mean to imply that discussions of bad policing should end and be replaced with this focus on good policing. We highlight above the need for more work on bad policing. There are still many questions to be answered about *bad cops* who get *jammed up*. Our point is simply that studies of good policing are not part of that research effort. Good policing represents an entirely different dialogue and one that is long overdue.

Appendix: Analyses from Chapter 5

Table A.1

Principal Component Analysis of Criminal History Variables

Criminal history	EV = 2.81; % variance explained = 20.1	EV = 2.00; % variance explained = 14.3	EV = 1.82; % variance explained = 13.0
Violent crime arrests	.684	–	–
Property crime arrests	.703	–	–
Juvenile delinquency	.514	–	–
Misdemeanor convict	.496	.398	–
Public order arrests	–	.948	–
Moving violations	–	–	.732
Parking summonses	–	–	.627
Driver's license suspension	–	–	.545

Work history	EV = 1.91; % variance explained = 31.9	EV = 1.04; % variance explained = 17.2
Jobs fired from	.765	–
Number of disciplinary actions	.748	–
Derogatory comments from prior employer	.718	–
Workman comp claims	–	.525
Number jobs held	–	.640
30-day (or longer) period unemployment	–	.685

Social conditions	EV = 2.47; % variance explained = 27.5	EV = 1.09; % variance explained = 12.1
Married	.916	–
Number of children	.704	–
Single (never married)	-.891	–
Active school enrollment	–	.546
Divorced	–	.706
Separated	–	.543
Living with partner	–	–

Note: EV = Eigenvalue

Logistic Regression

The logistic regression procedure is carried out in two steps, the first with no predictor variables (step 0) and the second with the predictor variables included (step 1). At step 0 the logistic procedure produced a −2 Log likelihood function of 2,128.61 and classified 51.6 percent of all cases correctly based on the intercept alone: essentially, no better than chance. At step 1 of the logistic regression analysis (during which all independent variables were simultaneously entered), the model produced a final –2 Log likelihood function of 1,604.77 (p < .001) and correctly classified 86.5 percent of all cases correctly. The final correct classification percentage coupled with the Cox and Snell R^2 and Nagelkerke R^2 (.55 and .73, respectively) suggest a highly internally reliable model with high predictive utility.

Multinomial Logistic Regression Analysis

A multinomial logistic regression model was then estimated to observe any possible significant differences among types of career-ending misconduct. Model diagnostics showed that the correct classification percentages were 98.9 for the comparison officers, 79.0 for crime/serious misconduct, 50.0 for administrative violations, and 82.1 for drug test failures/refusals. The model correctly classified 83.3 percent of the total cases and produced a composite pseudo-R^2 of .82. These goodness of fit indicators show a high degree of internal reliability.

Table A.2

Logistic Regression Estimates and Odds Ratios Predicting Police Misconduct

Variable	B	S.E.	Sig.	Odds
Dad NYPD officer	-.004	.001	.007	.996
Military service*				
Army	-.208	.175	.414	–
Navy	-.235	.267	.786	–
Air Force	.270	.262	.654	–
Marine Corps	.087	.306	.432	–
Command risk*				
Inspector precinct	.909	.296	.002	2.48
DI precinct	.813	.242	.001	2.26
Captain precinct	.705	.225	.002	2.02
Police Academy/FTU	.605	.288	.036	1.83
Proactive investigation	-.151	.476	.752	–
Detective/warrants	.290	.316	.358	–
OCCB field units	.830	.456	.069	–
Special patrol units	.106	.299	.724	–
Supervisory rank	-.639	.272	.019	.528
Age at appointment	-.055	.002	.016	.946
Mean complaints per year	1.11	.250	.001	3.03
Educational level at appointment*				
College study (no degree)	-.312	.143	.029	.732
Associate's degree	-1.241	.318	.001	.289
Bachelor's degree or higher	-.799	.313	.011	.450
Other post-secondary	-.218	.558	.696	–

Table A.2 (*continued*)

Variable	B	S.E.	Sig.	Odds
Officer sex	-.324	.203	.111	–
Racial composition*				
Black	1.185	.188	.001	3.27
Latino	.692	.228	.002	2.00
Other minority	1.001	.755	.185	–
Prior police service	-.241	.319	.355	–
Background investigator recommendation	.259	.230	.259	–
Mayor at time of separation*				
Beame (1975–77)	.032	.220	.884	–
Koch (1978–89)	-.485	.288	.092	–
Dinkins (1990–93)	-.509	.281	.070	–
Criminal history				
Traditional dimension	.199	.071	.005	1.22
Public order dimension	.577	.083	.001	1.78
Vehicle code dimension	.027	.065	.680	–
Years on the job	-2.952	.261	.001	.052
Social condition at appointment				
Conventional family dimension	.085	.198	.223	–
Second start dimension	.140	.798	.068	–
Employment history				
Disciplinary problem dimension	.318	.075	.001	1.37
Reliability dimension	.149	.069	.031	1.16

*Reference categories are as follows: military service (none); command risk (staff unit); educational level (high school diploma or less); Racial composition (white); Mayor at separation (Giuliani).
B = Standardized Coefficient; S.E. = Standard Error; Sig = Significance Level; Odds = Odds Ratio

Table A.3

Multinomial Regression Estimates Predicting Three Categories of Police Misconduct

Variable	Crime/Serious Misconduct (n = 581)		Administrative Misconduct (n = 430)		Drug Test Failures or Refusals (n = 420)	
	B	S.E.	B	S.E.	B	S.E.
Dad NYPD officer	-.05**	.001	.182	.668	.186	.668
Command risk [a]						
Inspector precinct	1.74**	.120	1.26**	.126	1.67**	.122
DI precinct	1.84**	.141	1.73**	.132	.812*	.410
Captain precinct	1.89*	.167	1.53**	.142	1.43*	.672
Police Academy/FTU	1.01*	.100	1.11*	.404	1.12	.711
Proactive investigation	-.251	.245	.365	.350	.261	.255
Detective/warrants	.842	.613	.985	.510	.852	.838
OCCB field units	.754	.533	.657	.541	.546	.412
Special patrol units	.643	.379	.512	.405	.521	.409

(*continued*)

Variable	Crime/Serious Misconduct (n = 581)		Administrative Misconduct (n = 430)		Drug Test Failures or Refusals (n = 420)	
	B	S.E.	B	S.E.	B	S.E.
Supervisory rank	-.633*	.303	.532	.306	-.549*	.171
Age at appointment	-.055*	.012	-.112	.113	-1.47*	.254
Mean complaints per year	1.58**	.126	.595*	.266	.598*	.256
Educational level at appointment [a]						
College study (no degree)	-1.28*	.449	.397	.475	.316	.449
Associate's degree	-1.62**	.145	.713	.477	.654	.451
Bachelor's degree or higher	-1.72**	.125	-.738	.548	-.709**	.050
Other post-secondary	-.876	.743	.534	.345	.521	.402
Racial composition [a]						
Black	1.92**	.161	.975	.751	.878**	.124
Latino	1.64**	.091	.717	.739	.754**	.143
Other minority	1.001	.927	.689	.620	.623	.421
Criminal history						
Traditional dimension	1.07*	.234	1.06*	.483	1.07*	.484
Public order dimension	1.43*	.255	1.70	.972	1.62*	.554
Vehicle code dimension	.027*	.007	1.68*	.612	.276*	.127
Years on the job	-.790*	.400	-.663	.413	-.760*	.368
Employment history						
Disciplinary problem dimension	1.22**	.062	1.26*	.279	1.18*	.520
Reliability dimension	.743*	.394	.677*	.257	.757	.731

[a] Reference categories are as follows: command risk (staff unit); educational level (high school diploma or less); racial composition (white). Reference category for outcome was comparison officers (n = 1542). B = Standardized Coefficient; S.E. = Standard Error.
*$p \leq .05$; **$p \leq .01$.

NOTES

Preface
1 Skogan, *Police and Community in Chicago.*
2 Guyot, *Policing.* Eck, "Science, Values."
3 Fyfe, "'Good' Policing."

Prologue
1 Skolnick and Fyfe, *Above the Law.*
2 Murphy and Pate, *Commissioner*, 237.
3 Murphy and Pate, *Commissioner.*
4 Skolnick and Fyfe, *Above the Law*, 180.
5 Skolnick and Fyfe, *Above the Law.*
6 Black, 1972.

Chapter 1
1 Mitchell Tisdale is a pseudonym, as are all other officer names used in this book.
2 In NYPD nomenclature, dispositions of *unsustained* are not the same as *not guilty*. They simply indicate that there was not enough evidence to infer guilt at an appropriate administrative standard. Dispositions of *unfounded* and *exonerated* are the not guilty dispositions.
3 Research for the *Bad Cops* study (Fyfe and Kane) was supported by the National Institute of Justice grant #1996IJCX0053.
4 For a detailed discussion of this procedure, the interested reader should see Fyfe and Kane, *Bad Cops*, as well as Kane and White, *Bad Cops.*
5 One indicator was whether officers resigned "with the permission of the police commissioner," the NYPD's term of art for departures in good standing. We pulled and reviewed any file that indicated that officers had resigned without the commissioner's permission, and wound up including most such cases in our files.
6 In this process, we also encountered a small number of cases in which probationary officers had been decertified when it was discovered that they had concealed pre-employment histories of criminal behavior or mental illness. These cases, too, were excluded on the reasoning that, although these officers were effectively living a lie after they were hired, they would have been screened out in a more thorough pre-employment investigatory process.
7 This data collection strategy almost certainly missed some small number of forced resignations and retirements that were due to misconduct. Nevertheless, the authors feel confident that we did everything reasonably possible to

capture them all, and that the few that may have been missed do not affect the direction or strength of our findings.

8 For example, if there were ten separated officers from the July 1980 recruit class, then ten control officers were also selected randomly from that class.

9 It should be noted that there were several cases where a randomly selected comparison officer could not be used in the study. For example, a few comparison officers had resigned from the NYPD within the first few days after their appointments, so that their files included insufficient information for comparisons of any kind. In other cases, the selected control officer had left the NYPD so long ago that his/her files had been destroyed in accord with the agency's 21-year document retention schedule. In all instances in which the original randomly selected control officer was determined to be unusable for analysis, the next available officer on the class roster was selected and included.

10 From this point forward, we refer to the current study as *Jammed Up* (rather than *Bad Cops*) for simplicity's sake.

11 Selznick, *T.V.A. and the Grassroots*.

12 Weber, *Theory of Economic and Social Organization*; Moskos, *Cop in the Hood*.

13 Perez, *Common Sense*.

14 Perez, *Common Sense*.

Chapter 2

1 Lardner and Repetto, *NYPD*, pp. 97, 263, 307.

2 Anechiarico and Jacobs, *The Pursuit of Absolute Integrity*.

3 Although discussions of theoretical frameworks would normally be found in the "prior research" chapter, this discussion can be found in chapter 7.

4 Kappeler et al., *Forces of Deviance*.

5 Goldstein, *Police Corruption*, p. 3.

6 Sherman, *Scandal and Reform*; Walker and Katz, *The Police in America*.

7 Stoddard, "The Informal 'Code' of Police Deviancy."

8 Sherman, *Scandal and Reform*.

9 Sherman, *Scandal and Reform*.

10 Sherman, *Scandal and Reform*.

11 Knapp Commission, *Report of the New York City Commission to Investigate Allegations of Police Corruption and the City's Anti-Corruption Procedures*.

12 Sherman, *Police Corruption*.

13 Sherman, *Police Corruption*.

14 Sherman, *Police Corruption*.

15 Sherman, *Police Corruption*.

16 Knapp Commission, *Report of the New York City Commission to Investigate Allegations of Police Corruption and the City's Anti-Corruption Procedures*, p. 4.

17 Sherman, *Scandal and Reform*.

18 Barker and Carter, *Police Deviance*, p. 7.

19 Barker and Carter, *Police Deviance*.

20 Carter, "Hispanic Perception of Police Performance."

21 National Commission on Law Observance and Enforcement, *Report on Lawlessness in Law Enforcement*, p. 1.

22 Del Carmen and Walker, *Confessions and Admissions*.

23 Worden and Catlin, "The Use and Abuse of Force by Police."

24 Worden and Catlin, "The Use and Abuse of Force by Police."

25 Kappeler et al., *Forces of Deviance*.

26 Crank and Caldero, *Police Ethics*.

27 Klockars, "The Dirty Harry Problem."

28 Matthews, "Racial Profiling," p. 38.

29 See RAND, *Do NYPD's Pedestrian Stop Data Indicate Racial Bias?*

30 See Rice and White, *Race, Ethnicity and Policing*, for a complete discussion of the issues surrounding racial profiling.

31 Fyfe, "Always Prepared." Fyfe subsequently reported a similar pattern of inappropriate off-duty police shootings—as well as lesser degrees of force—in Philadelphia.

32 At the time, the NYPD did not issue guns to officers, but instead required them to purchase and equip themselves with designated weapons. NYPD presently supplies officers with duty weapons, leaving them the option of buying one or more of several designated smaller weapons for use while off-duty or on plainclothes duty.

33 Sherman, *Scandal and Reform*.

34 Hale, "Ideology of Police Misbehavior."

35 McMullan, "A Theory of Corruption."

36 Sherman, *Scandal and Reform*, p. 30.

37 Fyfe, "The Split-second Syndrome."

38 Fyfe, "The Split-second Syndrome; see also Van Maanen, "The Asshole."

39 Fyfe, "The Split-second Syndrome."

40 Los Angeles Police Department, *Board of Inquiry into the Rampart Area Corruption Incident*; Philadelphia City Council, *Resolution 950757*.

41 Several researchers have suggested that police reluctance to release data on their officers' transgressions is part of a larger effort to control public perceptions. Manning argues that "the police self is shaped by mass media"; that police go to considerable lengths to control their image and how it is presented in the news media ("Policing and Reflection, p. 153). Similarly, Chermak notes that "police departments actively construct public images of themselves so that news presentation benefits the organization rather than harms it" ("Image Control," p. 21).

42 Chappell and Piquero ("Applying Social Learning Theory to Police Misconduct") offer a thorough discussion of the limitations of complaints as a

misconduct measure, particularly with regard to under- and over-reporting problems (i.e., most people who believe that they have been mistreated do not file a complaint, many complaints are not sustained, and, traditionally, many departments have not been vigorous in their investigations of such complaints).

43 Skolnick and Fyfe, *Above the Law*, p. 18.
44 National Commission on Law Observance and Enforcement, *Report on Lawlessness in Law Enforcement*.
45 Bureau of Justice Statistics, *Contacts Between Police and the Public*.
46 Walker and Katz, *The Police in America*.
47 Reiss, "Police Brutality."
48 Worden, "The Causes of Police Brutality."
49 Alpert and Dunham, *The Force Factor*.
50 Independent Commission on the Los Angeles Police Department.
51 Worden and Catlin, "The Use and Abuse of Force by Police."
52 I.e., the Knapp Commission, *Report of the New York City Commission to Investigate Allegations of Police Corruption and the City's Anti-Corruption Procedures*; Mollen Commission, *Anatomy of Failure, A Path for Success*.
53 E.g., Independent Commission on the Los Angeles Police Department.
54 Perhaps most notably, the recent Rampart scandal, in which Los Angeles police officers allegedly were involved in trafficking and stealing narcotics, and in related violence (Los Angeles Police Department, *Board of Inquiry into the Rampart Area Corruption Incident*). In addition, Philadelphia and New Orleans have, at various times, been marred by scandals involving profit-motivated misconduct and on-duty abuse (see, e.g., Fyfe, *Philadelphia Police Shootings*; New Orleans Mayor's Advisory Committee on Human Relations, *Report on Police Use of Force;* Skolnick and Fyfe, *Above the Law*; Thrasher et al., *Report of Investigation*; United States Civil Rights Commission, *Who Is Guarding the Guardians?*; *United States v. City of Philadelphia*, 1979; Williams, *Vice Squad*).
55 Bobb, *Five years Later*; Chevigny, *Edge of the Knife*; Chicago Police Department, *Chicago Police Problems*; Daley, *Prince of the City*; Domanick, *To Protect and Serve*; Fogelson, *Big-City Police*; Goldstein, *Policing a Free Society*; Kappeler et al., *Forces of Deviance*; The Knapp Commission, *Report of the New York City Commission to Investigate Allegations of Police Corruption and the City's Anti-Corruption Procedures*; Kolts, *The Los Angeles County Sheriff's Department*; Maas, *Serpico*; Mollen Commission, *Anatomy of Failure, A Path for Success*; Murphy and Pate, *Commissioner*; Rothmiller and Goldman, *L.A. Secret Police*; Rubinstein, *City Police*; Sherman, *Scandal and Reform*; Skolnick and Fyfe, *Above the Law*.
56 Daley, *Prince of the City;* Maas, *Serpico*; Mollen Commission, *Anatomy of Failure, A Path for Success;* Murphy and Pate, *Commissioner*.

57 Rubinstein, *City Police*.

58 Chevigny, *Edge of the Knife*, p. 85.

59 In the years since Chevigny wrote this, two notorious incidents (the sodomy inflicted upon Abner Louima in a precinct restroom and the Bronx shooting death of Amadou Diallo) have affected this benign image.

60 See also Fogelson, *Big-City Police*; Goldstein, *Policing a Free Society*, p. 214.

61 Kappeler et al., *Forces of Deviance*, pp. 145–67, 187–238.

62 Bobb et al., *Five Years Later*; Independent Commission on the Los Angeles Police Department; Domanick, *To Protect and Serve;* Rothmiller and Goldman, *L.A. Secret Police;* Skolnick and Fyfe, *Above the Law.*

63 Kolts, *The Los Angeles County Sheriff's Department*; Bobb et al., *Five Years Later.*

64 Cohen and Chaiken, *Police Background Characteristics and Performance.*

65 Wilson, "The Nature of Corruption," p. 162.

66 Mollen, *Anatomy of Failure, A Path for Success.*

67 E.g., Fogelson, *Big-City Police.*

68 Wilson, *Varieties of Police Behavior;* see also Sherman, *Scandal and Reform.*

69 Haller, "Historical Roots of Police Behavior."

70 Sherman, *Scandal and Reform.*

71 Miller, *Cops and Bobbies*; Murphy and Pate, *Commissioner.*

72 Maas, *Serpico.*

73 Knapp Commission, *Report of the New York City Commission to Investigate Allegations of Police Corruption and the City's Anti-Corruption Procedures.*

74 Knapp Commission, *Report of the New York City Commission to Investigate Allegations of Police Corruption and the City's Anti-Corruption Procedures.*

75 Chevigny, *Edge of the Knife;* Domanick, *To Protect and Serve.*

76 Wilson, *Varieties of Police Behavior.*

77 Herbert, "Police Subculture Reconsidered."

78 Herbert, "Police Subculture Reconsidered," p. 347.

79 Klinger, "Negotiating Order in Patrol Work."

80 Klinger, "Negotiating Order in Patrol Work."

81 Kane, "The Social Ecology of Police Misconduct," p. 871.

82 Kane, "The Social Ecology of Police Misconduct."

83 Kane, "The Social Ecology of Police Misconduct."

84 Earlier results from the NIJ-funded *Bad Cops* study were published by Kane and White in a 2009 issue of *Criminology and Public Policy* (Kane and White, "Bad Cops"). Chapter 5 here presents updated findings as well as our reactions to the response essays in that issue of *Criminology and Public Policy*.

85 Waugh, Ede, and Alley, "Police Culture."

86 Hickman, Piquero, and Greene, "Discretion and Gender Disproportionality" (but, cf. Fyfe et al., *Race, Gender and Discipline in the New York City Police Department*).

87 Felkenes, "Affirmative Action in the Los Angeles Police Department."

88 Bloch and Anderson, *Policewomen on Patrol*; Forst, Lucianovic, and Cox, *What Happens After Arrest?*; Melchionne, "The Changing Role of Police-women"; Sherman, "An Evaluation of Policewomen on Patrol"; Worden, "Situational and Attitudinal Explanations of Police Behavior."

89 Grennan, "Findings on the Role of Officer Gender"; Horvath, "The Police Use of Deadly Force."

90 It is unclear, however, that aggressive police posturing and the use of force actually represent misconduct.

91 E.g., Cohen and Chaiken, *Police Background Characteristics and Performance.*

92 Fyfe, *Philadelphia Police Shootings*; Geller and Karales, "Shootings of and by Chicago Police"; Bayley and Garafolo, "The Management of Violence."

93 Fyfe et al., *Race, Gender and Discipline in the New York City Police Department.*

94 Eterno, *Cadets and Policing*; Reuss-Ianni, *Two Cultures of Policing.*

95 Kappeler, Sapp, and Carter, "Police Officer Higher Education."

96 Truxillo, Bennett, and Collins, "College Education and Police Job Performance," p. 270.

97 Cohen and Chaiken, *Police Background Characteristics and Performance.*

98 Cohen and Chaiken, *Police Background Characteristics and Performance.*

99 Cohen and Chaiken, *Police Background Characteristics and Performance.*

100 Cohen and Chaiken, *Police Background Characteristics and Performance.* See also Grant and Grant, "Officer Selection and the Prevention of Abuse of Force."

101 Mollen Commission, *Anatomy of Failure, A Path for Success*, pp. 112–15.

102 Cohen and Chaiken, *Police Background Characteristics and Performance.*

103 In addition, much of the research on police misconduct has lacked a strong theoretical focus that would advance our thinking of causes of the problem. We address this issue in chapter 7.

104 Kane, "Collect and Release Data," p. 779.

105 Cohen and Chaiken, *Police Background Characteristics and Performance.*

106 Independent Commission on the Los Angeles Police Department; Mollen Commission, *Anatomy of Failure, A Path for Success.*

107 Independent Commission on the Los Angeles Police Department; Knapp Commission, *Report of the New York City Commission to Investigate Allegations of Police Corruption and the City's Anti-Corruption Procedures.*

Chapter 3

1 See, for example, Neiderhoffer, *Behind the Shield.*

2 NYPD/IAB, *Annual Report for Year 2000*, p. 4, 20.

3 Knapp Commission, *Report of the New York City Commission.*

4 NYPD/IAB, *Annual Report for Year 2000*, p. 15.

5 NYPD/IAB, *Annual Report for Year 2000.*

6 IAB uses COMPSTAT's computerized geographic information system methodologies to identify such patterns.

7 Employees are also free to bypass command discipline altogether and to insist instead on the filing of formal charges and specifications and resolution of the matter via formal administrative hearing.

8 Exceptions include wrongdoing by probationary officers, where the Police Commissioner has great discretion. Although some lesser cases against probationers do result in trial room proceedings, serious wrongdoing by probationers typically results in summary termination by the commissioner's fiat. In addition, many of the officers we studied resigned or retired rather than face dismissible charges, or were allowed to do so in return for their cooperation in testifying against other officers, or as part of negotiated case dispositions.

9 There are two exceptions to this general pattern. Extremely serious cases (e.g., those also involving criminal proceedings) often are handled by a Department Special Prosecutor rather than the Department Advocate (see NYPD, *Establishment of the Office of the Department Special Prosecutor*). In addition, cases substantiated by the Civilian Complaint Review Board and preferred against members in the rank of police officer are resolved before the Office of Administrative Trials and Hearings (OATH), a city agency independent of both the Personnel and Police departments.

10 The historical pieces of this section are generally based on Bolz and Hershey, *Hostage Cop*; Bouza, *Bronx Beat*; Daley, *Target Blue*, and *Prince of the City*; Knapp Commission, *Report of the New York City Commission*; Fogelson, *Big-City Police*; Gelb, *Varnished Brass*; Lardner, *Crusader*; Lardner and Reppetto, *NYPD*; McAlary, *Buddy Boys*; Melchionne, "The Changing Role of Policewomen"; Murphy, "Corruptive Influences"; Murphy and Pate, *Commissioner*; Reppetto, *The Blue Parade*; Reuss-Ianni, *Two Cultures of Policing*; Sherman, *Scandal and Reform*; Walker, *A Critical History*, and *Taming the System*; and on personal communications with James Fyfe.

11 See Daley, *Target Blue*; Fyfe, *Shots Fired*.

12 By way of comparison, a police officer's salary at the time of the Knapp Commission was about $1,000 per month.

13 Knapp Commission, *Report of the New York City Commission*.

14 Murphy introduced an "up or out" policy, which presumed that 20% of those at the rank of captain and above would be promoted or retire every year (see Murphy and Pate, *Commissioner*).

15 During 1971 and 1972, the department hired as police officers only police trainees (young men who held clerical police positions and who were appointed as police officers when they turned 21 years old) and returning military veterans who were in the service when they became eligible for police employment during earlier years.

16 McManus et al., *Police Training.*

17 Reuss-Ianni, *Two Cultures of Policing.*

18 At one point during this period, NYPD detectives needed a young female officer to serve as a decoy in a plan to arrest a dentist who reportedly molested young women patients while they were under anesthesia. The department could not identify a single suitable officer in its ranks, and the detectives were obliged to arrange a personnel loan from the neighboring Yonkers Police Department.

19 Expansion of the drug testing program during this period was made possible in large measure by two Supreme Court cases decided on the same day in 1989. In *Skinner v. Railway Labor Executives' Ass'n*, the Court ruled that drug testing employees who worked safety-sensitive assignments did not violate the Fourth Amendment protection against warrantless searches. In *National Treasury Employees Union v. Von Raab*, the Court held that the U.S. Customs Service's policy of drug testing without suspicion employees seeking transfer or promotion to drug enforcement related positions, or positions requiring the employee to carry a firearm, was permitted under the Constitution. Though these cases were not specific to local police agencies, both rulings addressed public employees and thus applied to police departments.

20 Sherman, *Police Corruption.*

21 McAlary, *Buddy Boys*, pp. 108, 172.

22 Kappeler et al., *Forces of Deviance.*

23 McAlary, *Buddy Boys*, pp. 185–86.

24 McAlary, *Buddy Boys.*

25 Daley, *Prince of the City*; Lardner and Reppetto, *NYPD.*

26 Kelly, *An Investigation into the Police Department's Conduct*; Mollen Commission, *Anatomy of Failure.*

27 Kelly, *An Investigation into the Police Department's Conduct*; McAlary, *Good Cop, Bad Cop*; Mollen, *Anatomy of Failure.*

28 Mollen Commission, *Anatomy of Failure.*

29 Mollen Commission, *Anatomy of Failure,* p. 10.

30 Loss of a shield has historically led to a five-day suspension for negligence. The officers separated for losing their badges have generally lost them under extraordinary circumstances, such as while patronizing a prostitute or ingesting drugs while on duty.

31 Kelling and Coles, *Fixing Broken Windows.*

32 Greene, "Zero Tolerance."

33 Fagan et al., "Street Stops and Broken Windows Revisited," p. 310. See also NYPD, *Reclaiming the Public Spaces.*

34 NYPD, *Getting Guns off the Streets.*

35 McDonald, *Managing Police Operations.*

36 New York City Mayor's Office, *The Mayor's Management Report.*

37 Bratton, *Turnaround.*

38 Weisburd et al., "Reforming to Preserve."

39 Fagan et al., "Street Stops and Broken Windows Revisited," p. 310.

40 Fagan and Davies, "Street Stops and Broken Windows."

41 Greene, "Zero Tolerance."

42 Greene, "Zero Tolerance."

43 Green, "Testimony of the Public Advocate"; Greene, "Zero Tolerance."

Chapter 4

1 Kane, *Urban Ecology and Police Malpractice.*

2 Kane, *Urban Ecology and Police Malpractice.*

3 Chevigny, *Edge of the Knife.*

4 Domanick, *To Protect and Serve.*

5 Matulia, *A Balance of Forces*; Geller and Scott, *Deadly Force.*

6 Skolnick and Fyfe, *Above the Law*; U.S. Department of Justice, Police Brutality Study.

7 Klockars, "A Theory of Excessive Force."

8 McAlary, "The Frightful Whisperings."

9 A small number of officers who served in the Coast Guard and in the militaries of foreign countries are excluded. It should be noted, however, that many former Marines have achieved great success in the NYPD. In fact, Distinguished Marine Corps alumni dominated the NYPD's top command at the time of the study, including the Police Commissioner, Deputy Commissioner for Counter Terrorism, Chief of Department, Chief of Patrol, Chief of Personnel, as well as many other top administrators.

10 Skolnick and Fyfe, *Above the Law*; White, "Identifying Good Cops."

11 In this analysis we excluded officers who were separated during their probationary period on the grounds that their academic and physical test performance might have affected decisions to terminate them for misconduct.

12 Our contention is strongly supported through anecdotal discussions with NYPD officials.

Chapter 5

1 Muir, *Police*; Christopher Commission, *Report of the Independent Commission.*

2 Waugh, Ede, and Alley, "Police Culture"; Hickman, Piquero, and Greene, "Discretion and Gender."

3 Cohen and Chaiken, *Police Background Characteristics*; Mollen Commission, *Anatomy of Failure.*

4 Cohen and Chaiken, *Police Background Characteristics*; Bowker, "A Theory of the Educational Needs"; Kappeler, Sapp, and Carter, "Police Officer Higher Education."

5 McManus, *Police Training*.

6 Grant and Grant, "Officer Selection."

7 Skolnick and Fyfe, *Above the Law*.

8 See also: Chevigny, *Police Power*, and *Edge of the Knife*.

9 Skolnick and Fyfe, *Above the Law*, 106.

10 E.g., Sherman, *Scandal and Reform*.

11 See also: Knapp Commission, *Report of the New York City Commission*; Mollen Commission, *Anatomy of Failure*.

12 All categorical variables were entered into the model using indicator contrasting, which designates a reference category against which the remaining categories are compared.

13 These categories are conceptually meaningful because they represent the primary dimensions of police misbehavior, but they are also complicated (and hence, somewhat methodologically undermined) by a certain degree of overlap. For example, in some cases where an officer was arrested for drug dealing but not convicted, he/she was often dismissed for "associating with known drug dealers"—an administrative rule violation. In cases where the official dismissal charge did not adequately represent the underlying behaviors that led to dismissal, the authors categorized the officer on the basis of the behaviors that led to the charge and not the charge itself.

14 Jones, Harris, Fader, and Grubstein, "Identifying Chronic Juvenile Offenders," 490.

15 See White and Ready, "Identifying Predictors of Effectiveness."

16 See the discussion of Inspector, Deputy Inspector, and Captain-led precincts in chapter 3.

17 When the slope is negative (i.e., variable is protective), the size of the effect is determined by dividing the odds ratio into 1. For example, the Associates' degree effect is 1/.289 – or 3.5.

18 The low-risk group is also characterized by the absence of risk factors: the background investigator recommended hiring; they had no prior criminal history, etc. Similarly, the high-risk group had few protective factors: they did not get married, they did not get promoted, they were not married at appointment, etc.

19 Martin, *Breaking and Entering*.

20 Hughes, "Dilemmas and Contradictions."

21 Fyfe et al., *Race, Gender and Discipline*.

22 Cohen and Chaiken, *Police Background Characteristics*; Mollen Commission, *Anatomy of Failure*.

23 See also White, "Identifying Good Cops."

24 Walker, *The New World of Police Accountability*, 118.

Chapter 6

1 Rosenfeld et al., "The Impact of Order-Maintenance Policing."
2 Greene, "Zero Tolerance;" Fagan et al., "Street Stops and Broken Windows Revisited."
3 Weitzer, "Incidents of Police Misconduct."
4 Kane, "The Social Ecology."
5 A composite indicator made up of percent population residing in poverty, having low educational attainment, and unemployed; as well as percent of households that were female headed with children and those receiving public assistance income.
6 This is defined as percent of the population that resided in their current residences for less than five years.
7 E.g., Dowd and Bengtson, "Aging in Minority Populations;" Ferraro and Farmer, "Double Jeopardy;" Ferraro, "Double Jeopardy."
8 Kane, "The Social Ecology."
9 Kane, "The Social Ecology," p. 891.
10 Kane, "The Social Ecology."
11 Kane, "Linking Compromised Police Legitimacy."
12 Anderson, *Code of the Street.*
13 Please see Kane ("Linking Compromised Police Legitimacy," p. 478) for a discussion of how he classified precincts by levels of structural disadvantage.
14 Kane, "Linking Compromised Police Legitimacy."
15 Sampson and Bartusch, "Legal Cynicism."
16 Weitzer, "Citizens' Perceptions."
17 Reisig and Parks, "Experience, Quality of Life"; Tyler, *Why People Obey the Law.*
18 Kane, "Linking Compromised Police Legitimacy."
19 Kane, "Linking Compromised Police Legitimacy."
20 E.g., Ahern et al., "Population Vulnerabilities"; Crane, "The Epidemic Theory"; Wilson, *The Truly Disadvantaged.*
21 Kane, "The Social Ecology" and "Linking Compromised Police Legitimacy."
22 Kane, "Linking Compromised Police Legitimacy."
23 Kane, "The Social Ecology."
24 Kane, "Linking Compromised Police Legitimacy."
25 Kane, "Linking Compromised Police Legitimacy."
26 Kane, "Linking Compromised Police Legitimacy."
27 Kane, "Linking Compromised Police Legitimacy," pp. 481–82.
28 Kane, "On the Limits."
29 This is different from Kane ("Linking Compromised Police Legitimacy."), which examined over- and under-policing on violent crime. Kane ("On the Limits") examined actual numbers of arrests on subsequent violent crime.
30 Kane, "On the Limits."

31 Kane, "Social Control in the Metropolis."

32 Kane, "Social Control in the Metropolis."

33 Kane, "Social Control in the Metropolis."

34 Liska and Chamlin, "Social Structure and Crime Control."

35 Kane, "The Social Ecology" and "Social Control in the Metropolis."

36 Jackson, *Minority Group Threat.*

37 Jargowsky, *Poverty and Place*; Wilson, *The Truly Disadvantaged* and *When Work Disappears.*

38 Kane, "The Social Ecology" and "Social Control in the Metropolis."

39 Kane, "The Social Ecology"; "Social Control in the Metropolis"; "Linking Compromised Police Legitimacy"; and "On the Limits."

40 Sampson, "Linking Time and Place."

41 Sampson, "Linking Time and Place," p. 432.

42 Klockars, "A Theory of Excessive Force."

43 Kane, "Linking Compromised Police Legitimacy."

44 See also Kubrin and Weitzer, "Retaliatory Homicide."

45 See Collins et al., *Evaluating Community Policing*; Kane, "Policing in Public Housing"; and "Permanent Beat Assignment."

Chapter 7

1 Contributing authors' names are listed alphabetically.

2 Klofas, Hipple, and McGarrell, *The New Criminal Justice.*

3 Barlow and Decker, *Criminology and Public Policy*. Indeed, the journal *Criminology & Public Policy* is dedicated to this very pursuit.

4 We recognize that life course criminology is not so much a theory of crime as it is a perspective within which to study, often from various theoretical perspectives, how personal turning points influence onset, persistence, duration, and desistance in patterns of criminal offending.

5 E.g., Chappell and Piquero, "Applying Social Learning Theory to Police Misconduct"; Kane, "The Social Ecology of Police Misconduct."

6 Knapp Commission, *Report of the New York City Commission to Investigate Allegations of Police Corruption and the City's Anti-Corruption Procedures.*

7 Walker and Katz, *The Police in America.*

8 I.e., to help others, job security and benefits, etc.—see Lester, "Why Do People Become Police Officers"; Raganella and White, "Race, Gender, and Motivation for Becoming a Police Officer."

9 Knapp Commission, *Report of the New York City Commission to Investigate Allegations of Police Corruption and the City's Anti-Corruption Procedures*, p. 1.

10 Kappeler et al., *Forces of Deviance.*

11 Skolnick and Fyfe, *Above the Law,* p.12.

12 Delattre, *Character and Cops.*

13 Mollen Commission, *Anatomy for Failure, A Path for Success.*

14 Chapell and Piquero, "Applying Social Learning Theory to Police Misconduct."

15 Chapell and Piquero, "Applying Social Learning Theory to Police Misconduct."

16 Hickman, Piquero, and Greene, "Discretion and Gender Disproportionality."

17 Klockars et al., *Measurement of Police Integrity*.

18 Hickman et al., "Discretion and Gender Disproportionality."

19 Pogarksy and Piquero, "Studying the Reach of Deterrence," p. 381.

20 Harris, *Pathways of Police Misconduct*.

21 E.g., Alpert and Dunham, *Force Factor*.

22 Adorno, *The Authoritarian Personality*; Neiderhoffer, *Behind the Shield*.

23 Bayley and Mendelsohn, *Minorities and the Police*; Stoddard, "The Informal 'Code' of Police Deviancy"; Van Maanen, "The Asshole."

24 See later discussion of ecological factors in the "correlates section" of this chapter and chapter 6.

25 Sherman, *Scandal and Reform*.

26 Skolnick and Fyfe, *Above the Law*.

27 Delattre, *Character and Cops*.

28 Crank and Caldero, *Police Ethics*.

29 Crank and Caldero, *Police Ethics*, p. 33.

30 Klockars, "Dirty Harry Problem."

31 Klockars, "Dirty Harry Problem."

32 Crank and Caldero, *Police Ethics*; Pomeroy, "The Sources of Police Legitimacy."

33 Crank and Caldero, *Police Ethics*, p. 76.

34 Kappeler et al., *Forces of Deviance*; see also Reuss-Ianni, *Two Cultures of Policing*.

35 Kappeler et al., *Forces of Deviance*.

36 Kappeler et al., *Forces of Deviance*, p. 61.

37 Ericson, "Rules for Police Deviance."

38 Kappeler et al., *Forces of Deviance*, p. 66.

39 Kappeler and Vaughn, "When Pursuit Becomes Criminal."

40 Walker and Katz, *The Police in America*.

41 Kappeler et al., *Forces of Deviance*.

42 Kappeler et al., *Forces of Deviance*.

43 Walker and Katz, *The Police in America*.

44 Kappeler et al., *Forces of Deviance*, p. 76.

45 Westley, "Secrecy and the Police" and *Violence and the Police*.

46 Skolnick, *Justice Without Trial*.

47 Van Maanen, "The Asshole."

48 Skolnick and Fyfe, *Above the Law*.

49 Skolnick and Fyfe, *Above the Law*.

50 Durkheim, *Suicide*.

51 Merton, "Social Structure and Anomie."

52 Lilly, Cullen, and Ball, *Criminological Theory: Context and Consequences*.

53 Merton, "Social Structure and Anomie"; Cohen, *Delinquent Boys: The Culture of the Gang*; Cloward and Ohlin, *Delinquency and Opportunity: A Theory of Delinquent Gangs*.

54 Messner and Rosenfeld, *Crime and the American Dream*.

55 Agnew, "Foundation for a General Strain Theory of Crime and Delinquency."

56 Agnew, "General Strain Theory."

57 Agnew, "General Strain Theory"; *Pressured into Crime: An Overview of General Strain Theory*.

58 Agnew, "Foundation for a General Strain Theory of Crime and Delinquency."

59 Agnew, "General Strain Theory"; Agnew, Brezina, Wright, and Cullen, "Strain, Personality Traits, and Delinquency: Extending General Strain Theory"; Adler and Laufer, *The Legacy of Anomie Theory*; Colvin, *Crime and Coercion: An Integrated Theory of Chronic Criminality*; Gibson, Swatt, and Jolicouer, "Assessing the Generality of General Strain Theory"; Jakupcak, "Masculine Gender Role Stress and Men's Fear of Emotions"; Paternoster and Mazerolle, "General Strain Theory and Delinquency: A Replication and Extension"; Sigfusdottir, Farkas, and Silver, "The Role of Depressed Mood and Anger"; Warner and Fowler, "Strain and Violence."

60 Muir, *Police*.

61 Van Maanen, "The Asshole."

62 Uchida, "The Development of the American Police"; Van Mannen, "Kinsmen in Repose."

63 Manning, "The Police: Mandate, Strategies, and Appearances."

64 Herbert, *Policing Space: Territoriality and the Los Angeles Police Department*.

65 Carte, "August Vollmer and the Origins of Police Professionalism"; Crank and Caldero, *Police Ethics: The Corruption of Noble Cause*; Raganella and White, "Race, Gender, and Motivation for Becoming a Police Officer"; White, Cooper, Saunders, and Raganella, "Motivations for Becoming a Police Officer."

66 Skolnick and Fyfe, *Above the Law*.

67 Skolnick and Fyfe, *Above the Law*.

68 Kappeler, Sluder, and Alpert, *Forces of Deviance*, p. 183.

69 Anshel, "A Conceptual Model and Implications for Coping."

70 Ayres and Flanagan, *Preventing Law Enforcement Stress*, pp. 4–5; see also Morash, Haarr, and Kwak, "Multilevel Influences on Police Stress"; Roberg, Kuykendall, and Novak, *Police Management*; White, Lawrence, Biggerstaff, and Grubb, "Factors of Stress among Police Officers."

71 Anshel, "A Conceptual Model and Implications for Coping"; Malloy and Mays, "The Police Stress Hypothesis: A Critical Evaluation."

72 Zhao, He, and Lovrich, "Predicting Five Dimensions of Police Officer Stress."

73 Burke and Descza, "Correlates of Psychological Burnout."

74 Niederhoffer, *Behind the Shield.*

75 Gershon et al., "Mental, Physical, and Behavioral Outcomes"; Roberg, Kuyk-endall, and Novak, *Police Management.*

76 Agnew, "General Strain Theory."

77 Agnew, "General Strain Theory."

78 Kappeler, Sluder, and Alpert, *Forces of Deviance.*

79 Zhao, Thurman, and He, "Predicting Five Dimensions of Police Officer Stress," p. 156.

80 Hughes, "Dilemmas and Contradictions of Status."

81 Lofkowitz, "Job Attitudes of Police"; Sherman, "Causes of Police Behavior."

82 Agnew, *Pressured into Crime.*

83 Walker, *The New World of Police Accountability.*

84 Kane, "Collect and Release Data on Coercive Police Actions."

85 Kane and White, "Bad Cops."

86 Akers, *Deviant Behavior.*

87 Cullen et al., *Taking Stock: The Status of Criminological Theory.*

88 Akers, *Social Structure and Social Learning.*

89 Cullen et al., *Taking Stock*, p. 39.

90 Barker, "Peer Group Support."

91 Chappell and Piquero, "Applying Social Learning Theory to Police Misconduct," p. 93.

92 Barker, "Peer Group Support "; Kappeler et al., *Forces of Deviance.*

93 Chappell and Piquero, "Applying Social Learning Theory to Police Misconduct."

94 Barker, "Peer Group Support "; Chappell and Piquero, "Applying Social Learning Theory to Police Misconduct."

95 Chappell and Piquero, "Applying Social Learning Theory to Police Misconduct."

96 Savitz, "The Dimensions of Police Loyalty."

97 See Sherman, *Police Corruption: A Sociological Perspective.*

98 Chappell and Piquero, "Applying Social Learning Theory to Police Misconduct"; Herbert, "Police Subculture Reconsidered"; Sherman, *Police Corruption*; Van Maanan, " Kinsmen in Repose."

99 Chappell and Piquero, "Applying Social Learning Theory to Police Misconduct."

100 Aultman, "A Social Psychological Approach to the Study of Police Corruption"; Conser, "A Literary Review of the Police Subculture."

101 Akers, *Social Structure and Social Learning.*

102 Chappell and Piquero, "Applying Social Learning Theory to Police Misconduct."

103 Chappell and Piquero, "Applying Social Learning Theory to Police Miscon-
    duct," p. 95.

104 Skolnick and Fyfe, *Above the Law*.

105 Gottfredson and Hirschi, *A General Theory of Crime*, pp. 89–91.

106 Arneklev et al., "Testing Gottfredson and Hirschi's 'Low Self-control' Stabil-
    ity Hypothesis "; Piquero and Bouffard, "Something Old, Something New";
    Turner and Piquero, "The Stability of Self-control."

107 Gottfredson and Hirschi, *A General Theory of Crime*, p. 3.

108 Lilly et al., *Criminological Theory*.

109 Brownfield and Sorenson, "Self-control and Juvenile Delinquency "; Burton
    et al., "Reconsidering Strain Theory "; Evans et al., "The Social Consequences
    of Self-control"; Grasmick et al., "Testing the Core Empirical Implications";
    Keane et al., "Drinking and Driving"; Nagin and Paternoster, "Enduring
    Individual Differences "; Wood, Pfefferbaum, and Arneklev, "Risk-taking and
    Self-control."

110 Pratt and Cullen, "The Empirical Status of Gottfredson and Hirschi's General
    Theory."

111 See Grasmick et al., "Testing the Core Empirical Implications."

112 See Piquero et al., "Does Self-control Affect Survey Response?"

113 See Evans et al., "The Social Consequences of Self-control"; Keane et al.,
    "Drinking and Driving"; Paternoster and Brame, "Structural Similarity of
    Processes"; Tittle et al., "Self-control and Crime/Deviance."

114 Grasmick et al., "Testing the Core Empirical Implications."

115 Chappell and Piquero, "Applying Social Learning Theory to Police
    Misconduct."

116 Bouffard and Kunzi, *forthcoming*; Muraven and Baumeister, "Self-regulation
    and Depletion of Limited Resources"; Muraven et al., "Daily Fluctuations
    in Self-control Demands and Alcohol Intake"; Muraven et al., " Self-control
    Depletion and the General Theory of Crime"; Piquero and Bouffard, "Some-
    thing Old, Something New."

117 Muraven et al., "Daily Fluctuations in Self-control Demands and Alcohol
    Intake."

118 Muraven et al., "Daily Fluctuations in Self-control Demands and Alcohol
    Intake."

119 Pratt, "Reconsidering Gottfredson and Hirschi's General Theory of Crime."

120 Sampson and Laub, *Crime in the Making*.

121 Kane and White, "Bad Cops."

122 Sampson and Laub, *Crime in the Making*; Farrington, "Building Developmen-
    tal and Life Course Theories of Offending."

123 Elder, "Perspectives on the Life Course."

124 Moffitt, "Adolescent-limited and Life-course-persistent Antisocial Behavior."

125 Sampson and Laub, *Crime in the Making*; Laub and Sampson, *Shared Beginnings, Divergent Lives: Delinquent Boys to Age*, 70.

126 Farrington, "Building Developmental and Life Course Theories of Offending."

127 Moffitt, "Adolescent-limited and Life-course-persistent Antisocial Behavior."

128 Sampson and Laub, *Crime in the Making*; Laub and Sampson, *Shared Beginnings, Divergent Lives: Delinquent Boys to Age*, 70.

129 Farrington, "Building Developmental and Life Course Theories of Offending."

130 Blumstein, Cohen, Roth, and Visher, *Criminal Careers and "Career Criminals."*

131 Moffitt, "Adolescence-limited and Life-course-persistent Antisocial Behavior"; Laub, Sampson, and Sweeten, "Assessing Sampson and Laub's Life-course Theory of Crime"; Farrington, "Building Developmental and Life Course Theories of Offending."

132 Harris, *Pathways of Police Misconduct.*

133 Van Maanen, "Kinsmen in Repose."

134 Harris, *Pathways of Police Misconduct.*

135 Walker, *The New World of Police Accountability.*

136 Harris, *Pathways of Police Misconduct.*

Chapter 8

1 Although the misconduct incident data span the 22-year period from 1975 to 1996, the research team gathered personal history information on all officers separated during that time. As a result, the research team gathered information on officers who were hired as early as 1945, which meant collecting departmental data from that point forward.

2 The study produced no direct evidence of this potential phenomenon.

3 Sampson et al., "Does Marriage Reduce Crime?"; King et al., "The Context of Marriage and Crime."

4 Manning, "Bad Cops."

5 This is not unique to the NYPD. Many, if not most, large police departments in the United States have difficulty maintaining records for their employees. This is especially the case for police departments prior to the year 2000, when most agencies did not have systematic access to desktop computing.

6 Manning, "Bad Cops."

7 A condensed version of this study was first published in the form of an article in the journal, *Criminology & Public Policy* (see: Kane and White, "Bad Cops"). It was in that same issue that Manning published a reaction essay in which he issued severe criticisms of the NYPD misconduct study.

8 Weber, *Theory of Economic and Social Organization*; Gulick and Urwick, *Papers on the Science of Administration.*

9 Manning, "Bad Cops," p. 789.

10 Gottfredson and Gottfredson, *Decision making*; Walker, *Sense and Nonsense*; Fyfe, "Blind Justice;" Kane, "Patterns of Arrest" and "Police Responses."

11 Manning, "Bad Cops."

12 E.g., Kane, "On the Limits."

13 E.g., Kane, "Linking Compromised Police Legitimacy."

14 E.g., Kane, "Social Control."

15 See generally Skolnick and Fyfe, *Above the Law*.

16 Grant and Grant, "Officer Selection."

17 E.g., Independent Commission, *Report of the Independent Commission*.

18 Jacob, "Black and White"; Kane, "Linking Compromised Police Legitimacy"; Kubrin and Weitzer, "Retaliatory Homicide."

19 E.g., Manning, *Policing Contingencies*.

20 E.g., Manning, *Narc's Game*.

21 Toch, "The Violence-Prone Officer."

22 Flowers, "Improving Strategic Leadership."

23 Skolnick and Fyfe, *Above the Law*.

24 Davis, *Discretionary Justice*.

REFERENCES

Abt Associates. 1973. *New York City police department street crime unit: An exemplary project*. Washington, DC: U.S. Government Printing Office.

Adler, Freda, and William B. Laufer. 1995. *The legacy of anomie theory*. New Brunswick, NJ: Transaction.

Adorno, Theodor W. 1950. *The authoritarian personality*. New York: Harper.

Agnew, Robert 1992. Foundation for a general strain theory of crime and delinquency. *Criminology* 30: 47–87.

Agnew, Robert. 2006. *Pressured into crime: An overview of general strain theory*. Los Angeles: Roxbury.

Agnew, Robert. 2008. General strain theory: Current status and directions for further research. In Francis T. Cullen, John P. Wright, and Kristen R. Blevins (eds.), *Taking stock: The status of criminological theory*. New Brunswick, NJ: Transaction, pp. 101–23.

Agnew, Robert, Timothy Brezina, John P. Wright, and Francis T. Cullen. 2002. Strain, personality traits, and delinquency: Extending general strain theory. *Criminology* 40: 43–72.

Ahern, J., Galea, S., Hubbard, A., and Karpati, A. 2008. Population vulnerabilities and capacities related to health: A test of a model. *Social Science & Medicine* 66: 691–703.

Akers, Ron L. 1985. *Deviant behavior: A social learning approach*. 3rd ed. Belmont, CA: Wadsworth.

Akers, Ron L. 1998. *Social structure and social learning*. Los Angeles: Roxbury.

Alex, Nicholas. 1969. *Black in blue*. New York: Appleton-Century Crofts.

Alpert, G. P., and R. G. Dunham. 1997. *The force factor: Measuring police use of force relative to suspect resistance*. Washington, DC: Police Executive Research Forum.

American Bar Association Project on Standards for Criminal Justice. 1973. *Standards relating to the urban police function*. New York: American Bar Association.

Anderson, Brian. 2003. Many charges refiled in Oakland "riders" police brutality case. *Contra Costa Times* (December 9).

Anderson, Elijah. 1999. *Code of the street*. New York: W. W. Norton.

Anechiarico, Frank, and James B. Jacobs. 1996. *The pursuit of absolute integrity*. Chicago: University of Chicago Press.

Anshel, Mark H. 2000. A conceptual model and implications for coping with stressful events in police work. *Criminal Justice and Behavior* 27: 375–400.

Arneklev, Bruce J., John K. Cochran, and Randy R. Gainey. 1998. Testing Gottfredson and Hirschi's "low self-control" stability hypothesis: An exploratory study. *American Journal of Criminal Justice* 23: 107–27.

Aultman, Madeline G. 1976. A social psychological approach to the study of police corruption. *Journal of Criminal Justice* 4: 323–32.

Ayres, Richard M., and George S. Flanagan. 1992. *Preventing law enforcement stress: The organization's role.* Washington, DC: Bureau of Justice Assistance.

Barker, Thomas 1977. Peer group support for police occupational deviance. *Criminology* 15: 353–66.

Barker, Thomas, and David L. Carter (eds.). 1994. *Police deviance.* 2nd ed. Cincinnati: Anderson.

Barlow, Hugh D., and Scott H. Decker. 2010. *Criminology and public policy: Putting theory to work.* Philadelphia: Temple University Press.

Bayley, David H., and James Garofalo. 1989. The management of violence by police patrol officers. *Criminology* 27: 1–25.

Bayley, David H., and Harold Mendelsohn. 1969. *Minorities and the police.* New York: Macmillan.

Black, Donald. 1972. The boundaries of legal sociology. *Yale Law Journal* 81: 1086–1100.

Bloch, Peter B., and Deborah Anderson. 1974. *Policewomen on patrol: Final report.* Washington, DC: Police Foundation.

Blumstein, Alfred, Jacqueline Cohen, Jeffrey A. Roth, Christy A. Visher. 1986. *Criminal careers and "career criminals."* Washington, DC: National Academy Press.

Bobb, Merrick, et al. 1996. *Five years later: A report to the Los Angeles Police Commission on the Los Angeles Police Department's implementation of independent commission recommendations.* Los Angeles: City of Los Angeles.

Bolz, Frank, and Edward Hershey. 1979. *Hostage cop.* New York: Rawson Wade.

Bouffard, Jeffrey A., and Tasha Kunzi. Forthcoming. Sexual arousal and self-control: Research note on an experimental test of the invariance proposition in the general theory of crime. *Crime and Delinquency.*

Bouza, Anthony V. 1990. *Bronx beat: Reflections of a police commander.* Chicago: Office of International Criminal Justice.

Bowker, Lee. 1980. A theory of the educational needs of law enforcement officers. *Journal of Contemporary Criminal Justice* 1:17–24.

Bratton, William. 1998. *Turnaround: How America's top cop reversed the crime epidemic.* New York: Random House.

Brownfield, David, and Ann M. Sorenson. 1993. Self-control and juvenile delinquency: Theoretical issues and an empirical assessment of selected elements of a general theory of crime. *Deviant Behavior* 4: 243–64.

Bureau of Justice Statistics. 2005. *Contacts between police and the public: Findings from the 2002 national survey.* Washington, DC: U.S. Department of Justice.

Burke, Ronald J., and Eugene Deszca. 1986. Correlates of psychological burnout phases among police officers. *Human Relations* 39: 487–501.

Burton, Velmer S., Jr., Francis T. Cullen, David Evans, and Gregory R. Dunaway.

1994. Reconsidering strain theory: Operationalization, rival theories, and adult criminality. *Journal of Quantitative Criminology* 10: 213–39.

Carte, Gene. 1986. August Vollmer and the origins of police professionalism. In Mark Pogrebin and Robert M. Regoli (eds.), *Police administrative issues: Techniques and functions.* Millwood, NY: Associated Faculty Press.

Carter, David. 1985. Hispanic perception of police performance: An empirical assessment. *Journal of Criminal Justice* 13: 487–500.

Chapman, Glenn. 2002. 'Riders' trial slated to start April 29 in Oakland. *Oakland Tribune* (February 2).

Chappell, Allison T., and Alex R. Piquero. 2004. Applying social learning theory to police misconduct. *Deviant Behavior* 25: 89–108.

Chermak, Steven. 1995. Image control: How police affect the presentation of crime news. *American Journal of Police* 14: 21–43.

Chevigny, Paul. 1969. *Police power: Police abuses in New York City.* New York: Pantheon Books.

Chevigny, Paul. 1995. *Edge of the knife: Police violence in the Americas.* New York: Free Press.

Chicago Police Department. 1931. *Chicago police problems.* Chicago: University of Chicago Press.

Christopher Commission. 1991. *Report of the Independent Commission on the Los Angeles Police Department.* Los Angeles: Christopher Commission.

Clark, Ramsey. 1970. *Crime in America.* New York: Simon & Schuster.

Cloward, Richard A., and Loyd E. Ohlin. 1960. *Delinquency and opportunity: A theory of delinquent gangs.* Glencoe, IL: Free Press.

Cohen, Albert K. 1955. *Delinquent boys: The culture of the gang.* Glencoe, IL: Free Press.

Cohen, Bernard, and Jan M. Chaiken. 1972. *Police background characteristics and performance.* New York: Rand Institute.

Cohen, Bernard, and Jan M. Chaiken. 1973. *Police background characteristics and performance.* Lexington, MA: Lexington Books.

Collins, Patricia, Jack Greene, Robert Kane, Robert Stokes, and Alex Piquero. 1998. *Evaluating community policing in public housing: Philadelphia's 11th street corridor program.* Washington, DC: National Institute of Justice.

Colvin, Mark 2000. *Crime and coercion: An integrated theory of chronic criminality.* New York City: St. Martin's Press.

Commission on Accreditation for Law Enforcement Agencies. 1994. *Standards for law enforcement agencies.* Fairfax VA: Commission on Accreditation for Law Enforcement Agencies.

Conser, James A. 1980. A literary review of the police subculture: Its characteristics, impact and policy implications. *Police Studies* 2: 46–54.

Counts, Laura, and Glenn Chapman. 2002. City pays $195,000 in suit over police "riders." *Oakland Tribune* (February 20).

Crane, J. 1991. The epidemic theory of ghettos and neighborhood effects on dropping out and teenage childbearing. *American Journal of Sociology* 96: 1226–59.

Crank, John P., and Michael A. Caldero. 2000. *Police ethics: The corruption of noble cause.* Cincinnati: Anderson.

Cullen, Francis T., John P. Wright, and Kristie R. Blevins. 2008. *Taking Stock: The Status of Criminological Theory*, vol. 15. New Brunswick, NJ: Transaction.

Daley, Robert. 1971. *Target blue.* New York: Delacorte.

Daley, Robert. 1978. *Prince of the city: The true story of a cop who knew too much.* Boston: Houghton-Mifflin.

Davis, Kenneth Culp. 1977. *Discretionary justice.* Champaign: University of Illinois Press.

Delattre, Edwin. 1989. *Character and cops: Ethics in policing.* Washington, DC: American Enterprise Institute for Public Policy Research.

Del Carmen, Rolando V., and Jeffrey Walker. 1991. *Confessions and admissions: Cases supporting Miranda.* Cincinnati: Anderson.

Di Grazia, Robert J. 1977. College education for police officers? *Liberal Education* 63: 154–58.

Domanick, Joe. 1994. *To protect and serve: The LAPD's century of war in the city of dreams.* New York: Pocket Books.

Dowd James J., and Vern L. Bengston. 1978. Aging in minority populations: An examination of the double jeopardy hypothesis. *Journal of Gerontology* 33: 427–36.

Durkheim, Emile. 1897/1951. *Suicide.* New York: Free Press.

Eck, John. 2005. Science, values and problem-oriented policing. In D. Weisburd and A. Braga (eds.), *Prospects and problems in an era of police innovation: Contrasting perspectives.* New York: Cambridge University Press.

Elder, Glen H. 1985. Perspectives on the life course. In Glen H. Elder (ed.), *Life Course Dynamics.* Ithaca, NY: Cornell University Press.

Ericson, R. V. 1981. Rules for police deviance. In C. D. Shearing (ed.), *Organizational police deviance.* Toronto, Canada: Butterworth.

Eskridge, Chris. 1989. College and the police: A review of the issues. In Dennis Jay Kenney (ed.), *Police and Policing: Contemporary Issues.* Westport, CT: Praeger, pp. 17–25.

Eterno, John. 1996. *Cadets and policing: An analysis of the New York City Police Department's cadet corps.* Academy of Criminal Justice Sciences Annual Meeting, Las Vegas, NV.

Evans, David, Francis T. Cullen, Velmer S. Burton, Gregory R. Dunaway, and Michael L. Benson. 1997. The social consequences of self-control: Testing the general theory of crime. *Criminology* 35: 475–501.

Fagan, Jeffrey A., and Garth Davies. 2000. Street stops and broken windows: *Terry,* race, and disorder in New York City. *Fordham Urban Law Journal* 28: 457–504.

Fagan, Jeffrey A., Amanda Geller, Garth Davies, and Valerie West. 2010. Street stops and broken windows revisited: The demography and logic of proactive policing in a safe and changing city. In Stephen Rice and Michael D. White (eds.), *Race, ethnicity and policing: New and essential readings.* New York: NYU Press.

Farrington, David P. 2008. Building developmental and life course theories of offending. In Francis T. Cullen, John P. Wright, and Kristen R. Blevins (eds.), *Taking stock: The status of criminological theory.* New Brunswick, NJ: Transaction, pp. 355–65.

Fazlollah, Mark. 1996. From prison, ex-cops call offenses routine. *Philadelphia Inquirer* (May 12).

Fazlollah, Mark. 1997. Phila. ordered to report on police. *Philadelphia Inquirer* (March 28).

Felkenes, George. 1991. Affirmative action in the Los Angeles Police Department. *Journal of Police Science and Administration* 15: 138–52.

Ferraro, Kenneth F. 1987. Double jeopardy to health among Black older adults?" *Journal of Gerontology* 42: 528–33.

Ferraro, Kenneth. F., and Melissa M. Farmer. 1996. Double jeopardy to health hypothesis for African Americans: Analysis and critique. *Journal of Health and Social Behavior* 37: 27–43.

Flowers, Michael. 2004. Improving strategic leadership. *Military Review*, March–April, 40–46.

Fogelson, Robert M. 1977. *Big-city police.* Cambridge: Harvard University Press.

Forst, Brian, Judith Lucianovic, and Sara J. Cox. 1977. *What happens after arrest? A court perspective of police operations in the District of Columbia.* Washington, DC: Institute for Law and Social Research.

Fosdick, Raymond. 1920. *American police systems.* New York: Century Co.

Frankel, B. 1993. Ex-NYC officer tells stark tale of cops gone bad. *USA Today*, September 28, p. A3.

Fyfe, James J. 1978. *Shots fired: An analysis of New York City police firearms discharges.* PhD dissertation. State University of New York at Albany (Ann Arbor: University Microfilms).

Fyfe, James J. 1980. Geographic correlates of police shooting: A Microanalysis. *Journal of Research in Crime and Delinquency* 17: 101–13.

Fyfe, James J. 1980a. Always prepared: Police off-duty guns. *Annals of the American Academy of Political and Social Science* 452: 72–81.

Fyfe, James J. 1980b. *Philadelphia police shootings, 1975–78: A system model analysis.* Washington, DC: Report for the Civil Rights Division, U.S. Department of Justice.

Fyfe, James J. 1981. Who shoots? A look at officer race and police shooting. *Journal of Police Science and Administration* 9: 367–82.

Fyfe, James J. 1982. Blind justice: Police shootings in Memphis. *Journal of Criminal Law and Criminology* 73: 707–22.

Fyfe, James J. 1986. The split-second syndrome and other determinants of police violence. In Anne T. Campbell and John J. Gibbs (eds.), *Violent Transactions*. Oxford: Basil Blackwell, pp. 207–25.

Fyfe, James. 1993. "Good" policing. In Brian Forst (ed.), *The socio-economics of crime and justice*. Armonk, NY: M.E. Sharpe.

Fyfe, James J., and Robert Kane. 2006. *Bad cops: A study of career-ending misconduct among New York City police officers*. Final Report. Washington, DC: National Institute of Justice.

Fyfe, James J., Robert Kane, George Grasso, and Michael Ansbro. 1998. *Race, gender and discipline in the New York City Police Department*. Paper presented at the Annual Meeting of the American Society of Criminology, Washington, DC.

Gelb, Barbara. 1983. *Varnished brass*. New York: G.P. Putnam's Sons.

Geller, William A., and Kevin Karales. 1981. Shootings of and by Chicago police: Uncommon crises–Part I. shootings by Chicago police. *Journal of Criminal Law and Criminology* 72: 1813–66.

Geller, William A., and Michael S. Scott. 1992. *Deadly force: What we know*. Washington, DC: Police Executive Research Forum.

Germann, A. C., Frank D. Day, and Robert Gallati. 1985. *Introduction to law enforcement and criminal justice*. Springfield, IL: Charles C. Thomas.

Gershon, Robyn R. M., Briana Barocas, Allison N. Canton, Xianbin Li, and David Vlahov. 2009. Mental, physical, and behavioral outcomes associated with perceived work stress in police officers. *Criminal Justice and Behavior* 36: 275–89.

Gibson, Chris L., Marc L. Swatt, and Jason R. Jolicoeur. 2001. Assessing the generality of general strain theory: The relationship among occupational stress experienced by male police officers and domestic forms of violence. *Journal of Crime & Justice* 24: 29–57.

Goldstein, Herman. 1975. *Police corruption: A perspective on its nature and control*. Washington, DC: Police Foundation.

Goldstein, Herman. 1977. *Policing a free society*. Cambridge, MA: Ballinger.

Gottfredson, Michael R., and Don M. Gottfredson. 1988. *Decision making in criminal justice: Toward the rational exercise of discretion*. New York: Plenum.

Gottfredson, Michael R., and Travis Hirschi. 1990. *A General Theory of Crime*. Stanford, CA: Stanford University Press.

Grant, J. Douglas, and Joan Grant. 1996. Officer selection and the prevention of abuse of force. In William Geller and Hans Toch (eds.), *Police violence: Understanding and controlling police abuse of force*. New Haven, CT: Yale University Press.

Grasmick, Harold G., Charles R. Tittle, Robert J. Bursik, and Bruce J. Arneklev. 1993. Testing the core empirical implications of Gottfredson and Hirschi's general theory of crime. *Journal of Research in Crime and Delinquency*, 305–29.

Green, Mark. 1997. *Testimony of the Public Advocate before the New York City Council Committee on Public Safety*. New York.

Greene, Judith A. 1999. Zero tolerance: A case study of police policies and practices in New York City. *Crime and Delinquency* 45: 171–87.

Grennan, Sean. 1987. Findings on the role of officer gender in violent encounters with citizens. *Journal of Police Science and Administration* 15: 78–85.

Gulick, Luther, and Lindal Urwick. 1937. *Papers on the science of administration.* New York: Institute of Public Administration, Columbia University.

Guyot, Dorothy. 1979. Bending granite: attempts to change the rank structure of American police departments. *Journal of Police Science and Administration* 7: 253–84.

Guyot, Dorothy. 1991. *Policing as though people matter.* Philadelphia: Temple University Press.

Hale, Donna. 1989. Ideology of police misbehavior: Analysis and recommendations. *Journal of Ideology* 13: 59–85.

Haller, Mark. 1976. Historical roots of police behavior: Chicago, 1890–1925. *Law and Society Review* 10: 303–23.

Harris, Christopher J. 2010. *Pathways of police misconduct: Problem behavior patterns and trajectories from two cohorts.* Durham, NC: Carolina Academic Press.

Hayeslip, David., Jr. 1989. Higher education and police performance revisited: The evidence examined through meta-analysis. *American Journal of Police* 8: 49–62.

Herbert, Steve. 1996. *Policing space: Territoriality and the Los Angeles Police Department.* Minneapolis: University of Minnesota Press.

Herbert, Steve. 1998. Police subculture reconsidered. *Criminology* 36: 343–68.

Hickman, Matthew J., Alex R. Piquero, and Jack R. Greene. 2000. Discretion and gender disproportionality in police disciplinary systems. *Policing: An International Journal of Police Strategies and Management* 23: 105–16.

Horvath, Frank. 1987. The police use of deadly force: A description of selected characteristics of intra-state incidents. *Journal of Police Science and Administration* 15: 226–28.

Hughes, Everett C. 1944. Dilemmas and contradictions of status. *American Journal of Sociology* 50: 353–59.

Independent Commission on the Los Angeles Police Department. 1991. *Report of the Independent commission on the Los Angeles Police Department.* Los Angeles: Independent Commission on the Los Angeles Police Department.

Jackson, Pamela. 1989. *Minority group threat, crime, and policing.* New York: Praeger.

Jacob, Herbert. 1971. Black and white perceptions of justice in the city. *Law & Society Review*: 69–89.

Jakupcak, Matthew. 2003. Masculine gender role stress and men's fear of emotions as predictors of self-reported aggression and violence. *Violence and Victims* 18: 533–41.

Jargowsky, P. 1997. *Poverty and place: Ghettos, barrios, and the American city.* New York: Russell Sage Foundation.

Johnson, Thomas A. 2000. Case evaluation: Higher education vs. prior military service. *Texas Police Journal:* 5–7.

Johnston, C. Wayne, and Sutham Cheurprakobkit. 2002. Educating our police: Perceptions of police administrators regarding the utility of a college education, police academy training and preferences in courses for officers. *International Journal of Police Science and Management* 4: 182–97.

Jones, Peter, Phillip Harris, Jamie Fader, and Lori Grubstein. 2001. Identifying chronic juvenile offenders. *Justice Quarterly* 18: 479–507.

Kane, Robert J. 1998. Policing in public housing: Using calls for service to examine incident-based workload in the Philadelphia Housing Authority. *Policing: An International Journal of Police Strategies and Management* 21: 618–31.

Kane, Robert J. 1999. Patterns of arrest in domestic violence encounters: Identifying a police decision-making model. *Journal of Criminal Justice* 27: 65–79.

Kane, Robert J. 2000. Police responses to restraining orders in domestic violence incidents: Identifying the custody-threshold thesis. *Criminal Justice and Behavior* 27: 561–80.

Kane, Robert J. 2000. Permanent beat assignment in association with community policing: Assessing the impact on police officer field activity. *Justice Quarterly* 17: 259–80.

Kane, Robert J. 2001. *Urban ecology and police malpractice: Identifying contexts for career-ending misconduct in the New York City Police Department.* Dissertation. Temple University.

Kane, Robert J. 2002. The social ecology of police misconduct. *Criminology* 40: 867–896.

Kane, Robert J. 2003. Social control in the metropolis: A community-level examination of the minority group-threat hypothesis. *Justice Quarterly* 20: 401–31.

Kane, Robert J. 2005. Linking compromised police legitimacy to violent crime in structurally disadvantaged communities. *Criminology* 43: 469–98.

Kane, Robert J. 2006. On the limits of social control: Structural deterrence and the policing of "suppressible" crimes. *Justice Quarterly* 23: 186–213.

Kane, Robert J. 2007. Collect and release data on coercive police actions. *Criminology & Public Policy* 6: 773–80.

Kane, Robert J., and Michael D. White. 2009. Bad cops: A study of career-ending misconduct among New York City police officers. *Criminology & Public Policy* 8: 737–69.

Kappeler, Victor E., Alan D. Sapp, and David L. Carter. 1992. Police officer higher education, citizen complaints and departmental rule violations. *American Journal of Police* 11: 37–54.

Kappeler, Victor, Richard D. Sluder, and Geoffrey P. Alpert. 1998. *Forces of deviance: Understanding the dark side of policing.* Prospect Heights, IL: Waveland Press.

Kappeler, Victor E., and Michael S. Vaughn. 1997. When pursuit becomes criminal: Municipal liability for police sexual violence. *Criminal Law Bulletin* 33: 467–88.

Keane, Carl, Paul S. Maxim, and James J. Teevan. 1993. Drinking and driving, self-control, and gender: Testing a general theory of crime. *Journal of Research in Crime and Delinquency* 30: 3–46.

Kelling, George L., and Catherine M. Coles. 1996. *Fixing broken windows: Restoring order and reducing crime in our communities.* New York: Free Press.

Kelly, Raymond W. 1992. An investigation into the police department's conduct of the Dowd case and an assessment of the police department's internal investigation capabilities. New York: New York City Police Department.

King, Ryan, Michael Massoglia, and Ross MacMillan. 2007. The context of marriage and crime: Gender, the propensity to marry, and offending in early adulthood. *Criminology* 45: 33–65.

Klinger, David A. 1997. Negotiating order in patrol work: An ecological theory of police response to deviance. *Criminology* 35: 277–306.

Klockars, Carl. 1980. The dirty harry problem. *Annals of the American Academy of Political and Social Science* 452: 33–47.

Klockars, Carl. 1996. A theory of excessive force and its control. In William A. Geller and Hans Toch (eds.), *Police violence.* New Haven, CT: Yale University Press, pp. 1–22.

Klockars, Carl B., Sanja K. Ivkovich, William E. Harver, and Maria R. Haberfeld. 2001. *Measurement of Police Integrity.* Washington, DC: National Institute of Justice.

Klofas, John M., Edmund F. McGarrell, and Natalie Kroovand Hipple (eds.). 2010. *The new criminal justice: American communities and the changing world of crime control.* New York: Routledge.

Knapp Commission. 1972. *Report of the New York City commission to investigate allegations of police corruption and the city's anti-corruption procedures.* New York: Bar Press.

Kolts, James G. 1992. *Report of the Special Counsel on the Los Angeles County Sheriff's Department.* Los Angeles: Kolts Commission.

Kramer, Michael. 1997. How cops go bad. *Time* (December 15).

Kubrin, Charis, and Ronald Weitzer. 2003. Retaliatory homicide: Concentrated disadvantage and neighborhood culture. *Social Problems* 50: 157–180.

Landrum, Lawrence W. 1947. The case of negro police. *New South* 11: 5–6.

Lardner, James. 1996. *Crusader: The hell-raising career of detective David Durk.* New York: Random House.

Lardner, James, and Thomas Repetto. 2000. *NYPD: A city and its police.* New York: Henry Holt.

Laub, John H., and Robert J. Sampson. 2003. *Shared beginnings, divergent lives: Delinquent boys to age 70.* Cambridge: Harvard University Press.

Laub, John, Robert J. Sampson, and Gary Sweeten. 2008. Assessing Sampson and

Laub's life-course theory of crime. In Francis T. Cullen, John P. Wright, and Kristen R. Blevins (eds.), *Taking stock: The status of criminological theory*. New Brunswick, NJ: Transaction, pp. 313–34.

Leonard, V. A., and Harry W. More. 1964. *Police organization and management*, 2nd ed. Mineola, NY: Foundation Press.

Lersch, Kim L., and Linda L. Kunzman. 2001. Misconduct allegations and higher education in a southern sheriff's department. *American Journal of Criminal Justice* 25: 161–72.

Lester, David. 1983. Why do people become police officers: A study of reasons and the predictions of success. *Journal of Police Science and Administration* 11: 170–74.

Lilly, J. Robert, Francis T. Cullen, and Richard A. Ball. 2007. *Criminological theory: Context and consequences*. Thousand Oaks, CA: Sage.

Liska, Allen E., and Mitchell B. Chamlin. 1984. Social structure and crime control among macrosocial units. *American Journal of Sociology* 90: 383–95.

Lofkowitz, Joel. 1974. Job Attitudes of police: Overall description and demographic correlates. *Journal of Vocational Behavior* 5: 221–30.

Los Angeles Police Department. 2000. *Board of Inquiry into the Rampart Area Corruption Incident Public Report* (Part I). Los Angeles: LAPD.

Maas, Peter. 1973. *Serpico: The cop who defied the system*. New York: Viking.

Malloy, Thomas E., and Larry G. Mays. 1984. The police stress hypothesis: A critical evaluation. *Criminal Justice and Behavior* 11: 197–224.

Manning, Peter K. 1978. The police: Mandate, strategies, and appearances. In Peter K. Manning and John Van Maanen (eds.), *Policing: A view from the street*. Santa Monica, CA: Goodyear, pp. 7–31.

Manning, Peter K. 1997. *Police work: The social organization of policing*. 2nd ed. Prospect Heights, IL: Waveland Press.

Manning, Peter K. 2003a. *Policing contingencies*. Chicago: University of Chicago Press.

Manning, Peter K. 2003b. *Narc's game*, 2nd ed. Prospect Heights, IL: Waveland Press.

Manning, Peter K. 2005. Policing and reflection. In Roger G. Dunham and Geoffrey Alpert (eds.), *Critical Issues in Policing*, 5th ed. Long Grove, IL: Waveland Press.

Manning, Peter K. 2009. Bad Cops. *Criminology and Public Policy* 8: 787–94.

Martin, Susan E. 1980. *Breaking and entering: Policewomen on patrol*. Berkeley: University of California Press.

Matthews, James 1999. Racial profiling: A law enforcement nemesis. *Police* 38–39.

Matulia, Kenneth J. 1982. *A balance of forces: A study of justifiable homicide by the police*. Gaithersburg, MD: International Association of Chiefs of Police.

Matulia, Kenneth J. 1985. *A balance of forces: Model deadly force policy and procedure*, 2nd ed. Gaithersburg, MD: International Association of Chiefs of Police.

McAlary, Mike. 1991. *Buddy boys.* New York: Charter Books.

McAlary, Mike. 1994. *Good cop, bad cop.* New York: Pocket Star Books.

McAlary, Mike. 1997. The frightful whisperings from a Coney Island hospital bed. *New York Daily News* (August 13).

McDonald, Phyllis P. 2002. *Managing police operations: Implementing the New York crime control model— CompStat.* Belmont, CA: Wadsworth.

McDougall, Christopher. 1997. Law and disorder. *Philadelphia Weekly* (June 18).

McManus, George E. 1969. *Police training and performance study.* Washington, DC: National Institute of Law Enforcement and Criminal Justice.

McManus, George P., John I. Griffin, William J. Wetteroth, Marvin Boland, and Pauline T. Hines. 1970. *Police training and performance study.* Washington, DC: National Institute of Law Enforcement and Criminal Justice.

McMullan, Michael. 1961. A theory of corruption. *Sociological Review* 9: 181–201.

Melchionne, Teresa M. 1974. The changing role of policewomen. *Police Journal* 47: 340–58.

Merton, Robert K. 1938. Social structure and anomie. *American Sociological Review* 3: 672–82.

Messner, Steven F. and Rosenfeld, Richard. 2006. *Crime and the American dream.* Belmont, CA: Wadsworth.

Miller, Wilbur R. 1977. *Cops and bobbies: Police authority in New York and London, 1830–1870.* Chicago: University of Chicago Press.

Moffitt, Terrie E. 1993. Adolescent-limited and life-course-persistent antisocial behavior: A developmental taxonomy. *Psychological Review* 100: 674–701.

Moffitt, Terrie E. 2008. A review of research on the taxonomy of life-course-persistent versus adolescence-limited antisocial behavior. In Francis T. Cullen, John P. Wright, and Kristen R. Blevins (eds.), *Taking stock: The status of criminological theory* . New Brunswick, NJ: Transaction, pp. 227–312.

Mollen Commission. 1994. *Anatomy of failure, a path for success: The report of the commission to investigate allegations of police corruption and the anti-corruption procedures of the New York City Police Department.* New York: City of New York.

Morash, Merry, Robin Haarr, and Dae-Hoon Kwak. 2006. Multilevel influences on police stress. *Journal of Contemporary Criminal Justice* 22: 26–43.

Muir, William K. 1977. *Police: street corner politicians.* Chicago: University of Chicago Press.

Muraven, Mark, and Roy F. Baumeister. 2000. Self-regulation and depletion of limited resources: Does self-control resemble a muscle? *Psychological Bulletin* 126: 247–59.

Muraven, Mark, Lorraine R. Collins, Saul Shiffman, and Jean A. Paty. 2005. Daily fluctuations in self-control demands and alcohol intake. *Psychology of Addictive Behaviors* 19: 140–47.

Muraven, Mark, Greg Pogarsky, and Dikla Shmueli. 2006. Self-control depletion and the general theory of crime. *Journal of Quantitative Criminology* 22: 263–77.

Murphy, Patrick V. 1977. Corruptive influences. In Bernard L. Garmire (ed.), *Local government police management*. Washington, DC: International City Management Association, pp. 65–86.

Murphy, Patrick V., and Tony Pate. 1977. *Commissioner: A view from the top of American law enforcement*. New York: Simon & Schuster.

Myrdal, Gunnar. 1944. *An American dilemma: The Negro problem and modern democracy*. New York: Harper and Brothers.

Nagin, Daniel S., and Raymond Paternoster. 1993. Enduring individual differences and rational choice theories of crime. *Law and Society Review* 3: 467–96.

National Advisory Commission on Civil Disorders. 1968. *Report of the National Advisory Commission on Civil Disorders*. New York: E.P. Dutton.

National Advisory Commission on Criminal Justice Standards and Goals. 1973. *Police*. Washington, DC: U.S. Government Printing Office.

National Commission on Law Observance and Enforcement [Wickersham Report]. 1931. *Report on lawlessness in law enforcement*. Washington, DC: U.S. Government Printing Office.

Neiderhoffer, Arthur. 1967. *Behind the shield: The police in urban society*. Garden City, NY: Doubleday.

New Orleans Mayor's Advisory Committee on Human Relations. 1993 *Report on Police Use of Force*. New Orleans: Mayor's Advisory Committee on Human Relations.

New York City Mayor's Office. 1998. *The Mayor's management report: Preliminary fiscal 1998 summary volume*. New York: Mayor's Office of Operations.

New York City Police Department. 1994. *Getting guns off the streets of New York*. Police Strategy, No. 1. New York: New York City Police Department.

New York City Police Department. 1994. *Reclaiming the public spaces of New York*. Police Strategy, No. 5. New York: New York City Police Department.

New York City Police Department. 1996. *Establishment of the office of the department special prosecutor*. Interim Order 22. New York: NYPD.

New York City Police Department, Internal Affairs Bureau. 2001. *Annual report for year 2000*. New York: NYPD.

O'Sullivan, William. 1994. *Proposed changes to New York City Police Department age and educational requirements*. New York: New York City Police Department, internal report.

Palombo, B. J. 1995. *Academic professionalism in law enforcement*. New York: Garland.

Paternoster, Raymond, and Robert Brame. 1998. Structural similarity of processes generating criminal and analogous behaviors. *Criminology* 36: 633–66.

Paternoster, Raymond, and Paul Mazerolle. 1994. General strain theory and delinquency: A replication and extension. *Journal of Research in Crime & Delinquency* 31: 235–63.

Payton, Brenda. 2003. Riders settlement won't rebuild trust. *Oakland Tribune* (February 21).

Perez, Douglas. 1995. *Common sense about police review*. Philadelphia: Temple University Press.

Philadelphia City Council. 1995. Resolution 950757 Regarding establishment of Philadelphia Commission to Study Police Corruption and its Effects on the Criminal Justice System, December 7.

Philadelphia Police Study Task Force. 1987. *Philadelphia and its police: Toward a new partnership*. Philadelphia: Roman and Haas.

Piquero, Alex R., and Jeffrey A. Bouffard. 2007. Something old, something new: A preliminary investigation of Hirschi's redefined self-control. *Justice Quarterly* 24: 1–26.

Piquero, Alex R., Randall MacIntosh, and Matthew Hickman. 2000. Does self-control affect survey response? Applying exploratory, confirmatory, and item response theory analysis to Grasmick et al.'s Self-Control Scale. *Criminology* 38: 897–930.

Pogarsky, Greg, and Alex R. Piquero. 2003. Studying the reach of deterrence: Can deterrence theory help explain police misconduct? *Journal of Criminal Justice* 32: 371–86.

Polk, O. Elmer, and David A. Armstrong. 2001. Higher education and law enforcement career paths: Is the road to success paved by degree? *Journal of Criminal Justice Education* 12: 77–99.

Pomeroy, Wesley A. Carroll. 1985. The sources of police legitimacy and a model for police misconduct review: A response to Wayne Kerstetter. In W. Geller (ed.), *Police Leadership in America: Crisis and Opportunity*. New York: Praeger, pp. 183–86.

Pratt, Travis C. (2009). Reconsidering Gottfredson and Hirschi's general theory of crime: Linking the micro- and macro-level sources of self-control and criminal behavior over the life course. In Joanne Savage (ed.), *The Development of Persistent Criminality*. New York: Oxford University Press.

Pratt, Travis C., and Francis T. Cullen. 2000. The empirical status of Gottfredson and Hirschi's general theory of crime: A meta-analysis. *Criminology* 38: 931–64.

President's Commission on Law Enforcement and Administration of Justice. 1967. *Task force report: The police*. Washington, DC: U.S. Government Printing Office.

Raganella, Anthony J., and Michael D. White. 2004. Race, gender, and motivation for becoming a police officer: Implications for building a representative police department. *Journal of Criminal Justice* 32: 501–13.

RAND. 2007. *Do NYPD's pedestrian stop data indicate racial bias?* Santa Monica, CA: RAND.

Reisig, Michael D., and Roger B. Parks. 2000. Experience, quality of life, and neighborhood context: A hierarchical analysis of satisfaction with police. *Justice Quarterly* 17: 607–30.

Reiss, Albert J. 1968. Police brutality: Answers to key questions. *Trans-Action*, 10–19.

Repetto, Thomas A.1978. *The blue parade.* New York: Macmillan-Free Press.

Reuss-Ianni, Elizabeth. 1983. *Two cultures of policing: Street cops and management cops.* New Brunswick, NJ: Transaction Books.

Rice, Stephen, and Michael D. White (eds.). 2010. *Race, ethnicity and policing: New and essential readings.* New York: NYU Press.

Roberg, Roy, Jack Kuykendall, and Kenneth Novak. 2002. *Police Management*, 3rd ed. New York: Oxford University Press.

Rosenfeld, Richard, Robert Fornango, and Andres F. Rengifo. 2007. The impact of order-maintenance policing on New York City homicide and robbery rates, 1998–2001. *Criminology* 45: 355–84.

Rothmiller, Mike, and Ivan G. Goldman. 1992. *L.A. secret police: Inside the LAPD elite spy network.* New York: Pocket Books.

Rubinstein, Jonathan. 1973. *City police.* New York: Farrar, Straus and Giroux.

Sampson, Robert J. 1993. Linking time and place: Dynamic contextualism and the future of criminological inquiry. *Journal of Research in Crime Delinquency.* 30: 426–44.

Sampson, Robert J., and Dawn Bartusch. 1998. Legal cynicism and (subcultural?) tolerance of deviance: The neighborhood context of neighborhood differences. *Law and Society Review* 32: 777–804.

Sampson, Robert J., and John H. Laub. 1993. *Crime in the making: Pathways and turning points in life.* Cambridge: Harvard University Press.

Sampson, Robert J., and John H. Laub. 2003. *Shared beginnings, divergent lives: Delinquent boys to age 70.* Cambridge: Harvard University Press.

Sampson, Robert, John Laub, and Christopher Wimer. 2006. Does marriage reduce crime? A counterfactual approach to within-individual causal effects. *Criminology* 44: 465–508.

Saunders, Charles B., Jr. 1970. *Upgrading the American police.* Washington, DC: Brookings Institution.

Savitz, Leonard. 1970. The dimensions of police loyalty. *American Behavioral Science* (Summer): 693–704.

Schecter, Leonard, and William Phillips. 1973. *On the pad.* New York: Berkeley Medallion Books.

Selznick, Philip. 1980. *TVA and the grassroots: a study of politics and organization.* Berkeley: University of California Press.

Sherman, Lawrence W. 1974. *Police corruption: A sociological perspective.* Garden City, NY: Anchor Books.

Sherman, Lawrence W. 1978. *Scandal and reform: Controlling police corruption.* Berkeley: University of California Press.

Sherman, Lawrence W. 1980. Causes of police behavior: The current state of quantitative research. *Journal of Research in Crime and Delinquency* 17: 69–100.

Sherman, Lawrence W., and the National Advisory Commission on Higher Education for Police Officers. 1978. *The quality of police education.* San Francisco: Jossey-Bass.

Sherman, Lewis J. 1975. An evaluation of policewomen on patrol in a suburban police department. *Journal of Police Science and Administration* 3: 434–38.

Sigfusdottir, Inga-Dora, George Farkas, and Eric Silver. 2004. The role of depressed mood and anger in the relationship between family conflict and delinquent behavior. *Journal of Youth and Adolescence* 33: 509–22.

Skogan, Wesley G. 2006. *Police and community in Chicago: A tale of three cities.* New York: Oxford University Press.

Skolnick, Jerome H. 1966. *Justice without trial: Law enforcement in a democratic society.* New York: John Wiley.

Skolnick, Jerome H., and James J. Fyfe. 1993. *Above the law: Police and the excessive use of force.* New York: Free Press.

Smith, Scott M., and Michael G. Aamodt. 1997. Relationship between education, experience, and police performance. *Journal of Police and Criminal Psychology* 12: 7–14.

Stoddard, Ellwyn R. 1968. The informal "code" of police deviancy: A group approach to "Blue-coat crime." *Journal of Criminal Law, Criminology, and Police Science* 59: 201–13.

Thrasher, Louis M., Charles D. Tiefer, Martha Fleetwood, and Stan Lechner. 1979. *Report of investigation of misconduct of Philadelphia Police Force and recommendation.* United States Justice Department, Civil Rights Division. Internal Memorandum to Assistant Attorney General Drew S. Days, III.

Tittle, Charles R., David A. Ward, and Harold G. Grasmick. 2003. Self-control and crime/deviance: Cognitive vs. behavioral measures. *Journal of Quantitative Criminology* 19: 333–65.

Toch, Hans. 1996. The violence-prone officer. In William Geller, and Hans Toch (eds.), *Police violence: Understanding and controlling police abuse of force.* New Haven, CT: Yale University Press.

Truxillo, Donald M., Suzanne R. Bennett, and Michelle L. Collins. 1998. College education and police job performance: A ten-year study. *Public Personnel Management* 27: 269–80.

Turner, Michael G., and Alex R. Piquero. 2002. The stability of self-control. *Journal of Criminal Justice* 30: 457–71.

Tyler, Tom R. 2006. *Why people obey the law.* Princeton, NJ: Princeton University Press.

Uchida, Craig D. 2005. The development of the American police: An historical overview. In Roger G. Dunham and Geoffrey P. Alpert (eds.), *Critical Issues in Policing: Contemporary Readings.* Long Grove, IL: Waveland Press, pp. 20–40.

United States Commission on Civil Rights. 1981. *Who is guarding the guardians?* Washington, DC: U.S. Government Printing Office.

United States Department of Justice, Civil Rights Division, Criminal Section. 1992. *Police brutality study* FY 1985–FY 1990. Washington, DC: U.S. Department of Justice.

United States of America v. City of Philadelphia et al. (U.S. District Court, Eastern District of Pennsylvania, CA 79-2937, 1979).

Van Maanen, John. 1978. The asshole. In Peter K. Manning and John Van Maanen (eds.), *Policing: A view from the street.* Santa Monica, CA: Goodyear.

Van Maanen, John. 2004. Kinsmen in repose: Occupational perspectives of patrolmen. In Victor E. Kappeler (ed.), *The police and society.* Long Grove, IL: Waveland Press, pp. 240–57.

Vollmer, August. 1972. *The police and modern society.* Montclair, NJ: Patterson Smith (reprint of original 1936 manuscript).

Walker, Samuel. 1977. *A critical history of police reform: The emergence of professionalism.* Lexington, MA: Lexington Books.

Walker, Samuel. 1992. *Sense and nonsense about crime and drugs: A policy guide,* 6th ed. New York: Wadsworth.

Walker, Samuel. 1993. *Taming the system.* New York: Oxford University Press.

Walker, Samuel. 2005. *The new world of police accountability.* Thousand Oaks, CA: Sage Publications.

Walker, Samuel, and Charles M. Katz. 2008. *The police in America: An introduction.* New York: McGraw-Hill.

Warner, Barbara D., and Shannon K. Fowler. 2003. Strain and violence: Testing a general strain theory model of community violence. *Journal of Criminal Justice*: 31: 511–21.

Waugh, Linda, Andrew Ede, and Avril Alley. 1988. Police culture, women police and attitudes towards misconduct. *Policing: An International Journal of Police Science and Management* 1: 288–330.

Weber, Max 1947. *Theory of economic and social organization.* (Talcott Parsons, trans. and ed.). Glencoe, IL: Free Press.

Weisburd, David, Stephen D. Mastrofski, Anne Marie McNally, Rosann Greenspan, and James J. Willis. 2003. Reforming to preserve: CompStat and strategic problem solving in American Policing. *Criminology and Public Policy* 2: 421–56.

Weitzer, Ronald. 1999. Citizens' perceptions of police misconduct: race and neighborhood context. *Justice Quarterly* 16: 819–46.

Weitzer, Ronald. 2002. Incidents of police misconduct and public opinion. *Journal of Criminal Justice* 30: 397–408.

Westley, William A. 1956. Secrecy and the police. *Social Forces* 34: 254–57.

Westley, William A. 1970. *Violence and the police: A sociological study of law, custom, and morality.* Cambridge: MIT Press.

White, Jacquelyn W., Scott P. Lawrence, Carolyn Biggerstaff, and Terry D. Grubb.

1985. Factors of stress among police officers. *Criminal Justice and Behavior* 12: 111–28.

White, Michael D. 2008. Identifying good cops early: Predicting recruit performance in the academy. *Police Quarterly* 11: 27–49.

White, Michael D., Jonathon A. Cooper, Jessica Saunders, and Anthony J. Raganella. 2010. Motivations for becoming a police officer: Re-assessing officer attitudes after six years on the street. *Journal of Criminal Justice* 38(4): 520–30.

White, Michael D., and Justin Ready. 2010. The impact of the TASER on suspect resistance: Identifying predictors of effectiveness. *Crime and Delinquency* 56: 70–102.

Williams, Robert H. 1974. *Vice Squad.* New York: Pinnacle Books.

Wilson, O. W. 1950. *Police administration.* New York: McGraw-Hill.

Wilson, James Q. 1968. *Varieties of police behavior.* Cambridge: Harvard University Press.

Wilson, James Q. 1985. The nature of corruption. In Robert E. Cleary (ed.), *The Role of Government in the United States.* Lanham, MD: University Press of America, pp. 160–64.

Wilson, William Julius. 1987. *The truly disadvantaged: The inner city, the underclass, and public policy.* Chicago: University of Chicago Press.

Wilson, William Julius. 1996. *When work disappears: The world of the new urban poor.* New York: Vintage Books.

Witham, Donald C. 1985. *The American law enforcement chief executive: A management profile.* Washington, DC: Police Executive Research Forum.

Wood, Peter B., Betty Pfefferbaum, and Bruce J. Arneklev. 1993. Risk-taking and self-control: Social psychological correlates of delinquency. *Journal of Crime and Justice* 16: 111–30.

Worden, Robert E. 1989. Situational and attitudinal explanations of police behavior: A theoretical reappraisal and empirical assessment. *Law and Society Review* 23:667–711.

Worden, Robert E. 1995. The causes of police brutality: Theory and evidence on police use of force. In William A. Geller and Hans Toch (eds.), *And justice for all: Understanding and controlling police abuse of force.* Washington, DC: Police Executive Research Forum.

Worden, Robert E., and Shelagh E. Catlin. 2002. The use and abuse of force by police. In Kim M. Lersch (ed.), *Policing and misconduct.* Upper Saddle River, NJ: Prentice Hall.

Zhao, Jihong, Ne He, and Nicholas Lovrich. 2002. Predicting five dimensions of police officer stress: Looking more deeply into organizational settings for sources of police stress. *Police Quarterly* 5: 43–62.

Zhao, Jihong, Q. T. Thurman, and Ne He. 1999. Sources of job satisfaction among police officers: A test of demographic and work environmental models. *Justice Quarterly* 15: 153–173.

INDEX

Martin, Susan, 99

Massogila, Michael, 193n3

Mastrofski, Stephen, 185n38

Matthews, James, 179n28

Matulia, Kenneth, 185n5

Maxim, Paul, 192n109, 192n113

Mays, Larry, 190n71

Mazerolle, Paul, 190n59

McAlary, Mike, 30, 53, 183n10, 184n21, 184n23, 184n24, 184n27, 185n8

McDonald, Phyllis, 62, 184n35

McGarrell, Edmund, 123

McManus, George, 87, 184n16

McMullan, Michael, 27

McNally, Anne Marrie, 185n38

Melchionne, Teresa, 182n88, 183n10

Mendelsohn, Harold, 189n23

Merton, Robert, 130, 131, 134, 190n53

Messner, Steven, 190n54

Miami River Cops, 126

Miller, Wilbur, 181n71

Minorities, targeting, 62. *See also* Race

Misconduct: administrative/failure to perform, 68, 71, 89–90, 93; availability of data, 28, 37; conduct-related probationary failures, 68, 71; defining, 6, 6–7, 8, 20–25, 28, 35–36, 65, 123; deviant nature of police, 123; education, 34; effects of police, 110; examples of, 5; frequency of, 36; geographic differences, 30, 31; life and career history, 34; measuring, 28; noble cause, 127; obstruction of justice, 69, 71; off duty, 25, 68, 71, 93; on duty, 68, 71, 72–73, 89, 93; organizational and environmental correlates/associations, 33, 108; police performance, 37; predictors of, 90–93, 93–94, 99, 101, 157–159; prevalence of, 68, 70; profit motivated, 1, 27, 28, 66, 68,

71, 73, 73–74, 89, 92, 165; protective factors against, 92–93, 94, 101–102, 159–160; theoretical explanation of police, 123–124; types of serious, 10. *See also* Abuse of authority; Buddy Boys; Career ending misconduct; Drugs; Education; Gender; Knapp Commission; Misconduct, patterns of; Mollen Commission; Police corruption; Police crime; Race; Theory

Misconduct, patterns of: 1975–1979, 49–50; 1980–1984, 51–52; 1985–1989, 54–56; 1990–1993, 56–58; 1994–1996, 58–59

Moffit, Terrie, 192n124, 193n127, 193n131

Mollen Commission, 19, 28, 30, 35, 126, 180n55, 180n56, 181n66, 182n106, 184n26, 184n28, 185n2, 186n11; drugs, 56–57; era, 56–58, 60; investigation, xvi, 58; misconduct during, 57–58, 61

Morash, Merry, 190n70

Muir, William, 185n1, 190n60

Muraven, Mark, 192n116–118

Murphy, Patrick, xvi, 30, 46, 177n2, 180n55, 180n56, 181n71, 183n10, 183n11

Nagin, Daniel, 192n109

Narcotics. *See* Drugs

National Commission on Law Observance and Enforcement, 179n21, 180n44

National Treasury Employees Union v. Von Raab, 184n19

Negotiated order framework, 33

Neiderhoffer, Arthur, 182n1, 189n22, 191n74

New Orleans Mayor's Committee on Human Relations, 180n54

167–170, 171; "Watchman Style" of, 32; "zero tolerance," 63, 107. *See also* "Bad" cops/policing; Crime prevention programs; "Good" cops/policing

Pomeroy, Wesley, 189n32

Pratt, Travis, 145, 192n110, 192n119

Presidential Commissions, 29

Race: civilian, 111–112; officers, 34, 75, 90, 91, 93, 94–97, 99, 100–101, 134–135, 141–142, 143, 147, 157–159, 159–160, 174, 175, 176; profiling, 24–25; racial threat perspective, 33; rank, 158; spatial distribution of, 112–117. See also Minorities, targeting

Racial profiling, 24–25. *See also* Race

Raganella, Anthony, 188n8, 190n65

Rampart scandal, 31, 180n54

RAND study, 179n29

Ready, Justin, 186n15

Recruits: career path, 47; hook system, 47; gender, 47; screening, 47, 105, 160, 166; training, 47

Reisig, Michael, 187n17

Reiss, Albert, 29

Rengifo, Andres, 187n1

Repetto, Thomas, 178n1, 183n10

Reuss-Ianni, Elizabeth, 48, 182n94, 183n10, 189n34

Rice, Stephen, 179n30

Roberg, Roy, 190n70, 191n75

Rockefeller, Governor Nelson, 47

Rosenfeld, Richard, 187n1, 190n54

Roth, Jeffery, 193n130

Rothmiller, Mike, 31, 180n55

Rubinstein, Jonathan, 30, 180n55

Sampson, Robert, 118, 187n15, 192n120, 192n122, 193n125, 193n128, 193n131, 193n3

Sapp, Alan, 34, 185n4

Saunders, Jessica, 190n65

Savitz, Leonard, 139

Schecter, Leonard, 30

Scott, Michael, 185n5

Self-control theory, 144- 145; applied, 145–147; future with police misconduct, 148–149; *Jammed Up* study, 147–148; limitations of, 146–147; self-control strength, 146

Selznick, Philip, 8

Serpico, 32; scandal, xv, 54; era, xvi

Sherman, Lawrence, xvii, 21–22, 27, 52, 178n6, 178n12–15, 178n17, 179n33, 180n55, 181n70, 183n10, 184n20, 186n10, 189n25, 191n81, 191n97, 191n98

Sherman, Lewis, 182n88

Silver, Eric, 190n59

Skinner v. Railway Labor Executives' Ass'n, 184n19

Skogan, Wesley, 177n1

Skolnick, Jerome, 29, 31, 71, 87, 125, 130, 132, 169, 177n5, 180n54, 180n55, 185n10, 186n9, 189n26, 189n49, 192n104

Sluder, Richard, 31, 190n68, 191n78

Social disorganization, 33, 127

Social learning theory, 126, 137; applied, 138–141; definitions, 137–138; differential association, 137; differential reinforcement, 138; future with police misconduct, 143–144; limitations of, 140–141; modeling/imitation, 138; *Jammed Up* study, 141–143

Sorenson, Ann, 192n109

Special Investigations Unit scandal, 54

Stoddard, Ellwyn, 22, 178n7, 189n23

Stokes, Robert, 188n54

Structural disadvantage, 108, 109, 110, 120

ABOUT THE AUTHORS

Robert J. Kane is Professor and Director of the Program in Criminal Justice at Drexel University, as well as a Senior Research Fellow at the Center for Violence Prevention and Community Safety at Arizona State University. He is a coeditor of the forthcoming book, *The Oxford Handbook of Police and Policing*.

Michael D. White is Associate Professor in the School of Criminology and Criminal Justice at Arizona State University, and is Associate Director at the Center for Violence Prevention and Community Safety at ASU. He is coeditor of *Race, Ethnicity, and Policing: New and Essential Readings*, and author of *Current Issues and Controversies in Policing*.